D1448035

Mathias Denecke, Anne Ganzert, Isabell Otto, F
ReClaiming Participation

Media Studies

MATHIAS DENECKE, ANNE GANZERT,
ISABELL OTTO, ROBERT STOCK (EDS.)

ReClaiming Participation

Technology – Mediation – Collectivity

[transcript]

Funded by the Young Scholar Fund at the University of Konstanz.

Bibliographic Information published by the Deutsche Nationalbibliothek
The Deutsche Nationalbibliothek lists this publication in the Deutsche Natio-
nalbibliografie; detailed bibliographic data are available in the Internet at
http://dnb.d-nb.de

Cover layout: Kordula Röckenhaus, Bielefeld
Proofread by Angela Whale
Printed in Germany
Print-ISBN 978-3-8376-2922-4
PDF-ISBN 978-3-8394-2922-8

Table of Contents

III. ART AND MEDIA: THEORY OF PARTAKING

PERSPECTIVES

Introduction

MATHIAS DENECKE/ANNE GANZERT/ROBERT STOCK

Participation has become the key issue in popular, economic, and academic notions of New Media. This book and its contributors seek to examine and unravel the debates of the 'Participation Age', while rejecting a mere appraisal of the impact of contemporary media on participation. Instead of perpetuating euphoric visions of social all-inclusion and web democracy and collaboration as well as pessimistic views of exclusion, top-down hierarchy, and the "digital divide", collectivity and participation are discussed as effects of technological, historical and political conditions and practices. This publication presents revised versions of the papers presented at the 2014 conference "ReClaiming Participation".

1   MEDIA AND PARTICIPATION

The collection of papers can also be considered the first product from the Research Group "Media and Participation. Between Demand and Entitlement", which has officially started in July 2015, and is funded by the German Research Foundation (DFG). The research group consists of several subprojects with principal investigators from universities in Hamburg, Konstanz, Lüneburg, and Zurich. Leading scholars from the fields of media studies, sociology, and art history are taking part in a compelling interdisciplinary research where 'medial participation' as a key concept is scrutinized in order to enable a differentiated debate about processes of participation located in media-cultural exchange processes. This reconceptualization is founded on a processual understanding of media, which allows the description of the relations between demand and entitlement in the assemblages of subjects, technological objects, practices, and communities. In order to fill the unmet need of grasping the relations between media and participation, the full scope of its socio-political and cultural implications has to be considered in order to enrich and differentiate the current approaches, which are mainly application oriented, with an analysis of participation from a media theoretic perspective.

2 CONFERENCE RECLAIMING PARTICIPATION

The international conference took place at the Zurich University of the Arts from May 7th – 9th, 2014 and was a cooperation of the University of Konstanz (Germany), the Institute for Critical Theory, Zurich University of the Arts, and the international research network "Media of Collective Intelligence", funded by the German Research Foundation (DFG). From the many submissions, the organization committee chose papers that offered a wide array of perspectives and encouraged in-depth discussions.

The three-day event started with the workshop: *Micropractices* by Wiktoria Furrer and Sebastian Dieterich (ZHdK Zurich). Over the course of the program Erin Manning, Claus Pias, and Erich Hörl gave keynote lectures, each relating to a thematically organized session which followed. An expert in the respective field chaired each of these sessions, giving a short introduction into the thematic horizon of the contributions on 'Art and Media: Theory of Partaking', 'Participatory Practices and Digital Media', and 'Participation and the Claims of Community'. The contributors were drawn from all over Germany, Switzerland, Austria, Sweden, Great Britain, Portugal, Lithuania, North America, and Canada. One speaker attended via Skype, while another presented a movie documentary. In a round of short presentations, members of the scientific network "Media of Collective Intelligence" discussed their research results under the title *Curiosities of Collective Intelligence*; namely, Nacim Ghanbari, Asko Lehmuskallio, Erika Linz, Sabine Niederer, Isabell Otto, Samantha Schramm, Marc Spaniol, and Tristan Thielmann.

The organization committee (Beate Ochsner, Isabell Otto, Mathias Denecke, Anne Ganzert) would like to take this opportunity and thank all the people involved for making this conference a success as well as for giving great papers and facilitating intriguing discussion:[1] Christina Friesch, Amelie Heinle, Christian Kleinwächter, Andrew Philipps, Veronika Pöhnl, Michel Schreiber, Markus Spöhrer, Robert Stock, and Katrin Stowasser. We warmly thank the DFG, the University of Konstanz, and the ZHdK for funding the conference. Furthermore, the editors of this collection thank Julia Ihls and Nikola Plohr for their help finalizing this volume. Finally, we thank the Young Scholar Fund of the University of Konstanz for generously funding the publication of this book.

3 CONTENT OF THIS BOOK

The selected papers in this collection focus on relational processes rather than a priori assumptions of politically, economically, culturally, and socially separated participants and communities. Many refer to concepts and theories by the likes of Jean-Luc Nancy, Gilbert Simondon, Louis Althusser, or Bernard Stiegler in order to reflect on the reciprocity of participatory processes or the possibilities and conditions of participation. At the same time, the methodological approaches vary: Some contributors consider theories and terminologies. Some describe promises of inclusion, exclusion, integration, and disintegration in participatory processes regarding their relational constitution, connection or separation; other articles present case studies on mechanisms of participation in the context of new media. Regardless of the method, each author discusses the role of media in affecting, enabling, or disabling participation, exclusion, or inclusion in the formation of particular (digital) communities.

The conference's three main panels also serve to structure this volume. The main part of the book is therefore divided into three sections which mirror the program of the conference. Each section is introduced by a text from the respective conference chair, followed by the keynote text and the corresponding case studies.

---

1 "Thank you." ReClaiming Participation, https://vimeo.com/94965326 (August 16, 2015).

Sabine Niederer (Amsterdam) opens the first section of the book by outlining the "logic of participation" as discussed by Bruno Latour, Noortje Marres, and Jyri Engeström. Claus Pias (Lüneburg) picks up this thread by comprehensively describing the relation of "Connectives, Collectives, and the 'Nonsense' of Participation". This discussion on media theory is followed by three different case studies. Sebastian Vehlken (Lüneburg) asks for the specific intermingling of technological condition and user practices in his text on "Multimodal Crowd Sensing". Arseli Dokumacı's (Montreal) contribution as well as the text by Pablo Abend and Benjamin Beil (Cologne) both approach participatory practices within a stronger ethnographical focus, each by putting a particular case study in the foreground. Dokumacı's "Blindness, Techno-Affordances, and Participation in Everyday Life" focuses on the relation between digital media, blindness, and "spatial problem-solving activities", while Abend and Beil take a closer look at the behavior of different groups of game players and the co-creative practices of editor games.

The second section puts the emphasis on "Participation and the Claims of Community" and is introduced by Christina Bartz (Paderborn). Erich Hörl's (Lüneburg) "Other Beginnings of Participative Sense Culture: Wild Media, Speculative Ecologies, Transgressions of the Cybernetic Hypothesis" therefore draws on the descriptions of 'animistic sense cultures' and Simondon's general ecology of participation with the background of our contemporary 'technological condition' in mind. Under the headline "Partial Visibilities, Affective Affinities: On (Not) Taking Sides" Arnoldas Stramskas (Kaunas) discusses whether political movement emerges from specific places where people meet and organize special activities, or vice versa. Nina Franz (Berlin) presents her findings from analyzing military text documents regarding their implicit notion of the human-weapon-relation in "'Man in the Loop': The Language of Participation and the New Technologies of War". Anne Kaun's (Södertörn/Pennsylvania) chapter "Crisis and Critique: Histories of Protest Media Participation" addresses the change from the age of "mechanical speed to digital immediacy in media practices", which she demonstrates via two different American protest movements. Also situated within the wider political framework is Martin Dege's (Konstanz) text "Liquid Democracy and Other Fixes to the Problem of Democracy", which refrains from the immediate rejection of the Internet's effects on the public. Instead, he suggests understanding technology as a consequence of social developments.

The last section "Art and Media: Theory of Partaking" is introduced by Samantha Schramm (Konstanz). There, the final keynote by Erin Manning (Montreal) is concerned with "Artfulness: Emergent Collectives and Processes of Individuation". Manning argues for an understanding of artistic practice and its relation to "new modes of existence". In "Art and Design as Social Collaborative Praxis. Engineering the Utopian Community or the Implosion of Techno-Aesthetic Reason", Maria Teresa Cruz (Lisbon) indicates that there is a "new contributive economy" on the horizon. Heading in another direction is Eva Axer's "'Choir of Minds'. Oral Media-Enthusiasm and Theories on Communal Creation (18th–20th Century)". Axer reviews a historic discourse and its specific relations of "oral media, communal creation, and the idea of a 'spirit of a people'". Seeking to explain contemporary phenomena and modes of participation is "Web Memes and Mobilisation: The Contagious Socio-Aesthetics of Participation", in which Sascha Simons (Lüneburg) analyzes these objects regarding the processes between "technology, sociality, and aesthetics". Christine Mitchel (Montreal) closes the third section with a text on "Who Will Translate the Web? Machines, Humans, and Reinventing Translation as a Participatory Practice". She discusses the promises and impositions regarding the translation chains of the 'sociocultural' and the 'technical'.

The edited volume is closed by an outlook, including remarks on the horizon of research goals and main lines of inquiry that have to be addressed in discussing media participation. Elke Bippus, Beate Ochsner, and Isabell Otto introduce some of the essential foci of the discourse and the research group. The resulting research questions are exemplified in case studies that each contributes to the reclaiming of participation for art and media studies through contemplating and critical reflection of co-existence (Mitsprechen), promise (Versprechen), and dissent (Widersprechen). The wide spectrum of approaches and contributions will hopefully contribute to the discussion about media and participation and add to futures debates in all the related areas.

I. Participatory Practices and Digital Media

Introduction: Objects of Citizen Participation

SABINE NIEDERER

1 INTRODUCTION

Discussions of participatory practices seem to thrive in a wide range of discourses: from citizen participation and DIY Citizenship (Ratto/Boler 2014), to the *Internet of Things* and its object-centered participation (Engeström 2005). What these practices and their theorization share is an effort to dissect the dynamics of participation. In this introduction, I would like to briefly address three concepts that look at the logic of participation: 'Group Formation' as theorized by philosopher and sociologist Bruno Latour, 'Material Participation' as developed by philosopher and digital sociologist Noortje Marres, and 'Object-centered Sociality' by *Internet of Things* designer Jyri Engeström.

2 CONCEPTS OF PARTICIPATION

Philosopher and anthropologist Bruno Latour, in his influential book *Reassembling the Social*, describes how there are no groups without a large retinue of 'group makers, group talkers, and group holders' (Latour 2005: 32). Not only are groups reliant on these active group-maintaining actors, groups are also never a given *over time*. Latour states that groups exist merely in instances of group formation. For researchers studying groups and group participation, this means a focus on retrieving traces of these cases of group formation. For instance, in a study of climate skepticism, I have studied the speakers at an annual conference of climate skeptics, their publications and related issues (Niederer 2013). Such gatherings and output are sources par excellence to study 'actor language', or the terminology used by members of the group, and interlinking (in terms of citations or co-authorship in publications, or in the form of hyperlinks on websites).

Philosopher and digital sociologist Noortje Marres has described the role of objects in participation around issues, arguing that material entities make an important positive contribution "to the organization of social, political, and moral life in industrialized societies" (2012: 6). In her book and previous writings she takes the case of the smart meters and other 'green home' technologies not as an example of the domestication of new technology, in the way Bruno Latour would describe public experiments as initiation rituals of technology making it into the home (Latour 1988 quoted in Marres 2009: 119), but as lightweight means of participation. In the case of climate change, the complexities of global warming do not need to be grasped fully in order to engage with the issue on a daily basis. Smart meters that reduce one's footprint instead provide a low-threshold way to make the issue part of your daily routine. That these green home experiments are both highly empirical and mediatized (through blogs and other public media) makes them a suitable site and object of study for investigating the role of devices, settings, and objects in the organization and performance of public engagement and participation. They also remind us that the traces of group formation are to be found both offline (in a kitchen cabinet) and online (on a blog for green home tips). And just as groups only exist in instances of group formation, these issue objects also exist in a moment in time and can quickly transform or lose their political or normative charge (ibid: 21).

How objects in turn can be social, or rather at the center of sociality, is described by designer and engineer Jyri Engeström, active in the field of *Internet of Things* technology. Engeström describes how social media are successful not because they gather people, but because they offer shared objects to people:

"The fallacy is to think that social networks are just made up of people. They're not; social networks consist of people who are connected by a shared object. That's why many sociologists [...] prefer to talk about 'socio-material networks', or just 'activities' or 'practices' (as I do) instead of social networks." (Engeström 2005)

In his blog post, he illustrates this phenomenon of people connecting through a shared object with the success of platforms such as *Flickr*, where photos are shared objects, the social bookmarking site of *del.icio.us*, where people share URLs, and event-websites such as *Upcoming.org*. He is critical of *LinkedIn*, because it focuses too much on "the 'social just means people' misunderstanding". However, the platform has been able to play with this by adding a competitive element, where the number of connections becomes a marker of reputation. This, he describes as the 'surrogate object' of *LinkedIn* (ibid.).

So as well as the traces of group formation and issue participation, we can study the objects that have been charged with issues, be they tangible objects for everyday use or the online content objects that are central to a social media platform. The papers in this section each examine participatory practices in connection to digital media objects, where apps and web platforms facilitate participation by offering socio-technical constructs.

3 PRACTICES OF PARTICIPATION

The contribution by Claus Pias (University of Luneburg, Germany) outlines the difficulties tied to adequately describing the rich relations between social organizational forms and material infrastructures that result from their heterogeneous inherent logics. Therefore, the first part of his keynote text asks "the question how connectives become collectives, or how they correlate". Situating this in a broader context, Pias emphasizes the need for reflecting upon historical and methodological aspects, specifically in their relation to the theoretical concepts in question. The final part discusses the terms 'transparency' and 'understanding' within a historical context. Hence, putting the concept of participation to the test he concludes pleading to think digital cultures differently from a pre-modern perspective, to be more exact in "the terms of the Arcanum".

Benjamin Beil and Pablo Abend (University of Cologne, Germany) study participation within the co-creative processes of computer game design in their paper titled "Editor Games: Scripts of Participation in Co-

Creative Media". Editor games such as *Minecraft* and *LittleBigPlanet* offer their players the means to construct the game world themselves. Beil and Abend analyze such participatory practices by distinguishing between "implicit" participation (scripted by the game software) and "explicit participation practices" (carried out by the players themselves) and explore the range of participatory practices that define participation in editor games.

The paper "Multimodal Crowd Sensing" by Sebastian Vehlken (University of Luneburg, Germany) discusses crowd-sensing technologies and their conceptual and media-technological importance as well as their actual user practices and the challenges these bring. Building on theories of mass behavior and mass psychology, for instance escape and panic behavior in crowds, Vehlken explores the use of sensory systems and computer simulation software to detect and simulate crowds and their dynamics. (Not only the simulation of human crowds, but also animal crowds such as herds and swarms.) Lastly, he discusses multimodal crowd sensing, or the possibility to combine different urban sensory data, such as detecting GPS-location traces from mobile phones and crowd capturing by CCTV, in order to simulate crowd behavior and bring the idea of citizen sensing to the level of 'the crowd as sensor', thereby generating big data. Just like Beil and Abend, Vehlken distinguishes between participatory sensing and (top-down) "opportunistic sensing", where crowds are sensed without the involvement of the individual users.

Closing this section is the paper "Micro-activist Affordances of Disability. Transformative Potential of Participation", by Arseli Dokumacı (Concordia University, Montreal, Canada), explores a blind individual's everyday life and investigates what new modes of participation emerge through his embodied engagement with mobile media and digital technologies. Fully intertwined with tools for accessing online content, the paper and its accompanying documentary (available at: performingdisability.com/video/bli ndness.mov) powerfully demonstrate how a blind Internet user deals with the object-centrality of online communication through usability tools.

4 CONCLUSION

The entanglement of participatory practices with digital tools and (offline or online) objects benefits highly from concepts that capture the essence of what one participates with and the dynamics of such participation and group formation. As we have seen from the papers, not only does an issue or an issue-charged object organize group formation and participation, but it can also be a game, invisible security data infrastructures, or a specific set of usability tools for online communication that involve or create groups – knowingly or unknowingly.

REFERENCES

Boler, Megan/Matt Ratto (eds.) (2014), DIY Citizenship: Critical Making and Social Media, Cambridge, MA: MIT Press.

Engeström, Jyri (2005): Why some social network services work and others don't. Or, the case for object-centered sociality, April 13, http://www. zengestrom.com/blog/2005/04/why-some-social-network-services-work-and-others-dont-or-the-case-for-object-centered-sociality.html (July 25, 2015).

Latour, Bruno (2005): Reassembling the Social, Oxford: Oxford University Press.

Marres, Noortje (2014): Material Participation: Technology, The Environment and Everyday Publics, Basingstoke: Palgrave.

Marres, Noortje (2009): "Testing Powers of Engagement: Green Living Experiments, the Ontological Turn and the Undoability of Involvement." In: European Journal of Social Theory February 2009 12/1, pp. 117-133.

Niederer, Sabine (2013): "'Global warming is not a crisis!': Studying climate change skepticism on the web." In: Necsus. European Journal of Media Studies 2/1, pp. 83-112, http://www.necsus-ejms.org/global-warming-is-not-a-crisis-studying-climate-change-skepticism-on-the-web/ (August 15, 2015).

Collectives, Connectives, and the 'Nonsense' of Participation

1

New forms of collectivity have increasingly shaped diagnoses of the times for many years. There is talk of swarms, smart mobs, networks, virtual collectives, and affect and risk communities; all of which have all become focal points of the current social sciences and cultural studies. These phenomena may be heterogenic, but these new logics of the collective are all distinctly different from classical social and cultural forms of identity.

The challenge is therefore twofold: On one hand there is the problem of a (however shaped) 'empirical' observation of these new phenomena,[1] on the other is the question of a methodological and theoretic vocabulary that is able to grasp those new logics. These logics concern different modalities of the production of collectivity, which are no longer (or at least no longer primarily) forms of representational constructions and identity politics, as they are viewed in cultural studies or theories of hegemony.[2]

---

1 For the constitution of swarms as epistemic object through the changing media of their 'empirical' observation see for example Vehlken 2012.

2 The following thoughts result from meetings with Urs Stäheli during the application for funds for the graduate center "Loose Couplings: Collectivity at the intersection of digital and urban space" (http://www.wiso.uni-hamburg.de/

For a long time – too long in my opinion, as I belong to a different school of thought – scholars of the humanities have understood collectivity in a continuation of the "linguistic turn" and in terms of representation. However, in doing so, they have failed to observe that the new collectivities have far superseded representational forms and that they are not constituted by shared myths, narratives, or other kinds of self-description. Instead, material and operational functionalities emerge with these new collectivities and it is the manifold forms of technological mediation, immediate connectivity, affective connection, and their infrastructures that determine which collectives evolve.

Then again, this kind of representation-bashing is neither particularly new nor original. Neither is the demand for an analysis of collectivity beyond representational models. In fact, this is the core business of any technology-conscious media studies. But, and this is my point on research strategies, it has become more and more apparent that a simple replacement of representational logics with operational logics is not the sole solution.

I do not mean to challenge the fact that it has been necessary and urgent to focus on the media-technological infrastructures or the affectivities of collective processes rather than continuously turning the wheels of representation. Neither do I mean to claim, that representational conflicts about identity have lost their relevance or could be replaced by heterogenic networks or assemblages. This is also just as little about denying the fact that classic conceptions of collective identity have also considered the importance of medial infrastructures. My aim is rather to grasp the material infrastructures as well as the modes of operation from their own logic (for example as local, swarm like coordination of affective infections), and therefore does not subordinate them, *a priori*, under processes of representation.

Instead of fighting in the trenches we should accept the challenge of conceptually opening or reconceptualizing the problem, in an effort to join operative, technical connectivity, on the one hand, with forms of collective self-description and experience, on the other hand. Or in short: Ask the

projekte/lose-verbindungen/graduiertenkolleg/) as well as from conversations with Dirk Baecker at the second DFG Symposium of Media Studies (Baxmann/Beyes/Pias 2014).

question how *connectives* and *collectives* relate to each other, or how they are intertwined.

The social sciences have developed some concepts – for example in the context of Bruno Latour's "actor network theory" – for thinking about new forms of "assembling" and of the "association" (Hardt/Negri 2002; Latour 2002, 2010; Agamben 2003; DeLanda 2006; Nancy 2008). But these concepts tend to leave out mediality and media technology, as is characteristic of social studies. What is needed is an analysis of new collectivities that is neither reduced to social nor technical networks or the modes of their cultural self-description but which is interested in the different configurations of their *correlation*.

Let me rephrase the problem: Even social identities are challenged in themselves by operative logics, by the modes of connecting to each other, in a way that can no longer be explained by identification processes, although these processes are still important in order to understand the correlation (and the drifting apart) of identities.

Considering these two logics is important: it cannot be merely about claiming that self-descriptions are confirmed or disavowed by the 'reality' of operating. That has been done already. Instead, it should really be about the interlocking of two different modes of collectivity creation. Only when we separate the representational and operative logics of collectivities can analytical potential be gained, as the theoretic and empiric understanding of the references and conflicts of each logic is thereby enabled. It also means avoiding simplifications, for example that an era of hegemony is succeeded by an era of post-hegemony. A mere replacement of the discursive creation of collectivities by focusing on the practices and actors would also not be satisfying for the situation, because both cases, 'era-creation' and premature theoretic substitution, lose sight of the tension between the two logics. More precisely, they lose sight of the problem that, while concepts of unity may be performatively at play, other non-representative modes are creating borders which cannot be reduced to semantics of unity.

In the perspective of the 'case studies' (oriented at phenomena) the historically 'new' consists in the first place of the prominent proliferation of the manifold modes of the new collectivities in diverse social areas. This includes, as it has been said plenty of times, a variety of things, from new forms of political protest, like the anti-globalization movement, the occupy movement, or online activism through to management techniques like the swarm based organization, crowd-sourcing, and the military doctrine of swarming, up to swarm like technologies of knowledge production in 'epistemic crowds'.

What the notorious (and scientific yet politically very useful) talk of the 'epochal shift' tends to overlook – and this is my historic point after the rather systematic previous remarks – is: All these forms of collectivity possess historic predecessors. It seems to me that this historic depth may be best captured through a genealogy of mass phenomena and mass semantics. New collectivities happen in the space between society and community, a space which conceptually announced itself for the social sciences in mass semantics long before media studies or cultural studies evolved.

A suspicion we followed in the DFG Symposium "Soziale Medien – Neue Massen" two years ago in Lüneburg is that it is possible to deduct from the theoretic destiny of the term of the 'mass' how such forms of the social have been reduced to mere remains of former societies or political battle cries and therefore have been theoretically and empirically excluded from the legitimate canon of the social and cultural sciences (Baxmann/Beyes/Pias 2014). Or put differently: If you want to talk about new collectivities you cannot avoid talking about old ones. Researching new collectivities is (at least to me as a media historian) not detachable from their knowledge-historical genealogy that repeatedly refers to the term of the 'mass'.

2

Let me elaborate a little on the question of old masses and new collectivities. If the question of the media of the social is posed, it is not aimed at *how* different media *serve* socially, but *which* media actually *spawn* and *inform* specific forms of sociality and mass. To what capacity can media be considered constitutive for these forms? In what way do they also mark a caesura in our own scholarly questioning, our methods, and our general epistemology? Even once new media like radio or film – as they were for Brecht or Vertov – did not debate mass as a matter of content or images but as a matter of media infrastructures, as modes of perception and organization, and meaning as *connectives*. And in this sense it has been, and will always be, 'old' media or connectives that appoint responsibility for changing social structures or collectives to the respectively 'new' media.

Connectivity to me is, as I have said, the operative, material mode of functioning; collectivity, on the other hand, is representational and symbolic. I am interested in how, from an epistemological perspective, certain forms of connectivity and collectivity bear historic correlation to the theories of media studies and sociological scholarship that are designed to describe them. In other words: Our own theory has always been and will always be deeply saturated with the phenomena it aims to describe. Look for example at the different epistemological interests in social sciences and media studies, or rather connectivity and collectivity sciences. This can be neatly summed up by a short anecdote made popular by Friedrich Kittler:

"Every attempt made in airport taxi cabs to explain to Luhmann that flip-flops, the components of digital circuitry, unlike social systems, cannot exist without input and output had gone unheard. 'Mr. Kittler', [Luhmann] then said, 'it has been like this since Babylon. A messenger rides through the gate. Some people (like you) ask, what kind of horse is he riding; others (like me), what message he brings."(Kittler 2004: 97)

For over 30 years media studies have given their attention to the operationality of media technology and therefore to the "materiality of communication" and their connectives. They have turned the pre-meaning, infrastructural level into their main research interest. This allowed remarkable gain in originality, esteem and contra-intuitive theses as well as the development of a vast archive of terms and case studies. Social sciences, on the other hand, have been shaped (for quite a while) by the duality of the terms "society and community". Community in this capacity is mostly imagined as a pure figure of sense – a collective, with medial conditions that are of little to no interest. This is still true today – even or especially in system theory which deals with new collectives only in regard to a quantitative increase of communication uncertainty. Technology is therefore indeed visible but it cannot be observed in its medial performance because it is always hidden behind the transfer of sense in the realm of meaning.

From the perspective of historical epistemology of sociology it can be said that the modern era assesses a loss of community in which the material dimension of collectivity merely appears as a faint scarecrow: an irrational and affective mass that counteracts the structure of the modern era but which still emerges at its very center. This also applies to cultural studies, where collectivity is only of interest as a phenomenon of the symbolic, normative, and discursive creation of identity, which for a long time resulted in the subordination, neglect, or even exclusion of material and media technological condition(s).

This is where (I again repeat) the research political application regarding new collectivities lies: between technology oriented media studies (horse) and sense centered social sciences (message). One could make three points – if it doesn't remind us too much of a third-party fund application:

I. Every present changes the past

Changes in the present are an opportunity to simultaneously re-contemplate the cultural history of the masses that shapes our view of the present. Our view of old media is influenced by the ever developing conditions of new media. Since the modern era (positive or negative) phantasms and utopias of mass have ignited diverse discourses and practices of social control, communication, interaction and the formation of communities.

Now there is talk (and there has been for quite some time now) of the end of mass and mass media, diffused publics, "social media", flash-mobs and multitudes, and the barely predictable dynamics and effects of digital technologies. But when the parameters of governance and communication as well as of interaction and the formation of communities shift in this way they also shed a different light on the established concepts of 'old' masses. These concepts used terms of the unconscious, non-addressability, or the irrational, and, in a way, constituted the 'dark side' of the subject of the so called civic public. New collectivities insist on a revision and historicization of those interpretation patterns, which are our own theoretic-genealogic condition through which we measure the present.

II. There has to be question of methodology

The search for terms and concepts necessary for analyzing new collectives speaks of a methodological uncertainty and poses the question of adequate methodologies for exploring contemporary socio-technical settings. This lack of appropriate methodology indicates an inability for communication studies (as another version of media studies) to continue any further, as an empirical social science, in this direction. (In itself, this question is most interesting as it constitutes the deepest rift in media studies.)

In order to derive 'representative' statements during the times of the mass, communication scholars had to presume even distribution and select at random. Mass media research was mostly advertisement research in the market of electronic linear media. This is now being replaced by algorithmic "big data" analysis using mass data collected from social networks, search engines, or online shopping platforms. However, the old methods fail – they are, simply rendered, redundant – even though they do not give up. In my opinion, looking at this example raises the basic questions of with which methods has the historically changing relation between masses and media been made observable and how that may be done in the future. The scope of new collectives' development, modes of operation, and effects will be inseparable from the key issue of revising the methodology. But it is also apparent that we are still at the very beginning of this revision.

III. Researching new collectives
is mainly done with old theoretical figures

This might be more of an observation than a thesis: A heterogenic quest for adequate terms and concepts, the methodology argument, is equally as noticeable as the fact that it is backfiring. We can refer to the works of the sociologist Gabriel Tarde, which are currently experiencing a renaissance in social and cultural studies and which claim a dominant position in the Anglophone discourse on contemporary mass phenomena. The elevated position of Tarde's works on mass and audience as well as on mimetic and infection mechanisms can be traced (apart from their explanatory capabilities) to movements in intellectual trends. In this case of Tarde's rehabilitation, theorists like Gilles Deleuze (1994), Peter Sloterdijk (2004), or Bruno Latour (2008) have been particularly effective since the 1990's. Tarde is useful because he delivers the approach to a form of theory that is not based on an Enlightenment concept of the subject. Indeed, we no longer want such a thing as that. On the other hand, we have to ask ourselves, to what capacity does using Tarde's terms allow for sufficient sensitivity regarding the new collectives' *media-technological*, connective conditions.

One part of the question is therefore if the quest for concepts and terms that would allow the description of the relation between media technology and new collectives can draw from other 'classic' concepts (such as Walter Benjamin's term of the mimetic faculty, which would enlarge Tarde's idea of imitation by the moment of emerging, the *poesis*). The second part of the question would be, if it may be finally time, to simply give thought to new concepts.

3

I apologize for not elaborating on participation earlier in the paper, and I am afraid I will not be able to make up for that. But maybe we can pose the question differently: The relation of connectives and collectives apparently becomes problematic in digital cultures. Something seems to be different here, and participation is of course at the center because it constitutes – on a systematic level – involvement in connectives and collectives as such. You participate *through* connectives and *in* collectives.

On a historic level, the whole matter is much more complicated. It is not only about hopes and disappointments in so many different kinds of participation and so many different areas, which always have to be regarded in relation to old or new media. It is also about, as previously mentioned, the diverse histories and designs of the theories that have been used in attempts to grasp participation. The assumption of digital culture's differentness challenges us to look for other terms and concepts. I therefore aim not to give any offers of understanding, but rather want to discuss possible conditions of understanding digital cultures. I don't give answers but suggest areas which should be problematized. I declare no point of view, but plead merely for other points of view.

All of this seems necessary in view of the increasing heat in debates on transparency, participation, and understanding of and within digital media. The demands for transparency are vociferous, the hopes for participation high, and the number of media-whisperers is far too large. But I am of the opinion that all these terms and concepts have their own, indelible, historic index. They are inventions of the modern era; specifically, the *saddle period* from 1750 to 1850. Therefore, they are all subject to a paradox: the claim, that, although everything is changing completely (keyword "digital revolution"), we still seek to understand and evaluate this entirely other in terms and concepts which, precisely because of this complete change, are already outdated. In short: digital cultures themselves have already made our terms obsolete.

That is why I have recently focused on decidedly *pre-modern* terms – to see if they can maybe be of use here. We can of course repeat time and time again, that Habermas has been outdated (and maybe was never really useful); we can habitually dismiss the subject of the Enlightenment; we can re-iterate the failed hopes for participation of once new media or carry the torch for hope in now new media – but this game gets tiresome. It is tiresome because the rejection of the terms and concepts, in this never ending critique of the Enlightenment era, is also and particularly bound to the modern era. The battle zone was simply chosen wrongly. Let me suggest two things, more as an experiment, not in detail, not as an explanation, merely as an impulse for thought.

Firstly: How modern forms of participation are designed seems to be clear to all, from Enlightenment to "communicative rationality" (Habermas 1984): Transparency, Equality, Publics, etc., etc. – whatever the terminology may be. Participation is embedded in or a product of a modern order that is oriented towards the future. Otherwise participation – in our understanding that is deeply shaped by modernity – would be completely useless as it takes place between is and ought: between how the world *is* and how it *ought* to be (different).

The 18th century invented new forms of historicity and therefore invented history itself: it made the present, the crucial place between "realm of experience" and "horizon of expectation" (Kosellek 1985), and it made it the scene of a principally *open* future and the birthplace of the modern subject. Pre-modern forms of 'participation' (that strictly speaking did not exist in this view) appeared differently. For example, there is no way – if we look at the political field – to simply retrace modern parliamentarism back to the "assembly of estates", the *états* and *cortes*, the country and county parliaments, that were typical from the late middle ages until the 18th century. For instance, were all of these assemblies rituals of *consensus* and not (as in the modern era) of *dissent*. It has to be said that pre-modern participation processes were rituals – a description that is now only used with defamatory intent. Rituals are empty to us: mere theatre, symbolical politics, something that has nothing to do with the political or the participation of a partaking public based on arguments and transparency. That also means that we, living in the modern era, believe that participation can only make sense if decisions are principally *open*. Otherwise, what else would you need participation for? Participating without the possibility of change makes no sense in our modern views, it seems absurd.

The pre-modern ritual survives on formalization, repeatability, and a performative character; it is based on the repeated, formally 'correct' execution of certain actions and its outcome is already predetermined. The modern era has replaced it with the decision and its procedures, and only in these does participation make sense, as a decision's impact is only negotiated in the process of making the decision. That is why the outcome is not predetermined but generated in the process (Krischer 2010).

So let me turn the question on its head and use the strangeness of the pre-modern: Why can we not simply claim that digital cultures establish a new temporal order? (Beyes/Pias 2014) A temporal order that is different from the chronotope, which originated between 1750 and 1850, in which we still somehow believe and in which we still move around thinking. This is not a new thesis. Among others we can find it in Marshall McLuhan's writings, and it also trails, becoming ever more apparent, through the entire modern discourse on electricity and immediate communication (Sprenger 2012). Nevertheless, I think that it changed again after 1945 with cybernetics. That is, with feedback and self-regulatory systems, with prediction and digital computers, and as Norbert Wiener assumed, the question of time has changed (Wiener 1948).

Through the digitalization of large areas of our environment, specifically the almost insurmountable number of apparatuses that communicate via subjects without detour and which control each other and give each other feedback on the smallest and the largest scales, these special, cybernetic temporal orders have made themselves absolute. They create a temporal order, in which modern historicity collapses. Maybe, using Musil's terminology, we could call this "absolutism of the present" (Hagen 2003). This cybernetic absolutism of the present puts the question of historic times back up for discussion. Again, I merely repeat an old answer, this time by quoting a diagnosis Vilém Flusser delivered almost 25 years ago.

If there really is a bond of cybernetic machines that interlink through feedback, that behave adaptively, and that process disturbances autonomously, then – following Flusser – the relation between is and ought collapses and with it the concept of future. He called this state (as others have before him and after him) "posthistoire" or "post-history". In this new temporal order there can no longer be an argument, critique, or politic for simple reasons of logic. That is why participation is (literally) 'nonsense'.

Flusser's answer to the diagnosis of a rule of cybernetic function circularity was, if a direct quote is permitted, a theory of types:

"One can function in various ways. With personal commitment: One loves the apparatus, as its functions one is working (this is the [...] functionary [...]). In despair: One rotates in a circle within the apparatus, until one withdraws [...]. With a method: One functions within the apparatus, even if you change its functions by internal feedback and interconnection with other devices (this is the technocrat). In protest stance: One abhors the apparatus and tries to destroy it, an attempt that is recuperated by the apparatus and transformed in its functioning (that's the terrorist). Hopeful: One tries to dismantle the apparatus slowly to breach into it, that is, one tries to reduce the quantity of functioning in order to increase the 'quality of life', that automatically becomes a new feature of the apparatus (these are the environmentalists)." (Flusser 1991: 35-36)

The functionary, the despaired, the terrorist, the technocrat, the environmentalist – these are the socio-types of a present (a "broad present" perhaps (Gumbrecht 2014)) in which participation has become virtually impossible. I want to oppose this dark, phenomenological attempt – as I have tried – with another attempt, an experimental-historical one that consists of not thinking of the present of digital cultures in modern terms but with premodern terms.

Let me briefly make the *second* and last argument for this position. Friedrich Kittler, whom I still hold in high regard, coined the well-known phrase that "media determine our situation, which [still and precisely] – in spite or because of it – deserves a description" (Kittler 1997: xxxix). But this determined and very fruitful undertaking has always been characterized by melancholia. This topography of the situation occurs in a moment in which it is almost no longer possible. Or in Kittler's own words:

"The general digitization [...] erases the difference between individual media. [...] a total media link on a digital base will erase the very concept of medium. Instead of

wiring people and technologies, absolute knowledge will run as an endless loop."
(Kittler 1997: 1-2)

It is becoming clearer and clearer how much Kittler's demand for a domination of media technologies is bound to a media historic place. The early
1980s were shaped by home computers, PC and Macintosh, by laser printers, ISDN, and censuses – relating this alleged learning-to-understand "the
digital itself" to very specific technologies. The perception of the digital itself is triggered by the specificity of these historic technologies. And that is
why this theory could not deal with the Internet for example, a fact that was
criticized as early as the late 1990s, only five or six years later. Programming your home computer in assembly language or C does not help much
with understanding the effects of the – also digital – World Wide Web.
Having said that, Kittler himself was not very interested in it. My counter-
proposal (and as a pupil of Kittler I am allowed to make one) takes this diagnosis very seriously. Whereas Kittler required some residual understanding – for example that one should learn computer code – I would rather follow his second and more radical thesis: that understanding has meanwhile
become impossible.

My favorite example is climatology, where researchers themselves no
longer understand or can explain what happens within their incredibly
complex software but still obtain results upon which global actions are oriented. You could extend this model to all areas in which the level of interconnectivity, processing power, and software development have reached a
level of complexity that surpasses understanding or traceability. This is no
longer the 286-processor computer you could program using Assembler
and understand its code. Nevertheless, the code of climate research is not
hidden: as open source software it is free to anyone who wants to read it. In
a sense it is a secret and not a secret and at the same time: it is open to everyone's eyes and is yet incommensurable.

If, as the climate example shows, the political twines around a center of
not-understanding, there can no longer be a modern concept of transparency of knowledge, no participation through "a voice in the matter". This can
also be phrased in a pre-modern manner: computer-simulated scenarios and
strategies of legitimization belong to the pre-modern political register of
sovereignty and thus might hold the properties of a new *science royale*. Data-processing has taken the systematic position that previously belonged to

the wisdom (or caprice) of the sovereign, a position that was protected by a metaphysical limit to knowledge. The sovereignty of data-processing draws another border around something that withdraws itself constitutively because it is 'by nature' a secret; except that it is now technology rather than nature or cosmology.

This used to be called *Arcanum* – in reference to the sovereign rule. And I plead – in line with my pre-modern thesis – for trying to think of digital cultures in the terms of the Arcanum. This is already useful because the pre-modern era was aware of different kinds of secrets with different terms, methods, and rationalities: the *arcana cordis* (secrets of the heart), the *arcana dei* (religious secrets), the *arcana imperii* (secrets of the state) etc.

If you read about current debates on data privacy and personality rights you will instantly see that they are about extremely reduced varieties of the secret; namely, the secret that *can* be told. As soon as we move into this modern category the secret can only be either told or not, revealed or concealed. This is the secret of the idea of the transparency of the so called "civic public", the secret that can be and has to be exposed – and, at the same time, the secret with which it is not clear whether the state should be afraid of its people or vice versa.

The pre-modern on the other hand offers a different kind of secret in the Arcanum, one which has – contrary to other rumors – never entirely vanished from the modern era. This is the un-revealable secret. The un-revealable secret is the center of the *arcana imperii*, it is surrounded by many other small and large secrets that have to be protected, can be revealed, and can be stolen. It is the secret of the decisions and actions of the sovereign that are plainly visible but have a motivation that is not revealed and therefore cannot be discussed. This is precisely why the sovereign is the sovereign. The modern era has moved the location of the un-revealable secret of the sovereign to time. The future is a secret to all of us and one which cannot be revealed. Moreover, it indissolubly connects the un-revealable secret of the future to the idea of participation – the idea that we can shape the open future by participating. If this temporal order indeed becomes problematic, it seems to be an intellectual challenge to think of digital cultures not in categories of transparency and participation but under the banner of fundamental non-transparency and the Arcanum.

Translated from German by Anne Ganzert.

REFERENCES

Agamben, Giorgio (2003): Die kommende Gemeinschaft, Berlin: Merve.

Baxmann, Inge/Beyes, Timon/Pias, Claus (eds.) (2014): Soziale Medien – Neue Massen, Zürich: diaphanes.

Beyes, Timon/Pias, Claus (2014): "Transparenz und Geheimnis." In: Zeitschrift für Kulturwissenschaft 8/2, pp. 111-117.

DeLanda, Manuel (2006): A new Philosophy of Society. Assemblage Theory and Social Complexity, London: Continuum.

Deleuze, Gilles (1994): Difference and Repitition, London: Athlone Press.

Flusser, Vilém (1991): Gesten. Versuch einer Phänomenologie, Düsseldorf: Bollmann.

Geulen, Christian (2010): "Plädoyer für eine Geschichte der Grundbegriffe des 20. Jahrhunderts." In: Zeithistorische Forschungen/Studies in Contemporary History 7, pp. 79-97.

Gumbrecht, Hans Ulrich (2014): Our Broad Present. Time and Contemporary Culture, New York, NY: Columbia University Press.

Hardt, Michael/Negri, Antonio (2002): Empire. Die neue Weltordnung, Frankfurt/Main: Campus.

Habermas, Jürgen (1984): Theory of Communicative Action. Translated by Thomas McCarthy, Boston, MA: Beacon Press.

Hagen, Wolfgang (2003): Gegenwartsvergessenheit. Lazarsfeld – Adorno – Innis – Luhmann, Berlin: Merve.

Kittler, Friedrich (1997): Gramophone, Film, Typewriter, translated by Geoff Winthrop-Young and Michael Wutz, Stanford, CA: Stanford University Press.

Kittler, Friedrich (2004): Unsterbliche: Nachrufe, Erinnerungen, Geistergespräche, München.

Koselleck, Reinhart (1985): Futures Past. On the Semantics of Historical Time, translated by Keith Tribe, Cambridge, MA: MIT Press.

Krischer, André (2010): "Das Problem des Entscheidens in systematischer und historischer Perspektive." In: Idem/Barbara Stollberg-Rilinger (eds.), Herstellung und Darstellung von Entscheidungen. Verfahren, Verwalten und Verhandeln in der Vormoderne, Zeitschrift für Historische Forschung 44, pp. 35-64.

Latour, Bruno (2002), "Gabriel Tarde and the End of the Social." In: Patrick Joyce (ed.), The Social in Question. New Bearings in History and the Social Sciences, London: Routledge.

Latour, Bruno (2010): Das Parlament der Dinge. Für eine politische Ökologie, Frankfurt/Main: Suhrkamp.

Latour, Bruno (2008): "Einleitung." In: Idem, Gabriel Tarde, Monadologie und Soziologie, Frankfurt/Main: Suhrkamp, pp. 7-16.

Nancy, Jean-Luc (2008): The Inoperative Community, Minneapolis, MN: University of Minnesota Press.

Sloterdijk, Peter (2004): Sphären III: Schäume. Plurale Sphärologie, Frankfurt/Main: Suhrkamp.

Sprenger, Florian (2012): Medien des Immediaten. Elektrizität, Telegraphie, McLuhan, Berlin: Kadmos.

Vehlken, Sebastian (2012): Zootechnologien. Eine Mediengeschichte der Schwarmforschung, Zürich: diaphanes.

Wiener, Norbert (1948): "Newtonian and Bergsonian Time." In: Idem, Cybernetics, or: Control and Communication in the Animal and the Machine, Cambridge, MA: MIT Press.

Editors of Play

Scripts of Participation in Co-Creative Media

PABLO ABEND/BENJAMIN BEIL

Video games like *Minecraft*[1], *LittleBigPlanet*[2], *Garry's Mod*[3], or, most recently, *Disney's Infinity*[4] open up action spaces for participatory practices to a wide circle of users. A process of popularizing co-creative practices is taking place, with the potential to alter and even transcend 'classical' forms of participative media culture (cf. Jenkins 1992/2006). These practices are related to and emerged from the "community-based creative design" (Sotamaa 2005: 2) of the larger game modding scene since the games themselves have their roots in editor software that is used to take part in game design and content creation. But whereas numerous sophisticated modding practices require the use of image editing and modelling software and even demand advanced programming skills (modding in the narrow sense), in editor games, which seem to be closer to the early construction sets (e.g. Bill Budge's *Pinball Construction Set* from 1983), modding found its way into the gameplay itself (modding in a broader sense). These playboxes or sandboxes pose new questions regarding the player's motivation(s) and the appeal of a gameplay that consists of building a game world rather than

---

1   Game Developer/Publisher: Mojang 2011.
2   Game Developer: Media Molecule; Publisher: Sony Computer Entertainment 2008.
3   Game Developer: Facepunch Studios; Publisher: Valve Corporation 2004.
4   Game Developer: Avalance Studio; Publisher Microsoft Studios 2013.

playing within it. Editor games or 'co-creative open worlds' confront gamers and researchers with a new level of uncertainty and contingency.

In this chapter, we want to investigate these issues not only in theoretical terms but also within a case study of the games *Minecraft* and *LittleBigPlanet*. After a short overview of the characteristic features of both games, we want to discuss some methodological issues before introducing an ethnographically informed approach to study editor games.

1 LEGO VS. PLAYMOBIL

Computer games can be described as assemblages (cf. Taylor 2009) which, to use a term from Science and Technology studies, provide different "scripts" (cf. Akrich 1992) that set the scene for user practices and encounter these practices in the course of play. All well as the game's set of rules, these scripts include the game world's possibilities and restrictions and the degree of freedom provided to the users by the overall gameplay. To describe the scripts used in the editor games *Minecraft* and *LittleBigPlanet*, we want to draw an analogy between the scripts of these two games and the specifics of the 'philosophies of toys' like *LEGO* and *Playmobil*.

Minecraft can be characterized as an open-world *LEGO* building set in which the players move through blocky 3D landscapes that are procedurally generated at the start of every new game. These blocks represent different materials which the player has to 'mine' in order to 'craft' items. *Minecraft* offers two different game modes: the *creative mode*, which focuses on the creation of complex structures by providing the player with an unlimited amount of blocks (resources), and the *survival mode*, which compels the player to acquire and manage resources with the purpose of building a shelter to protect him/herself from the monsters that populate the game world at night. But, even the latter, more 'classical' gameplay mode, relies strongly on editing mechanics.

At first sight, *Minecraft* may almost look like an alternative draft to current trends in the gaming industry, since the 'pixelated' game world appears dated in contrast to the almost photorealistic graphics of the latest games. The action takes place in a sparse, empty, and relatively inanimate sandbox that adjusts its size according to the user's space of action. Even the open, rather rudimentary gaming mechanic seems odd in its 'dramaturgy' when compared to the narratively complex representatives of other gaming genres: *"Minecraft* never tells the players what to do. They do not have a story objective, whether short-term or long term [sic!]. How come *Minecraft* is not a mere level editor?" (Léja-Six 2012) The action in *Minecraft* is neither structured through an obvious gameplay nor prescribed through narrative paths. Rules exist, but are unclear, and the player has to uncover them through experimentation, learn them through observation, or acquire them by reading information pages (like Wikis). If nothing else, it is this 'unmarkedness' that poses new questions for game studies regarding the player's motivation and action.

In *LittleBigPlanet*, the second game we want to analyze, the scripts of interaction must be problematized differently since they span a different frame around the players' possibilities for action. *LittleBigPlanet*, released for Playstation 3 in 2008, is one of the most prominent examples of the growing impact of user-generated content on the game market, especially in the console domain. The story mode in *LittleBigPlanet* can take from six to eight hours of gameplay and can be played by up to four players simultaneously. Nonetheless, the level editor is advertised as the central feature of the game, offering a unique and ample array of functionalities – at least for console game standards. Users can publish their creations on the Playstation Network through an easy-to-use sharing system, making them available to all members of the *LittleBigPlanet* community. On the one hand, the meticulously organized editor structure provided by the developer appears to contradict the principle of "bottom-up modularization by users" (Jeppesen 2004: 10). On the other hand, Media Molecule's system adopts many characteristic aspects of web communities since it implements a sophisticated database system which is organized through comment sections and Web 2.0 tag clouds.[5]

---

5   In fact, one can include *LittleBigPlanet* in the wider category of digital mashups since it lets players or users seamlessly combine popular cultural objects onto one single surface.

2   EDITOR GAMES AND THE SCRIPTS OF PARTICIPATION

Consumer co-creative design has significantly opened up to the mainstream market through games like *Minecraft* and *LittleBigPlanet*. Nevertheless, the question remains as to which 'scripts of participation' – using Madeleine Akrich's concept (1992) – are inscribed in these different forms of editor games. An analytical comparison between implicit participation, within the scripts of the software, and explicit participation practices, as suggested by Mirko Tobias Schäfer (2011), seems promising as a means to clarify the often conflicting nature of participative media cultures. While implicit participation is part of an underlying design principle, for example the sharing of links or the semantic annotation of contents, and is not bound to the deliberate decision to contribute, explicit participation depends on motivational factors and requires further commitment from the subject, for example active participation in a modding community.

In analyzing *LittleBigPlanet*'s editor, Christian Trapp argues:

"Though, at first glance, *LittleBigPlanet*'s editor seems to exhibit a strong 'modding character' through its in-game integration, on a second look, the level editor performs as a limited feature that only allows for a restricted and controlled degree of modification. The player essentially 'plays' the game as he designs levels within the boundaries of the given scope of action." (Trapp 2011: 133)

This difference between the interface analysis and the praxeological perspective constitutes a demand for a stronger consideration of the tools, since they inscribe the degrees of freedom in the gameplay, and the actual practices, since they show how the scripts are followed, counteracted, or even subverted, during the research of editor games. To date, research on the (cultural) history of co-creative games is scarce, and, at best, it merely plays a role in the footnotes of texts on modding communities (cf. Barton/Loguidice 2009). Consequently, discussing mods implies the existence of editing tools, but then again, usually just the end-products stand in the centre of the debate, i.e. finished mods, instead of their development process. These "result-oriented consideration[s]" (Gethmann/Hauser 2009: 9) misjudge the actuator status – the *agency* – of modding tools and their importance in design and editing processes. Currently, the 'popularization' of modding cultures through the use of level editors generates novel forms of participatory media cultures.

3 Research Design

Espen Aarseth argues that playing games is the only effective method to conduct research in Game Studies. He highly recommends that researchers should play to gain first-hand experience of the material. However, Aarseth also takes into account the use of paratexts, additional materials like manuals, reviews, and, more recently, *Let's Play* videos.[6] In addition, he briefly mentions "observing others play" (Aarseth 2003: 6) as a resource for conducting research. Since the characteristics of editor games undermine the claim of an implicit player – which Aarseth takes for granted in his writings – who is inscribed into the fabric of every game and becomes visible as the script, we believe that it is not sufficient to intrinsically analyze these games. Since there are many possibilities to play these games, the scripts in editor games are not strictly defined but are subject to negotiation processes between the player and the game time after time.

To deal with this uncertainty in editor games we wanted to heed Aarseths advice and observe other people play. Therefore, we conducted a focus group analysis (Summer Institute Cologne 2013) with nine participants whom we split in two groups: one played *Minecraft* and the other *LittleBigPlanet*. During the course of one workshop day, the two groups used five computers and one Playstation console. There were Students and PhD candidates in media and theater studies, philosophy, and history.

In order to get comparable results – in this case comparable process routines – we gave each team an objective. The task included, but was not limited to, building a castle. We specified the task and narrowed it down to Castle Wahn, a late baroque style, former moated castle. The castle was the

---

6   *Let's Play* videos have become a popular form of fan culture. It involves the presentation and commentating of playing video games usually done through screen and audio capturing. The finished videos are frequently shared online on video platforms. As distinguished from walkthrough videos, *Let's Plays* usually foreground the individual experience of playing.

venue where the workshop took place, and, as such, it was both the gaming location and the desired outcome of play. We also limited the games modes used, prescribing the creative mode in *Minecraft* and the level editor in *LittleBigPlanet*.

We conducted the experimental case study with the two focus groups of players and one observer group. There were four people in the *LittleBigPlanet* group and five in the *Minecraft* group, while the observer group consisted of four people who were not playing at all. The uneven distribution in the groups did not constitute an obstacle since the *LittleBigPlanet* group used one console with two controllers, and the *Minecraft* group had one computer per player. These computers were connected by a Local Area Network so that the *Minecraft* players could collaborate on one project.

The observation group used various documentation techniques: camera recordings (audio/video), to document the off-screen action; audio recordings, to conduct interviews and to document the discussions within the respective groups; and screen capturing technology, to document on-screen activities. In addition to the recording devices, the observer group also took notes while watching the others play.

There was an overall methodological interest in the comparison between the participatory structure inscribed into the aesthetics of the game and the actual participation acted out by the participants in situ. Furthermore, there were concrete research questions we wanted to direct towards the collected data. The most general question was in which way people approach these 'co-creative open world games'. Where are the differences in the unmarked game of *Minecraft* compared to the rather prescribed world of *LittleBigPlanet*? Beyond that, what pre-sets, rules, and modes of production will be agreed upon in the respective groups? For example, will there be group dynamics or individual efforts to find a solution to overcome the unmarkedness of the interfaces?

4 FINDINGS AND CONCLUSION

In this chapter, we can only demonstrate a small selection of the results of our focus group analysis. We will concentrate on certain level design functionalities of *LittleBigPlanet* and *Minecraft* as well as on the different 'labor division' strategies of the two groups.

4.1 Design Strategies

As stated above, *LittleBigPlanet* and *Minecraft* offer different scripts for participation. *LittleBigPlanet* has a platformer aesthetics – a gameplay mechanic that is also inherited in the editor mode of the game. Even though the interface seems to be intuitive, handling the avatars that have to be used to build structures and to assign textures proved difficult. This is largely due to the handling of the menus using a controller that involves extensive switching through all the various items, colors, and textures via left/right/up/down operations and by rotating the control stick on the gamepad. In order to learn all the different operations, the game urges users to try out all the functionalities within tutorials, which seemed helpful at first but quickly became cumbersome by delaying the time when the actual building process could begin. Since the editor mode in *LittleBigPlanet* was designed as a level editor for the game, there is an implicit appeal to build a playable construction. For example, because structures need to be climbable, distinct elements have to be joined by staircases and bridges. Another aspect inscribed into the platformer editor is that the temporal structure is bound to causality and therefore screen space expands in a linear manner. The script urges builders to work from left to right. This is even reflected in the delete function. Instead of the possibility to delete certain isolated objects and leave the rest intact, one has to rewind (and by this means going back in time), revoking the last steps. This led to a constant movement from left to right and when the players decided to start over and build a new structure, they moved to the right and opened up a new empty space.

In *Minecraft's* creative mode there is no tutorial guidance at all and only a few traces of the survival mode remain in the editor. The players are 'spawned' in an open and empty game space, ready to go in all directions. The handling of *Minecraft* seemed to pose fewer problems to the participants of the study. The menus in the building mode are clearly structured and compartmentalized. Additionally, making choices with the help of the mouse proved much easier as compared to the controller.

The main distinctions of the scripts lay in the player's degrees of freedom, the underlying physics, and the overall orientation of the game world. *LittleBigPlanet* relies on platformer mechanisms, which makes handling in the editor mode much harder at first. Users who want to 'build' something are more concerned with the mechanics of the avatar – who is subject to artificial gravitational forces – and the game space, than with the translation and transformation of their ideas onto the screen and into the game world. The *Minecraft* avatars appear easier to handle, the setting is much 'calmer' – there is no background voice giving instructions – and the physics are much more discreet.

4.2 Co-operation and Division of Labor

In *Minecraft*, players started to cooperate right from the beginning. At first, they encountered several technical issues, like getting the game to work on every computer and setting up the LAN. When the actual building process started, a clear division of labor took place after a short period of time. A skilled player took command and oversaw the development without destroying the group effort to crowd-source design solutions and to work out the ideal way to transform the castle into a digital model. The analytical approach continued taking shape till the end of the experiment despite some attempts at counter-gaming where one participant tried to counteract the overall constructively minded approach of the rest of the group by experimenting with TNT and trying to destroy what the others had built. For the rest, the modus operandi was intriguing: The cooperation on the *Minecraft* project clearly resembled team work in a professional environment.

With *LittleBigPlanet* the circumstances were different. Given that the players had to work on the same screen, it was difficult to distribute tasks. Players were creating and working at the same time and were frequently distracted by their own actions. In this way it is hard to establish an overview of the overall structure. The participative environment of the game simply did not afford it (Gibson 1977; 1979; Gaver 1991).

In *Minecraft*, the distributions of the group's efforts led to a situation where playing was coordinated towards efficiency. There was an accepted and strictly adhered division of labor among the *Minecraft* builders and every member of the group had a segment to work on, e.g. details of the façade, the roof, or the interior of the castle.

While *LittleBigPlanet* contains many elements that represent known and often popular artefacts, *Minecraft* only offers blocks with different textures and functions, like a box of *LEGO*. This does not mean that there is a higher degree of participation and creativity within *Minecraft*. Instead, it shows that there are different premises concerning the praxeological range of participation and creativity in editor games and perhaps in the wider context of digital media. While *Minecraft* can be described as a digital remediation (Bolter/Grusin 2000) of analogue *LEGO*, the praxeological dimension is to use abstract and reduced building blocks to create structures that resemble their template's dimensions and on-site measurement. *Little-BigPlanet* seems to resemble a rather loose combination of different elements that are more or less fully formed. While the creative mode of *Minecraft* resembles playing with toy building blocks or *LEGO*, the editor mode in *LittleBigPlanet* relies on the paradigm of compilation, remixing, and mashing-up to create collage-like surfaces associated with the content sharing platforms of the so called Web 2.0. Since the scripts of *LittleBigPlanet* do not directly afford the reversal of moves, the players have to leave behind their existing structures and move on to an empty space in the game world to continue building – this shows a cumulative character of the game. It is about constantly adding things, again a similarity to participative practices in the Web 2.0, where people keep on adding content and filling in blank spaces rather than overwriting or deleting old or even outdated contributions.

5 OUTLOOK

Within the praxeological comparison of two editor games, our on- and off-screen captures and direct observation of player interaction indicated great differences in the scripts of participation. *Minecraft* became apparent as a multi-tool, highly adoptable, and open for social negotiation processes. This was supported by the appearance of the building blocks whose design left plenty of room for the ascription of specific roles in the overall construction. At large, a cooperative script was provided by the technical structure since the game affords cooperation in an open source like manner where everybody can open up a server, which functions as a distributed co-working space, and freely share content by distributing creations via a download link. Related to this highly cooperative structure, the analysis of the produced data through a praxeological perspective also revealed a strong tendency of the *Minecraft* group towards a social organization based on the division of labor within the setting of the experiment. We traced this intermingling of play and labor back to the script that is hidden in the organization of the game space. It is the grid-like structure and the blocky elements, which encourage players to take a very analytical approach using the blocks as the basis for a conversion table, to adjust and translate the 'real' world to the grid (cf. Gehmann/Reiche 2014).

In contrast, *LittleBigPlanet* is a platform technology for playful level design rather than a tool of construction. The menus, the overall setting, and the fully formed shapes do not primarily allow building things from scratch but rather combining and mashing-up existing cultural objects. Additionally, the technical pre-sets seem to be an obstacle for working on the same project simultaneously since the automatic navigation of the virtual camera makes it hard to keep track of both avatars at once. The editor mode prescribes the design and construction of a linear structure in the form of a platformer game, the depth on the z-axis is limited, and it is not possible to directly delete particular elements. Therefore, the praxeological perspective reveals a rather accumulative practice where things are constantly added while covering empty game space from left to right – just like on a weblog or on the Facebook timeline where nothing ever gets deleted but new things are constantly being added. The technical structure of *LittleBigPlanet* also supports sharing, but, in contrast to *Minecraft,* only via the central agency of the publisher, who in turn benefits from co-creative action since user-generated levels extend the lifecycle of the game.

This essay is a fraction of a work in progress. There are as yet no definite answers to the overall question "What is participation?" But research into the scripts and practices of editor games offers many starting points. A praxeological approach that included affordances – the functionally relevant and invariable properties in the scripts of the artefact in question in combination with the anticipated ascriptions (Gibson 1979: 138) of the media users in question – and took actual user implementation into account proved valuable in beginning to define the terrain of contemporary participatory culture.

By including affordances and considering user participation, this study offers a starting point from which to approach contemporary participatory culture.

REFERENCES

Akrich, Madeleine (1992): "The De-Scription of Technical Objects." In: Wiebe E. Bijker/John Law (eds.), Shaping Technology/Building Society. Studies in Sociotechnical Change, Cambridge, MA: MIT Press, pp. 205-224.

Aarseth, Espen (2003): "Playing Research: Methodological Approaches to Game Analysis." In: Digital Arts & Culture 2003, pp. 1-7.

Barton, Matt/Loguidice, Bill (2009): "The History of the Pinball Construction Set. Launching Millions of Creative Possibilities", http://www.gamasutra.com/view/feature/3923/the_history_of_the_pinball_.php (August 14, 2015).

Bolter, Jay/Grusin, Richard (2000): Remediation. Understanding New Media, Cambridge, MA: MIT Press.

Gaver, William W. (1991): "Technology affordances", in: Scott Robertson/Gary Olson/Judith Olson (eds.), Proceedings of the SIGCHI Conference on Human Factors in Computing Systems. Reaching Through Technology, New Orleans, LA, pp. 79-84.

Gehmann, Ulrich/Reiche, Martin (2014): "The World as Grid." In: Ulrich Gehmann/Martin Reiche (eds.), Real Virtuality. About the Destruction and Multiplication of World. Bielefeld: transcript, pp. 443-451.

Gethmann, Daniel/Hauser, Susanne (2009): "Einleitung." In: Daniel Gethmann/Susanne Hauser (eds.), Kulturtechnik Entwerfen, Bielefeld: transcript, pp. 9-15.

Gibson, James J. (1977): "The Theory of Affordances." In: Robert Shaw/John Bransford (eds.), Perceiving, Acting, and Knowing: Toward an Ecological Psychology, Hillsdale, NJ: Lawrence Erlbaum, pp. 67-82.

Gibson, James J. (1979): The Ecological Approach to Visual Perception, Boston, MA: Houghton Mifflin.

Jenkins, Henry (1992): Textual Poachers. Television Fans & Participatory Culture, New York: Routledge.

Jenkins, Henry (2006): Fans, Bloggers, and Gamers: Exploring Participatory Culture, New York, NY: New York Univ. Press.

Jeppesen, Lars Bo (2004): "Profiting from Innovative User Communities. How Firms Organize the Production of User Modifications in the Computer Games Industry", http://openarchive.cbs.dk/bitstream/handle/10398/7227/wp%202004-03_main%20doc.pdf (August 14, 2015).

Léja-Six, Eddy (2012): "How Can Gameplay Allow Players to Get Creative?", http://www.gamasutra.com/view/feature/181915/how_can_game play_allow_players_to_.php (August 14, 2015).

Schäfer, Mirko Tobias (2011): Bastard Culture! How User Participation Transforms Cultural Production, Amsterdam: Amsterdam University Press.

Sotamaa, Olli (2003): "Computer Game Modding, Intermediality and Participatory Culture", http://www.yorku.ca/caitlin/futurecinemas/course pack2009/Sotamaa_modding.pdf (August 14, 2015).

Summer Institute Cologne (2013): "[Techniques of Imagination] New Perspectives in the Historiography of Art, Media Culture, and Theatre", http://sic.phil-fak.uni-koeln.de/19843.html (August 14, 2015).

Taylor, T.L. (2009): "The Assemblage of Play." In: Games and Culture 4/4, pp. 331-339.

Trapp, Christian (2011): "Aktant – Spieler." In: Benjamin Beil/Thomas Hensel (eds.), Game Laboratory Studies, Siegen: universi, pp. 131-134.

Multimodal Crowd Sensing

Sebastian Vehlken

Introduction

The behavior of human crowds has always been compared to the behavior of animal collectives, most notably resulting in the popular denouncements of 'the mass' in the writings of mass psychology at the end of the 19th century. Participation in such collectives – according to the unanimous opinion of authors like Gabriel de Tarde (1896), Gustave LeBon (1901), and Scipio Sighele (1901) – turned well-behaved and conscious individuals into 'mobsters' who reacted irrationally, unconsciously, or purely instinctively and were devoid of everything that would characterize a self-determined subject. Adopting insights taken from contemporary natural history, the advocates of mass psychology laid the ground for at least half a century of a predominantly socio-psychological research practice in mass behavior (McPhail 1991; Sime 1995).

Although, affected by the insufficient methods of experiment-based socio-psychological studies in mass behavior, the two last decades have seen a boom in computer simulations of collective dynamics, whose mostly agent-based models (ABM) stem from a different techno-scientific background: From the mid-1990s onwards, the field of Computational Swarm Intelligence not only amalgamated biological findings on the functional (self-) organization of animal collectives like flocks, swarms and schools with novel programming techniques and modes of parallel computing (Engelbrecht 2005). It also spawned a growing discourse in the form of such expressions as 'smart majorities' (Fisher 2010; Miller 2010), 'swarming in the battlefield' (Arquila/Ronfeldt 2000), 'the wisdom of crowds'

(Surowiecki 2004), and simply 'multitude' (Hardt/Negri 2004). Swarms have become a metaphor for the coordination processes of an engineered present, a present in which flexible adaptation to ever-changing conditions can be associated with the alleged potential for freedom inherent in 'autonomous individuals'. With the help of ever more dynamic forms of interconnectedness, as the swarm metaphor suggests, we are able to use an instantaneous infrastructure of decision-making to our own advantage. To achieve certain goals, it is thought, we are thereby able to coordinate temporarily with those of the same mind. This ephemeral and apparently 'grass-roots democratic' conception of collectivity has promised to uncouple political, economic and social behavior from the structures of entrenched systems and social organizations such as nations, political parties and labor unions as well as turning mobs and crowds into 'smart mobs' (Rheingold 2002). Over the last fifteen years, it seems swarming has established itself both technologically and socially as a means of collaboration superior to traditional forms of collective organization. And this discourse, by reconceptualizing notions of participation (cf. Bippus/Ochsner/Otto, in this book; Evert et al. 2012), initiated distinctions between collectivity and connectivity (Thacker 2004; Baxmann/Beyes/Pias 2014) as well as cooperation (Schüttpelz/Gießmann 2014) in media studies and sociology (Stäheli 2012; Wiedemann 2015).

This article will concentrate on a complementary development in computational swarm intelligence: In recent years, ABM have been employed to investigate, quantify and 'manage' crowd behavior. Crowd simulations are epistemic tools that conceptualize mass behavior as mathematically and physically specifiable aggregated motion of particles or autonomous individuals in time and space. ABM thus operationalize the relation between quantified, non-linear, locally specified agent behaviors and the emergent qualities of the crowd on a global level. In contrast to the emotional (Le Bon) and affective (de Tarde) crowds of mass psychology, these computer simulations replace psychological *affects* and emotions with physical *effects* and motions (Helbing/Johansson 2009). They conceptually and media-technically turn human masses and crowds from collectives into mere quantifiable 'connectives' (Wiedemann 2015). This computational operationalization of crowd dynamics has recently been elevated to a new level: Media technologies of Multimodal Crowd Sensing make use of data feeds from multiple devices in a crowd. These on the one hand improve current ABM with 'empirical' on-site data. But on the other, by feeding back movement data directly to individuals in the crowd in real time, such applications irrevocably transform its traditional perception: The uncontrollable entity with unpredictable and animalistic behavior transmogrifies into a 'self-reflective', techno-biological collective that optimizes its global movements via a distributed, individualized communication infrastructure. Human crowds turn into context-sensitive, techno-social sensor networks that regulate themselves, but also provide real-time information about environmental conditions and infrastructures.

In the following, my article first presents a concept from biological swarm studies termed "Sensory Integration Systems" (Schilt/Norris 1997) as a conceptual background for actual multimodal crowd sensing applications. The second part briefly discusses the replacement of mass-psychological approaches by crowd capturing and agent-based crowd simulation techniques. Whilst these connectives still refer to the management and 'control' of crowds, the third part, exemplified by some leading-edge multimodal crowd sensing applications, depicts the second conceptual turn regarding crowds and masses, a shift into 'self-reflective' connectives. Whilst this turns traditional notions of the mass upside down, the incorporated modes of participation certainly raise novel governmental and privacy issues, for instance if methods of *participatory sensing* contrast with *opportunistic sensing* or if novel media technologies not only pose the problem of *how to take part* in their development or usage but also *take the user as a part* (and eventually even *take him apart*) in the construction of distributed sensor networks.

1 SENSORY INTEGRATION SYSTEMS

Around 1900, thoughts on the 'animalistic behavior' of crowds coincided with a contemporary notion of swarming characterized by either chaos and disturbance or mystical coordination, such as meta-physical thought-transference (Selous 1931). As an effect of the more recent *zoo-technological* transformation of biological swarm studies (Vehlken 2012), both human and animal collectives are viewed differently, connected not only via a merely metaphorical but also a media-technological understanding of their respective dynamics. It thus seems rather expectable that a concept taken from a biological paper provides compelling insights into the constituents of crowd control and crowd sensing applications.

In 1997, biologists Carl R. Schilt and Kenneth S. Norris proposed a novel bio-physical concept for animal collectives, more precisely for fish schools: Sensory Integration Systems (SIS). In order to organize themselves collectively, members of a swarm constantly process information on the dynamically changing environmental conditions and quickly distribute relevant information, including to distant members with no direct access to the environmental condition. Only this guarantees an adequate collective response. For instance, although only the individuals on one edge of the swarm can detect the approach of a single predator, this information has to be distributed further into the swarm to initiate a collective escape maneuver:

"The fundamental tenets of sensory integration systems are: 1. transduction of environmental stimuli external to the group via the sensory capacities of many individuals; 2. propagation of resulting social signals across the group, possibly with attenuation or amplification or other signal conditioning; 3. coordinated group response based on a summation of these social signals from various sources in various directions *at any moment*." (Schilt/Norris 1997: 229)

As an "interacting array of sensors and effectors" (ibid: 228), swarms exhibit the capacity to integrate and process a far greater amount of information compared to a single individual or small group. They generate access to a distributed set of parallel processed environmental information from all around the collective.

Furthermore, Schilt and Norris depict SIS as dynamic network systems of different senses whose incoming information is summed up or filtered in the process of distribution into the collective. In fish, for example, the lateral organ complements vision with information about hydrodynamic conditions. This information is distributed into the collective by transferring "social signals" (ibid: 229) to nearby individuals – that is, by propagating certain bodily movements like direction or speed changes or flashes that emerge from sunlight reflections on the silvery lower sides of the bodies of certain species of schooling fish. These so-called "waves of propagation" (Radakov 1973: 82) spread out like physical waves, like on a water surface, signaling direction changes to more distant parts of the school:

"In sensory integration systems, individuals receive, process, and respond to stimuli from the environment. Their responses may influence (change) other near neighbors, which may in turn influence still others. The signal thereby generated may die out or may, by propagation and summation, change the greater group's behavior. Group members may also generate social signals (i.e. internally derived) that propagate through the group. We use the word 'integration' in the sense of combining or blinding into a unified response. The functional result of such a process is that the individuals in the group can respond in a coordinated manner to stimuli to which most of them have no direct access." (Schilt/Norris 1997: 229)

The time-spatial self-organization of fish schools relies on a "rhythmic cadence of signals, [...] related to locomotory movements, that keep the mutual monitoring system engaged and operating" (ibid: 242). Broken down to their basic functionality and their underlying chains of co-operation and implemented as a *zoo-technology* (Vehlken 2012), such a form of swarm intelligence displays a chiasm where information produces the formation of the collective, which at the same time produces novel information through its formation. This coupling of formation and information can be utilized to co-ordinate multimodal processes in a variety of fields, such as coordinating traffic flows, solving logistics problems or optimizing human crowd behavior using computer simulation.

2 CROWD CAPTURING AND AGENT-BASED SIMULATION

Humans are not fish – except in some particular cases: When moving in large crowds, the possible behavior of humans can also be described according to a set of rather simple rules of movement (Helbing/Johannson 2009). In the case of mass panic and crowd disasters, the possible modes and (consensus-free) chains of co-operation (Schüttpelz/Gießmann 2014) are also reduced and restricted to a rather small set of basic vectors and (verbal and behavioral) interactional cues between nearby individuals immediately reacting to environmental stimuli, mostly without the time for thorough reflection and rational contemplation of the situation.

This setting also posed insurmountable impediments for the experimental cultures of socio-psychology which entailed the early writings of mass psychology and tried to find scientifically solid principles of human crowd behavior. But, as Dirk Helbing and Anders Johansson write in a seminal article (2012: 6484), "despite of the frequent reports in the media and many published investigations of crowd disasters, a quantitative under-standing of the observed phenomena [...] was lacking for a long time." However, the collective dynamics of large crowds and agglomerates has been studied using novel techniques such as computer simulations since the mid-1990s. These approaches aimed at complementing socio-psychological findings with computer models that would provide the means to define and predict specific parameters of crowd dynamics and disasters (Vehlken 2014). In the so-called Agent-based Computer Simulations or ABM, agents can act as individual or group decision makers. Individual agents can be de-scribed by a variety of different and differing *agent attributes* and *agent methods*. The former define the internal dispositions of an agent, the latter determine the capabilities of an agent to interact with others and the environ-ment (Macal/North 2006).

ABM operate in a highly distributed fashion, and therefore epistemical-ly generate collective behavior in crowds as an accumulation of intrinsic individualized influence factors such as agent velocities, collision proba-bilities, acceleration or pressure forces, or simulated perceptual constraints. These studies continue – under the conditions of advanced object-oriented software models – in the movement away from vague concepts and notions such as *asocial* or *irrational*. They convey a regulatory approach that much more neutrally deals with something which now is rather baptized "non-adaptive behavior" (Helbing/Farkas/Viczek 2000; Mintz 1951). ABM coa-lesce formerly separated areas of psychological behavioral studies and mechanistic modeling approaches and couple earlier mechanistic references with bio-physical groundings of collective behavior. As an effect, they clar-ify the relations between certain spatial environments and realistic human crowd behavior, insofar as also the environments can now be very neutrally conceptualized as "an information system through which people move" (Sime 1995: 10). Hence, they enable a quantitative account of mass panic which shows novel qualities, for instance emerging pressure waves in the crowd which precede crowd disasters as typical patterns.

Some groundbreaking work in ABM derives from the simulation of bio-logical systems such as swarms, flocks and herds, which show how com-plex behavior on a collective scale can emerge even from a set of very few and simple decision and behavior rules in each individual (Reeves 1983; Reynolds 1987). Shao and Terzepoulos (2007), Magnenant-Thalmann and Thalmann (2004), and Helbing (1994), for instance, started to model human crowds and equipped their agents with ever more detailed *artificial senses* and biophysical control. Some models use agents with an ability to learn from previous experiences and memorize information by way of evolutionary or genetic algorithms; others are pre-programmed with certain preferred *cultural determinants* or *social forces* (Helbing/Johansson 2009: 6478), for example with conventions on how to avoid other pedestrians or to choose a certain side when walking along a corridor (ibid: 6487-6489). Instead of assigning instances like a *group mind* or *collective consciousness* to human crowds, these computer-based simulation studies seek to develop certain typical global patterns as an effect of various local and individual movements and movement decisions. These dynamics only emerge synthetically in the runtime of their simulation models and are not observable by real-life experimentation or by sheer mathematical-analytical approaches.

As an outcome, a large enough number of such *lifelike autonomous agents*, put together in a virtual spatial environment, would show a collective behavior similar to real life in specific situations. And this holds true especially for evacuation scenarios with high densities, where human behavior is much easier to model and to predict due to environmental and perceptional constraints. Modulating the parameters identifies relevant factors, which can then be tuned by experimenting with the simulation model.

As an effect, human crowd behavior can no longer be described as a degeneration of men into animals. Rather, the computational abstraction of biological movement rules enables an operative and quantitative description of crowd dynamics in humans.

Over the last decade researchers have applied newly developed algorithms that can simultaneously handle thousands, tens of thousands or even more 'lifelike' agents to *calculate disasters* using ABM. More specifically, they seek to calculate survival strategies and prevent real life disasters by running disastrous crowd scenarios in their computer simulations. Such simulations involve the behavior of pedestrians in various spatial environments and with differing velocities and grades of density. Subsequently, one can, for instance, identify feasible architectural interventions to improve the evacuation speed of a certain building. These simulations can guide the modelers to counter-intuitive solutions, such as placing a column directly in front of an exit substantially increases evacuation speed. The situations can be tested under different environmental conditions, for example by adding smoke or fires, further constraining the orientation of the agents. Moreover, in combination with advanced methods of *crowd capturing*, simulations can help event organizers and emergency response personnel to detect emerging, potentially critical crowd situations at an early stage. This technique involves inserting live feedback data, generated by the automated analysis of digital video images of mass phenomena, into the ABM. Once typical patterns (for example, so-called *movement waves*, structurally comparable to the abovementioned *waves of agitation* in fish schools) indicating catastrophic outcomes at a later stage are identified, various countermeasures can be tested in the computer model to identify the optimal reaction strategy. This simulation software can then be seamlessly coupled with video-based Crowd Capturing technology to model future, real-life crowd events.

3 SELF-REFLEXIVE CROWDS AND HOT-WIRED PETTY-BOURGEOISIES

Although the combination of "virtual" Crowd Simulations and "real-world" Crowd Capturing by CCTV analysis provides researchers and managers of mass events with first steps towards a real-time interaction for dealing with crowd dynamics, even more refined systems are under way. These generate dynamic visualizations of crowd dynamics by using embedded technologies. One example is a project by the German Research Centre for Artificial Intelligence (Wirz et al. 2012) that creates pedestrian-behavior models by inferring and visualizing crowd conditions from pedestrians' GPS location traces. The system was tested in the field in 2011 and applied during the 2012 London Olympic Games. It is able to infer and visualize crowd density, turbulence, velocity and pressure in real-time by calculating data from a feed of location updates (Pluta 2012). These data derive from a mobile phone app that the researchers distributed among a certain number of ticket holders in advance of the event. On the one hand this program supplied the users with event-related information, on the other hand, it periodically logged the device's location, orientation and movement speed measured using GPS and the built-in gyroscope and sent the data to the model. The system allegedly helped organizers assess occurring crowd conditions and locate critical situations faster than traditional video-based methods (Wirz et al. 2012). However, one must still question the applicability of the proposed feedback loop, as most people equipped with the crowd sensing app would be unlikely to read the (individualized) directives appearing on their smartphones in case of panic.

The emerging field of Mobile Crowd Sensing (Ganti et al. 2011), or Multimodal Crowd Sensing (Roitman et al. 2012), employs the multiple sensory capacities of today's smartphones for a variety of personal, group and community-scale sensing applications. Such programs collectively share data and extract information to measure and map phenomena of personal (for instance, relating to the discourse of the Quantified Self) and common interest. An overview paper by a team from the IBM Research Center distinguishes between three areas: First, environmental data like air pollution. Second, infrastructural data like traffic congestion, road conditions or honking levels on city streets – the latter app, as it seems, is very popular in India. And third, data of social processes, like the abovementioned crowd management or healthcare or sports activities (Ganti et al. 2011). All of these apps tend to be used in contexts with scarce resources and high population density, such as in urban spaces; therefore, not only do they contribute to a more sustainable use of resources, but they also allude to an overall logic of optimization lingering behind the apps' capacitive surfaces.

The extent of involvement in crowd sensing can be discriminated between two principles: *participatory sensing* (Burke et al. 2006) and *opportunistic sensing* (Lane et al. 2010). The former requires the active involvement of individuals to contribute sensory data related to a large-scale phenomenon (like taking photographs, giving context information). This brings 'human sensory capacities' into play, which help applications to collect higher-quality or semantically complex data that would otherwise require sophisticated hard- and software, e.g. for pattern recognition. Such 'sousveillance' information can also be indirectly harvested from aggregates of social network feeds like Twitter. However, as Boulos et al. (2010) state, the "variable amounts of 'noise', misinformation and bias [...] usually require some advanced forms of filtering and verification by both machine-based algorithms and human experts before becoming reliable enough for use in decision-making." And as the user commitment will be negotiated against, for example, privacy concerns, it is often based on forms of incentive structures that persuade people to involve themselves (Lane et al. 2010: 144).

Opportunistic sensing, on the other hand, is more autonomous, and user involvement is reduced to a minimum (e.g. continuous location sampling), adding technical sensory capacities to the network. But this also requires that a critical number of users be persuaded to contribute their movement data, for instance by a guaranteed process of anonymization.

Moreover, as a group from Dartmouth College states, other problems emerge, like the device's context problem. For example, a city noise mapping app is designed to take a sound sample for a city noise, but is only capable of doing so if the phone is out of the user's bag or pocket. This can be solved by the participation of other phone sensors in the process: The accelerometer or the light sensors can determine whether the phone is in the open (Lane et al. 2010: 146-147).

Another main issue with multimodal sensing, according to the IBM researchers, consists of the wide variety of mobile devices and forms of data that have to be integrated to generate useful information. The type of sensory data which the devices produce and the quality of data in terms of accuracy, latency and confidence can be subject to constant change due to the device's mobility, variations in energy levels and communication channels, and owners' preferences (Ganti et al. 2011: 36-37). In order to enable the integration of various raw data, these have to be locally pre-processed on the mobile device, which at the same time helps to avoid network flooding by compressing the data (ibid: 35-36).

Consequently, all these data can be collected in data centers and then put out as visualized dynamics on interactive (heat) maps (Boulos et al. 2011: 22). Such information environments can thereby deal with a variety of different data and dynamics as well as integrate modelling, simulation and sensing applications with the help of visual displays to support actions, assessments and decision-making by experts (Goodchild 2007). Or, they can simply use one special type of sensory data, as in a Copenhagen CO_2- measurement example. In this case, a mobile network of only ten bicycle messengers, equipped with air quality sensors, was able to produce far more detailed data about the dynamics of CO_2 pollution and its dependency on not only traffic congestion but also on humidity, temperature and wind direction than a classical system comprising a larger number of fixed physical sensors (Boulos 2011: 15-17). Similar examples are a variety of geolo-cation-aware social health networks for sickness forecasting like *Sick-weather* (see URL: http://sickweather.com) or a crowdsourced, real-time radiation map developed after the Fukushima disaster (Saenz 2011).

Such information can be fed back to individual users who commute within a certain space. Moreover, a lot of crowd sensing applications func-tion on a distributed basis, even when it comes to evaluation: For mid-size groups like local neighborhoods, applications can automatically feed cer-tain monitored data back to the individuals, leading to autonomous decision making. For example, the recycling rate of a university campus can be op-timized by collectively sharing information about the locations of various garbage bins. However, these examples all demonstrate the disconcerting way how "crowd-enabled systems are revolutionizing the way we tackle problems and allowing us to monitor and act upon almost anything, any-where, in real-time" (Boulos et al. 2011: 2). The ubiquitous effort of opti-mizing the organization of, as Foucault has it, "the dust of events, actions, behaviors, opinions" (1977: 213), which is inherent in all these applica-tions, coalesces with the more alarming dispositions of petty bourgeois thinking. Voluntary or opportunistic modes of techno-social participation in mobile crowd sensing applications, on the one hand, produce more exact data about environmental conditions than classical fixed network systems, thereby contributing to the improvement of public spaces and the realiza-tion of common goals as long as the abovementioned technological and in-formational challenges are met. However, on the other hand, they instanti-ate a form of governmentality that imposes a techno-savvy *Hermeneutics of the Subject* (Foucault 2005) on all sorts of everyday practices. This (semi)-automated form of normalization in a relational system consisting of "the instinct of the experts, the wisdom of the crowds, and the power of algo-rithms" (Boulos 2011: 8) runs the risk of literally taking apart the individu-als who participate in these novel forms of self-reflective crowds.

The first transformation from mass-psychological conceptions to agent-based computer simulation models replaced a psychological foundation of the behavior of individuals in crowds with the physics of bodily movement vectors in environments with scarce resources. The traditional mass, its dangerous 'thermodynamic' and explosive amalgam (Schäfer/Vogl 2004) dissolved into the computable individual actions of simulated agent connec-tives. With the second transformation to the sensing, self-reflective crowd, media-technological applications no longer restrict individual actions to mere abstract (collective) movements but incorporate all sorts of 'sensor data' from humans ('qualitative' data from social network feeds etc.) and mobile devices ('quantitative' technical sensor data), thus mapping a whole spectrum of complex real-life behaviors and interconnected environmental dynamics. These can be externally monitored or be fed back to the 'autonomous individuals' in the crowd almost in real time. In addition to the first dissolution, now the 'lifelike agents' also dissolve into a set of data streams. The reverse side of partaking in crowd sensing thus irreducibly reduces the individual to a 'dividual' state (Deleuze 1992). And this fundamental dissolution not only effectuates the techno-social crowd as a productive force but also imposes a totality of governmental self-optimization. Thus, the most convincing reclaiming of participation quite paradoxically might be a cutting of links and a hedging of "non-connected islands" (Stäheli 2014) as a last resort for dreaming the dream of a critique that has not yet "run out of steam" (Latour 2004) in the 21st century.

The author thanks Clara Lotte Warnsholdt (MECS) for her assistance in copy-editing this article.

REFERENCES

Arquilla, John/Ronfeldt, David (2000): Swarming and the Future of Conflict, Santa Monica, CA: Rand Corporation.

Baxmann, Inge/Beyes, Timon/Pias, Claus (2014): Soziale Medien – Neue Massen, Medienwissenschaftliche Symposien der DFG, Berlin: Diaphanes.

Borch, Christian (2012): The Politics of Crowds. An Alternative History of Sociology, Cambridge, MA: Cambridge University Press.

Boulos, Kamel et al. (2011): "Crowdsourcing, Citizen Sensing and Sensor Web Technologies for Public and Environmental Health Surveillance and Crisis Management: Trends, OGC Standards and Application Examples". In: International Journal of Health Geographics 10/67, http://www.ij-healthgeographics.com/content/10/1/67 (December 3, 2014).

Burke, Jeff et al. (2006): "Participatory Sensing". In: Workshop World-Sensor-Web, Collocated with ACM SenSys, https://escholarship.org/uc/item/19h777qd (August 17, 2015).

Cunningham, Christopher/Zichermann, Gabe (2011): Gamification by Design: Implementing Game Mechanics in Web and Mobile Apps, Sebastopol, CA: O'Reilly.

de Tarde, Gabriel (1901): L'Opinion et la foule, Paris: Félix Alcan.

Deleuze, Gilles (1992): "Postscript on the Societies of Control." In: October 59, pp. 3-7.

Engelbrecht, Andries P. (2005): Fundamentals of Computational Swarm Intelligence, New York, NY: Wiley.

Evert, Kerstin/Burri, Regula/Peters, Sibylle/Ziemer, Gesa (2012): "Versammlung und Teilhabe. Urbane Öffentlichkeiten und performative Künste", http://www.versammlung-und-teilhabe.de/cms (August 17, 2015).

Fisher, Len (2010): The Perfect Swarm: The Science of Complexity in Everyday Life, New York, NY: Perseus.

Foucault, Michel (1977): Discipline and Punish. The Birth of the Prison, New York, NY: Vintage.

Foucault, Michel (2005): Hermeneutics of the Subject. Lectures at the Collège de France 1981-82, New York, NY: Palgrave MacMillan.

Fuchs, Mathias et al. (2013): Rethinking Gamification, Lüneburg: Meson Press, open access: http://meson.press/books/rethinking-gamification/ (August 17, 2015).

Ganti, Raghu K./Ye, Fan/Lei, Hui (2011): "Mobile Crowdsensing: Current State and Future Challenges." In: IEEE Communications Magazine, November 2011, p. 32-39.

Goodchild, Michael (2007): "Citizens as Sensors: the World of Volunteered Geography." In: GeoJournal 69/4, pp. 211-221.

Hardt, Michael/Negri, Antonio (2004): Multitude: War and Democracy in the Age of Empire, New York, NY: Penguin.

Helbing, Dirk (1994): "A Mathematical Model for the Behavior of Individuals in a Social Field." In: Journal of Mathematical Sociology 19/3, pp. 189-219.

Helbing, Dirk/Farkas, Illés/Vicsek, Tamás (2000): "Simulation dynamical features of escape panic." In: Nature 407, pp. 487-490.

Helbing, Dirk/Johansson, Anders (2009): "Pedestrian, Crowd and Evacuation Dynamics." In: Robert A. Meyers (ed.), Encyclopedia of Complexity and Systems Science, New York, NY: Springer, pp. 6476-6495.

Lane, Nicholas D. et al. (2010): "A Survey of Mobile Phone Sensing." In: IEEE Communication Magazine 48/9, pp. 140-150.

Latour, Bruno (2004): "Why Has Critique Run Out of Steam? From Matters of Fact to Matters of Concern." In: Critical Inquiry 30/2, Special Issue on the Future of Critique, pp. 225-248.

Le Bon, Gustave (1896): The Crowd: A Study of the Popular Mind, London: T. Fisher Unwin.

Macal, Charles M./North, Michael J. (2006): "Tutorial on Agent-Based Modeling and Simulation. Part 2: How to Model with Agents." In: L.F. Perrone et al. (eds.), Proceedings of the 2006 IEEE Winter Simulation Conference, pp. 73-83.

Magnenat-Thalmann, Nadia/Thalmann, Daniel (2004): Handbook of Virtual Humans, New York, NY: John Wiley.

McPhail, Clark (1991): The Myth of the Madding Crowd, New York, NY: de Gruyter.

Miller, Peter (2010): The Smart Swarm: How Understanding Flocks, Schools, and Colonies Can Make Us Better at Communicating, Decision Making, and Getting Things Done, New York, NY: Avery.

Mintz, Alexander (1951): "Non-Adaptive Group Behavior." In: Journal of Abnormal Social Psychology 46, pp. 150-159.

Pluta, Werner (2013): "Crowd Management. Smartphone soll Massenpanik verhindern", http://www.golem.de/news/crowd-management-smartphone-soll-massenpanik-verhindern-1209-94331.html (August 17, 2015).

Radakov, Dimitri V. (1973): Schooling in the Ecology of Fish, New York, NY: Wiley.

Reeves, William T. (1983): "Particle Systems: A Technique for Modeling a Class of Fuzzy Objects." In: ACM Transactions on Graphics 2(2), pp. 91-108.

Reynolds, Craig W. (1987): "Flocks, Herds, and Schools: A Distributed Behavioral Model." In: Computer Graphics 21, pp. 25-34.

Rheingold, Howard (2002): Smart Mobs: The Next Social Revolution, Cambridge, MA: Basic Books.

Roitman, Haggai et al. (2012): "Harnessing the Crowds for Smart City Sensing." In: Proceedings of the 1st International Workshop on Multimodal Crowd Sensing (CrowdSens '12), ACM, New York, NY, pp. 17-18.

Saenz, A. (2011): "Japan's Nuclear Woes Give Rise to Crowd-Sourced Radiation Maps In Asia and US", http://singularityhub.com/2011/03/24/japans-nuclear-woes-give-rise-to-crowd-sourced-radiation-maps-in-asia-and-us (August 17, 2015).

Schäfer, Armin/Vogl, Joseph (2004): "Feuer und Flamme. Über ein Ereignis des 19. Jahrhunderts." In: Henning Schmidgen/Peter Geimer/Sven Dierig (eds.), Kultur im Experiment, Berlin: Kadmos, pp. 191-211.

Schilt, Carl R./Norris, Kenneth S. (1997): "Perspectives on Sensory Integration Systems: Problems, Opportunities, and Predictions." In: Julia K. Parrish/Willliam H. Hamner (eds.), Animal Groups in Three Dimensions, Cambridge, MA: Cambridge University Press, pp. 225-244.

Schüttpelz, Erhard/Gießmann, Sebastian: "Medien der Kooperation." In: Navigationen 15/1, pp. 7-54.

Selous, Edmund (1931): Thought Transference (Or What?) in Birds, London: Constable.

Shao, Wei/Terzopoulos, Demetri (2007): "Autonomous Pedestrians." In: Graphical Models 69(5-6), pp. 246-274.

Sighele, Scipio (1901): La foule criminelle. Essai de psychologie criminelle, Paris: Alcan.

Sime, Jonathan D. (1995): "Crowd Psychology and Engineering." In: Safety Science 21, pp. 1-14.

Stäheli, Urs (2014): "Entnetzt Euch!" In: Deutschlandradio Kultur, January 24, http://www.deutschlandradiokultur.de/kommunikation-entnetzt-euch.954.de.html?dram:article_id=275523 (August 17, 2015).

Stäheli, Urs (2012): "Infrastrukturen des Kollektiven: alte Medien – neue Kollektive?" In: Zeitschrift für Medienphilosophie und Kulturtechnikforschung 1, pp. 99-116.

Surowiecki, James (2004): The Wisdom of Crowds: Why the Many are Smarter than the Few and How Collective Wisdom Shapes Business, Economies, Societies and Nations, London: Anchor.

Thacker, Eugene (2004): "Networks, Swarms, Multitudes." In: CTheory, May 18, http://www.ctheory.net/articles.aspx?id=423 (August 17, 2015).

Vehlken, Sebastian (2013): "Zootechnologies. 'Swarming' as a Cultural Technique." In: Geoffrey Winthrop-Young/Jussi Parikka/Ilinca Irascu (eds.), Theory, Culture and Society 30/6, Special Issue Cultural Techniques, pp. 110-131.

Vehlken, Sebastian (2014): "After Affects. Zealous Zombies, Panic Prevention, Crowd Simulation." In: Marie-Luise Angerer et al. (eds.): The Timing of Affect, Berlin and Zurich: Diaphanes, pp. 303-320.

Wiedemann, Carolin (2015): "Digital Swarming and Affective Infrastructures. A New Materialist Approach to 4chan." In: Sebastian Vehlken/Tobias Harks (eds.), Neighborhood Technologies. Media and Mathematics of Dynamic Networks, Berlin: Diaphanes.

Wirz, Martin et al. (2012): "Inferring Crowd Conditions from Pedestrians' Location Traces for Real-Time Crowd Monitoring during City-Scale Mass Gatherings." In: Proceedings of the 2012 IEEE 21st International Workshop on Enabling Technologies: Infrastructure for Collaborative Enterprises, Toulouse: WETICE, pp. 367-372.

Micro-activist Affordances of Disability. Transformative Potential of Participation

ARSELI DOKUMACI

> "What does it take for each of us to partici-
> pate in this very media environment? I see
> letters, perceive words, read them out loud;
> you hear what I say and see what I show
> and perceive what all these signs are sup-
> posed to signify."[1]
> DOKUMACI (2014)

INTRODUCTION

As we are immersed in our routinized activities, rarely do corporeal details such as the above become the focus of our awareness.[2] This, however, seldom is the case for the disabled body whose corporeal differences have, as feminist scholar Rosemarie Garland-Thomson writes, "rendered it out of

---

1 The quote is taken from the documentary "Blindness, Techno-Affordances and Participation in Everyday Life" that this article is based upon. The film can be viewed online at: performingdisability.com/video/blindness (August 14, 2015).

2 For a phenomenological reflection on the disappearance and reappearance of corporeal awareness, see Drew Leder's seminal essay "The Absent Body" (1990).

sync with its environment" (2006: 267). For the blind before text, for the d/Deaf before spoken words, or for the arthritic, such as myself, before a keyboard to type these words[3], it may not be the ends but the very process of a participatory activity that first and foremost matters.

Participation, since its emergence as a concept in the late 20th century, has been widely debated in relation to a wide variety of frameworks ranging from democratic theory to citizenship, from new media to game theory, from communication to aesthetic practice (cf. Popper 1975; Jenkins 2006; Cammaerts 2008; Dezeuze 2010; Carpentier 2011; Bishop 2012; Loader/Marcea 2012; Delwiche/Henderson 2013). Disability, however, has remained at the margins of these discussions – discussions, which paradoxically focused on the 'inclusion' of what remained beyond. This article seeks to address this gap by exploring the question of participation in relation to blindness – a form of embodiment as well as a social phenomenon that challenges the functioning of digital media in the most forceful ways. In the paper, I draw on the materials of my ongoing ethnographic research in which I, as a sighted researcher, follow my research participant/collaborator Jérôme Plante, who is blind from birth, and investigate what it means to participate along with in and through which bodily and material means we *practice* participation.

The testimonies that I use in the article are taken from the interviews that I have done with Jérôme throughout the year of 2013-2014. The interviews were videotaped at Jérôme's home, located in Longueuil (Québec), and during his daily commute to Montréal (Québec) where he studies. The interviews were conducted in English, which is neither Jérôme's nor my mother tongue. In order not to overlook the effects of language on our communication, I leave Jérôme's sentences in their original.

I shall also underline that my embodied learning process in this research is ongoing, and in this paper I share with you what I have, thanks to Jérôme, learned so far. In the first part of this paper, I present my ethnographic knowledge under two interrelated rubrics: a) digital wayfinding in

---

3 My examples are inspired by Rosemarie Garland-Thomson's explanation of how everyday life and its arrangements disable subjects who do not fit into a narrowly defined bodily standard (1997: 24).

physical environments and b) physical wayfinding in digital environments. Then I apply James Gibson's (1979) "theory of affordances" to the context of disability studies in order to explore how these ethnographic materials may inform us about the socio-technical nature of participation.

DIGITAL WAYFINDING IN PHYSICAL ENVIRONMENTS

Put in a simple way, the embodied process of wayfinding involves three interrelated layers of bodily activity: motion, perception, and cognition. In order to navigate, one needs to be able to move and infer one's changing location at the same time as well as doing this in relation to a destination already set. Now this may sound rather intuitive to some readers. The reason I reiterate it though is to problematize the taken-for-grantedness itself and outline ways of thinking about this "spatial problem-solving" activity (Arthur/Passini 1992) that go beyond the privileges of sightedness.

Let me begin with asking: what are some of the non-visual perceptual cues and cognitive "tactics" – to use de Certeau's term (1984) – that can mediate navigation? First of all, sounds are often indicative of what and where their origins are and, if mobile, toward which direction they are going (Saerberg 2010: 370). Places such as a park, an airport, a highway, a forest, have their own distinctive soundscapes and architectural features, such as an exit at the end of a corridor, that can be revealed in the way they shape and funnel sound (ibid: 370-371). Similarly, geographical events help to disclose spatial structures. The sound of falling rain, for instance, "throws a coloured blanket over previously invisible things" (Hull 1990: 26) while the sensation of the wind, as in Inuit wayfinding practices, creates "a wind-compass" that can be used to situate things (Aporta and Higgs 2005: 731 in Saerberg 2010: 379). Further "because sound is first and foremost vibration" (Rodaway 1994: 97), it partakes in the shaping of various synaesthetic experiences. In echo-location, sound waves bounce off objects and spatial elements, informing the traveller of what affords safe-passage (or danger for that matter) on her path.[4] The tapping or sweeping

---

4   For further discussion on echo-location, cf. Kish (2013).

sound of a cane, being echo-location cues, extend the proximal haptic reach into a distal acoustic one with which one can more readily discern the environmental structure (Giudice/Legge 2008: 484). Through such sounds, one can figure out (if not muffed by other sounds) the corridors or exit ahead of oneself or (if outside) whether one is walking on a concrete (sidewalk) or an asphalt (street) surface (cf. Figure 1). Further, the texture, layout, and irregularities of the ground provide "a kinesthetically felt structure" while distinct smells, coexistent in the same place, can be used to build "an olfactory map" (Saerberg 2010: 371). On top of these multimodalities, one always has a sense of what Paul Rodaway calls "global touch", that is an obscure and often passive feeling of one's overall locatedness in space, which "can be enhanced by the movement of the body through space, across surfaces, through the air and water" as well as by skin sensations of "temperature, [and] humidity" (1994: 49).

Navigational cues, needless to say, are also gathered directly through one's hands and indirectly through the mediation of an instrument like a cane[5]. As examples of epistemic tactics, the traveller may count her steps, build cognitive maps, and memorize spatial regularities as she navigates (ibid: 53). Finally at moments of uncertainty where all of the aforementioned navigational methods fail, the traveller may resort to "farther-reaching cognitive structures", such as theorizing, trial and error, "memory- and history keeping" and "backtracking in error searches" (Saerberg 2011: 21).

---

5   For a phenomenological reflection on how the materiality of a cane extends the sensuous space of a moving body, cf. Merleau-Ponty (2002: 165).

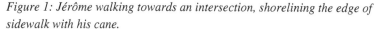

Figure 1: Jérôme walking towards an intersection, shorelining the edge of sidewalk with his cane.

Still from the documentary "Blindness, Techno-Affordances and Participation in Everyday Life" (2014). All images © Arseli Dokumacı, 2014

Siegfried Saerberg terms all these non-visual methods of navigation as "blind style of perception" and (one may add) of action (ibid: 17). This style evidently requires a rigorous "disciplining of the body" and its senses and a continuous attentiveness to one's body and environment (ibid: 17). Unlike sighted (and overall able-bodied) style of perception, in which spatial problem-solving usually occurs in an automatic way, blind navigation often entails "conscious moment-to-moment problem solving" – a process that can take up a good amount of the traveller's "cognitive and attentional resources" (Giudice/Legge 2008: 482).[6] And this even more within built

---

6   This is not to imply that blind and visually impaired individuals do not get habituated to performing navigational tasks. My point here aims to emphasize that it is much easier for a sighted and able-bodied person to become habituated to everyday tasks (including navigation) in an ableist environ-

environments and public systems that take the perceptual capacities of a sighted traveller as given.

In consideration of the non-sighted navigational tactics summarized above, the question that I would now like to ask is: Which further tactics and skills come into play when blind navigation occurs in unfamiliar outdoor settings that bring on further cognitively demanding tasks, such as "accessing the names of the shops being passed, the name of the street being crossed, or the state of the traffic signal at a busy intersection" (ibid: 480)?

Figure 2: Jérôme travelling on the bus, which lacks audio cues, and using the iPhone GPS application in order to infer his whereabouts.

Still from "Blindness, Techno-Affordances and Participation in Everyday Life" (2014).

Jérôme: We use a lot of applications to localize like everyone. The difference is that for us it can help a lot more than everyone. I have an adapted GPS that is not on the phone that is a real GPS [...] but on phone, technology advance fast and today we can use some GPS applications to help us to localize and even to do some projects [...] For example, I use an application called Blind Square. [...] It uses information from the social network

---

ment than it is for a blind person, given that both individuals share similar living circumstances and social characteristics.

Four Square and the cartography of the iPhone. It can help me to obtain a project; it can give me the information about the intersections and interest points that are on my way and it helps a lot when my other GPS doesn't work or doesn't work properly or when I don't have it. With this application I have always an access to the information about my localization. So it's really useful [...] And we can use other applications for the bus, such as information about bus stops and bus circuits, when it will pass at our stop [...] So localization is something really useful for us.

Arseli: Before the GPS or the iPhone came out, what were you doing? How were you finding your way?

Jérôme: [smiling] I just ask to the driver [...] And today too! By precaution normally, I ask to the driver to tell me at the stop because I cannot be sure that the GPS will tell me [the bus stop] sufficiently in advance [...] It's also important to ask to the driver before the last time than possible; because the problem with the driver is that they have a lot of information to remember so they can forget.

In their article "Storied Spaces", Joanna Brewer and Paul Dourish write: "Mobile technology is not [...] simply operating within a spatial environment; it is implicated in the production of spatiality and spatial experience" (2008: 3). Indeed, developments like internet-enabled mobile devices and location-based services have largely challenged earlier theories of Internet that had assumed digital and physical spaces to be separate. As Adriana Silva argues in her concept of "hybrid space", mobile interfaces have blurred this boundary to such an extent that one could no longer think of the two spaces as independent of one another (2006: 262). As mobile-internet users continue to map actual spaces with digital information (and vice versa), these spaces begin to take on new meanings and mediate navigators' movements in ever elaborate ways. This transformation becomes all the more so evident in a blind user's wayfinding process. As can be observed in Jérôme's use of location-aware applications, the entwining of the mobile, the physical and the digital not only reconfigures the way space is experienced but also the way it is, in the words of de Certeau, "practiced".[7]

---

7   Michel de Certeau defines space as "a practiced place" (1984: 117).

If auditory, tactile, cognitive, olfactory, and synaesthetic experiences help expand the embodied space of blind individuals beyond the immediate radius of their bodies, as Saerberg and Rodaway point out, then location-aware mobile technologies, I add, further multiply that expanded radius, producing what one may call *digitally-mediated touch*. By this I do not mean that these technologies once and for all render accessible an otherwise inaccessible physical world. If it had, Jérôme would not have to resort to such precautions as asking the bus driver. Yet he has to; because digital participation, while offering new solutions to navigational tasks, does not overcome all the possible problems of and barriers to navigation[8]. In fact, a GPS device or application, as Jérôme notes, has its own limitations and impositions. Akin to the way that a bus driver may forget to announce the bus stop that you have requested for, a GPS app or device may not operate "real-time" enough to alert you of your stop. What is of importance here is not the shortcomings of each navigational technique and tactic (e.g. interpersonal communication, digital participation, auditory and haptic experience) but the ways in which they come into play and act upon the limitations of one another: Where buses lack audio cues, digital participation comes in to provide locational cues; where digital participation lags, speech interaction serves as a back-up for bus stop alerts. This interplay and coactions of tactics and techniques not only render visible how a participatory activity occurs through complex socio-technological processes but also expose how these processes are deeply enmeshed with multi-sensuous, mobile, cognitive, and epistemic registers.

---

8 In many cases, these obstacles arise from the ableist assumptions that underlie the built environments and systems, such as public transports lacking wheelchair accesses and audio and visual cues. In fact, as of 2014, none of the public buses operated by the local transport authorities in Longueuil and Montréal provide audio cues or stop signals for their travellers. Only the metro system in Montréal provides audio cues.

Physical Wayfinding in Digital Environments

For a sighted internet user, the perception of what is on the screen and the gesture that follows this perception happen in a matter of seconds since the visual contents remain as readily available objects of perception within the same temporal frame. This, however, is not quite the case for Jérôme, whose digital navigation relies on the operation of the screenreader.

Jérôme: Generally, the problem for someone that is seeing and observing us is that the cursor just does not follow for us the same aspect than for a seeing person. For example, if I go down the arrow [he presses the arrow on keyboard and the screenreader reads the contents] I will see each link separately and I will see the page from the top to the bottom. I cannot see the page in a single view at one time. I have some shortcuts to go directly to the code that I want or the link that I want, if I know the website. But if I do not know the website, I have to explore the page completely. That is really longer.

Figure 3: Jérôme in front of his computer, visiting the website of TVA. The heavily graphic-based contents of the page are loading.

Still from the documentary "Blindness, Techno-Affordances and Participation in Everyday Life" (2014).

Grond and Hermann write that "sound as signs", because of their ephemeral nature, "cannot coexist next to each other in the same sense as two static visual signs can" and when they attempt to do so, they may begin to blend, conceal, and even offset each other entirely (2014: 47). In the context of digital navigation, this means that a blind user has to manually perform what visual signs achieve by way of their co-existence. For instance, to figure out the contents of a Web page, Jérôme has to literally move, via keyboard commands, through its architecture heading-by-heading and item-by-item (listening to what the screen-reader says). When making navigational choices, he might have to go back and listen to the screen-reader again because the transient nature of sound-signs and the impossibility of perceiving them all at once prevent them from being reachable within the same timeframe. If one were to make an analogy to illustrate the situation: In sighted style of internet navigation, a cursor is moved around on the screen as if it were a plane flying through traversable clouds; whereas in (following Saerberg) "blind style" of navigation, the screen-reader and keyboard commands remain bound to the structure of web-scape in the way a car is to the materiality of landscape. As any object lying on the path of a car can turn into an obstacle, any visual content of Web 2.0 (from automatically loading audio to heavily graphic-based interfaces) may interfere with the operation of screenreader, which is in a way Jérôme's hands and arms in digital space.

Arseli: How do you find websites in terms of their accessibility?

Jérôme: There is an improvement since a few years but the majority of websites don't meet any accessibility criteria. [He types the web address of TVA, a popular TV channel in Québec (see figure 3)] Here in this website, it is really not easy to navigate. It is enormous. It is huge and not easy. Other medias are also not friendly but are a little bit accessible like the website of *La Presse* [a popular newspaper in Québec] that is a real challenge for us. It is accessible. No, a little bit accessible. Basically accessible but it is enormous and really difficult for us [...] [He opens the website of La Presse] So in this website I can navigate easily from title to title or list to list. There is a lot of ways to find myself in the page but I have to be familiar with the computer in order to be able to navigate here. Because it is enormous.

Arseli: You mean by enormous, the amount of information is too much?

Jérôme: There is a lot of information and often in these websites, information is not always clearly classified.

In their book "Disability and New Media" Katie Ellis and Mike Kent (2011) discuss how the transition from web to web 2.0 has impacted disabled users. The earlier version, the authors contend, was largely text-based and thus friendly to assistive technologies and it has, in a way, attested to its inventor Tim Berner-Lee's vision of it being an accessible "platform" for all (ibid: 45-46). Web 2.0, on the other hand, with its user-defined, graphic-based and multi-media rich content and plug-ins, the authors add, has brought along both enactive and restrictive potentialities for the disabled (ibid: 132). While there are Web 2.0 accessibility standards in place, aimed for the consideration of webmasters, the use of such standards remain voluntary. Moreover, these guidelines cannot always meet differing and at times conflicting accessibility requirements of different impairments. In lieu of this, Ellis and Kent suggest using the term "Accessibility 2.0". The idea behind the term is, its coiner Brian Kelly explains: going beyond giving simple accessibility formulas and checklists to webmasters who, once complying with them, might assume that accessibility is achieved once and for all (Kelly 2008 in Ellis/Kent 2010: 26). The idea, Ellis and Kent add, is to take impairment variations and their differing relations to technology into account and consider accessibility as "a process rather than a finite solution" (ibid: 26). Accessibility 2.0 thus promotes an understanding of access not as coercing people into doing things in certain ways but as giving them options to choose from that suit their bodily differences (ibid: 49). As its name implies, it "embraces the underpinning philosophy of web 2.0" and offers the "user choice" principle that enabled the participation of many in the creation of web content to the viewers of those contents (ibid: 28). This way users with different impairments could have a chance to directly remove barriers to access themselves rather depending on some third party to decide and act on their behalf. As can be observed in the following testimony, even the different options available to navigate a website (such as multiple browsers, responsive websites and native mobile applications) may have certain accessibility implications – implications that the creators of those sites might have not originally thought about.

Jérôme: Generally I prefer when it is possible to use the mobile version of one website. The best example I can show you is Facebook. [He logs into his Facebook account.] So I am on the Facebook ordinary website and that is complicated. [As he presses the arrow key and the screenreader reads the contents of wherever the tab moves towards] I see that I do not have any requests but it is menu; same thing for the messages, same thing for the notifications. And I have a form to search for something. With a lot of information that I do not need…

Arseli: You mean part of the information is advertisements and stuff?

Jérôme: There is advertisement. There is information about my profile… If I want to check my profile, I can but I do not want necessarily to see all this information in the same page and I cannot use a lot of keyboard shortcuts. I cannot use them here; it is too complicated. In contrast, if I use the mobile version [he types the address for Facebook mobile on the navigation bar] I have just [screenreader begins to read the contents as Facebook mobile loads] a small menu with the home, the profile, the friends, the messages, the notifications and I can change my status and after that it's the last news of my friends. And it is so simple!… It is really more simple than the ordinary facebook site!

Being able to choose between the mobile and desktop versions of a website does not, in this case, arise out of a need to overcome device compatibility issues. Instead, it is taken up by a disabled user as a way to mitigate the impact of, if not entirely obviate, digital barriers to access. In this sense, it helps to exemplify how Accessibility 2.0 may take place, especially through the reclaiming of user-choices in ways that complement the materiality of the user's body rather than that of the device.

MICRO-ACTIVIST AFFORDANCES OF DISABILITY

"The verb to afford is found in the dictionary, but the noun affordance is not […] I mean by it something that refers to both the environment and the animal in a way that no existing term does" (Gibson 1979: 127).

James Gibson (1979) proposed his "theory of affordances" as part of his ecological approach to perception and since its inception in 1980s; the theory has been taken up by a variety of fields, including design and human computer interaction. Despite its extreme relevance to a critical disability perspective, however, the theory of affordances has not yet been rigorously explored in this field, particularly in relation to the ableist presumptions that are embodied in the collective "body techniques" of societies. What I summarize below is my own interpretation of the theory of affordances as I read it from a critical disability perspective. Speaking from this lens, I am going to propose to consider affordances as micro-activists practices, as potentially transformative actions in the world.

What exactly are affordances? Simply put, they are the offerings inherent in the physicality of an environment. Or to be more precise, they are possibilities for action, the actualization of which depends upon the complementary relations between an organism and its environment. Upon seeing a flat, rigid, and knee-high surface, I *directly* see the possibility of sitting embodied in its material. But, in that same substance, another person may detect an entirely different possibility. Affordances are properties of the environment taken in reference to the perceiver (Gibson 1979: 143). Yet they exist in the environment independently of any individual, whether they are perceived or not (ibid: 139). This very duality gives affordances a historical character and Gibson's term "niche" reflects this most plainly (ibid: 128). Niche is a set of affordances actualized in an environment yet the same historical environment, Gibson says, may harbor many other offerings "that have *not* been taken advantage of, that is, niches not yet occupied" (ibid: 129). These latent affordances continue to remain so, as long as occupants of that environment can easily find world-counterparts for their bodily states and are in no urgent need of going beyond the limits of what has already been actualized in their environments. As a result of this contentment with "the actual" (rather than the latent), both their bodies and the material infrastructures surrounding them, sink into complete silence. It is precisely this silence, this *taken-for-grantedness*, I claim that the disabled body breaks. Disability, by definition, is the rupture of the complementarity between the body and the environment. Disabled individuals, either because their bodies are physically suffering and/or not complying with the norms of an ableist environment, are forced to seek new niches to occupy and create new affordances within which their corporeal differences would be accommodated. They may, for instance, deploy various multisensuous affordances of geographies, instruments, and digital technologies in such ways that they add up to an otherwise way of affording navigation that defies the limits of the one that is taken as given (thanks to the normalcy of sightedness). Or they may, as in the cases of Accessibility 2.0, come up with digital affordances by way of actively seeking user-choice alternatives that do not stand in the way of the operations of assistive technologies. Putting affordances theory in dialogue with critical disability studies, I call these highly creative choreographies of the mundane; and these solutions that often get buried in the banal minutiae of everyday life, as *micro-activist affordances of disability*. I make this proposal because these improvisations are *not* simply a matter of inventing day-to-day strategies that would make one's life easier and more convenient, when this life is already provided with the basics of subsistence, and lived in health and free of pain. Neither are they the 'achievements' of a disabled person 'despite' 'his/her' limitations; nor the proofs of an extraordinary human resilience. I term these non-normative ways of moving, sensing, and being in the everyday as *micro-activist affordances of disability* precisely because they are potentially transformative actions in the world. Even if they may not manifest themselves in the form of activities that are usually associated with activism (i.e. intentional, and often taking place on the street), they still have an inherently political character. They do so because: disabled individuals, immaterializing their corporeal differences, discomforts, and pains in the form of *otherwise unimaginable affordances*, at the same time, make a political claim towards the many possible ways of sharing their single environment. Their *micro-activist affordances of disability* are the subversions of the collective way that we, as a society, have decided to share this world, and make use of its material offerings; the way that we, as a public, have come to make *this particular niche* – one that takes certain bodies and abilities for granted – out of all its endless possibilities.

To further this argument by applying it in the context of participation: it is precisely in the emergences of such *micro-activist affordances of disability,* that is, in the failures of normalcy and simultaneous *reclaimings* of bodily agency that the socio-technological character of participation becomes most visible and most concrete. In a way, non-ableist ways of affording participation – with their highly transformative potential – render visible the coupling between the body and the technical that underlies all participatory practices, and gives them their particular forms of affordances.

In "Rethinking Disability" Michael Schillmeier writes: "Being blind means getting in touch with the invisible, moving within a rather complex set of practices, objects and relations that make the materiality of social relations traceable" (2010: 43). As I have written elsewhere (Dokumacı 2014a), *"disability as a method"*, as a critical mode of inquiry with which one could pry open many phenomena that are otherwise not so easily traceable, including the performativity of bodies, selves, the habitus, and in this case, participation. By co-exploring the sensuous environments that the disabled body navigates, one may gain access to a broader understanding of historically-mediated nature of participation and answer the question of "how participation can be thought of as a socio-technological process"[9] with its negation: When could it ever be thought of not as one?

ACKNOWLEDGEMENTS

I would like to thank my participant Jérôme Plante for his time, kindness, and the incredible generosity with which he shared his knowledge with me, and welcomed me to his home and his everyday life. This article draws on the materials of my postdoctoral research that I undertook at Concordia University's Mobile Media Lab. The research was made possible by funding from the Canadian Consortium on Performance and Politics in the Americas and GRAND Networks of Centres of Excellence *Program*.

REFERENCES

Arthur, Paul/Passini, Romedi (1992): Wayfinding-People, Signs, and Architecture, New York, NY: McGraw-Hill.

Bishop, Claire (2012): Artificial Hells: Participatory Art and the Politics of Spectatorship, London: Verso.

Brewer, Joanna/Dourish, Paul (2008): "Storied Spaces: Cultural Accounts of Mobility, Technology, and Environmental Knowing." In: International Journal of Human Computer Studies 66/12, pp. 963-976.

Cammaerts, Bart (2008): Internet-Mediated Participation Beyond the Nation State, Manchester: Manchester University Press.

---

9   "ReClaiming Participation. Technology, Mediation, Collectivity." Call for Papers, www.reclaimingparticipation.files.wordpress.com/2013/09/cfp-reclaiming-participation.pdf (August 18, 2015).

Carpentier, Nico (2011): Media and Participation: A Site of Ideological-democratic Struggle, Bristol: Intellect.

de Certeau, Michel (1984 [1980]): The Practice of Everyday Life, translated by Steven Rendall, Berkeley, CA: University of California Press.

de Souza e Silva, Adriana (2006): "From Cyber to Hybrid: Mobile Technologies as Interfaces of Hybrid Spaces." In: Space and Culture 9/3, pp. 261-278.

Delwiche, Aaron/Henderson, Jennifer (2013): The Participatory Cultures Handbook, New York, NY: Routledge.

Dezeuze, Anna (2010): The 'do-it-yourself' Artwork: Participation from Fluxus to New Media, Manchester: Manchester University Press.

Dokumacı, Arseli (2014a): "Habitus of the Disabled Body." In: Marin Blažević/Lada Feldman (eds.), Misperformance: Essays in Shifting Perspectives, Ljubljana: Maska Publishing.

Dokumacı, Arseli (2014b): "Blindness, Techno-Affordances and Participation in Everday Life" [Director: Arseli Dokumacı].

Ellis, Katie/Kent, Mike (2011): Disability and New Media, New York, NY: Routledge.

Gibson, James (1979): The Ecological Approach To Visual Perception, Hillsdale, NJ: Lawrence Erlbaum Associates.

Giudice, Nicholas/Legge, Gordon (2008): "Blind Navigation and the Role of Technology." In: Abdelsalam Helal/Mounir Mokhtari/Bessam Abdulrazak (eds.), Engineering Handbook of Smart Technology for Aging, Disability, and Independence, New Jersey, NJ: John Wiley & Sons, pp. 479-500.

Garland-Thomson, Rosemary (1997): Extraordinary Bodies: Figuring Physical Disability in American Culture and Literature, New York, NY: Columbia University Press.

Garland-Thomson, Rosemary (2006): "Integrating Disability, Transforming Feminist Theory." In: Lennard Davis (ed.), The Disability Studies Reader, 2nd edition, New York, NY and London: Routledge, pp. 257-273.

Grond, Florian/Hermann, Thomas (2014): "Interactive Sonification for Data Exploration, How Listening Modes and Display Purposes Define Design Guidelines." In: Organised Sound 19/1, pp. 41-51.

Hull, John (1990): Touching the Rock: An Experience of Blindness, London: SPCK Publishing.

Jenkins, Henry (2006): Fans, Bloggers, and Gamers: Exploring Participatory Culture, New York, NY: New York University Press.

Kish, Daniel (2013): "Experience: I taught myself to see." In: The Guardian July 13, http://www.theguardian.com/lifeandstyle/2013/jul/13/experience-blindness-echolocation-daniel-kish (August 16, 2015).

Leder, Drew (1990): The Absent Body, Chicago, IL: University of Chicago Press.

Loader, Brian/Marcea, Dan (2012): Social Media and Democracy: Innovations in Participatory Politics, Oxon: Routledge.

Merleau-Ponty, Maurice (2002 [1945]): Phenomenology of Perception, New York, NY: Routledge.

Popper, Frank (1975): Art – Action and Participation, London: Studio Vista.

Rodaway, Paul (1994): Sensuous Geographies: Body, Sense and Place, London: Routledge.

Saerberg, Siegfried (2010): "'Just go straight ahead': How Blind and Sighted Pedestrians Negotiate Space." In: Senses & Society 5/3, pp. 364-381.

Saerberg, Siegfried (2011): "The Sensorification of the Invisible: Science, Blindness and the Life-world." In: Science, Technology & Innovation Studies, 7/1, pp. 9-28.

Schillmeier, Michael (2010): Rethinking Disability: Bodies, Senses, and Things, New York, NY: Routledge.

II. Participation and the Claims of Community

Introduction: Questioning Community

CHRISTINA BARTZ

Just like 'participation', 'community' is one of the shining words in public and scientific debates hailing the Internet. This relationship can be traced back to its founding documents where community plays a vital role. In 1968 the two ARPA-research directors Joseph Carl Robnett Licklider and Robert W. Taylor aimed to optimize the organization of scientific work by creating "on-line communities" (Licklider/Taylor 1968: 31) to connect geographically distanced colleagues endeavoring to solve similar intellectual problems and thereby assist scholarly exchange. Licklider and Taylor outlined the requirements for augmenting cooperation between colleagues and subsequently fostering "a working sense of community" (ibid: 31). The core element of such a cooperation is a "single multi-access computer with the aid of telephone line" (ibid: 28) that brings close intellectual contact through sharing individual researchers' resources. Hence the computer was conceptualized as a communication device, or rather, a medium (Friedewald 2000: 10).

This dream of a 'working sense of community' reemerged with the advent of the World Wide Web, for instance in Howard Rheingold's famous book *Virtual Community*, published in 1993. Under this descriptive title, Rheingold examined a new form of social life brought about through computer based communication. According to Rheingold, the Internet is a tool for regaining an earlier type of community: one based on shared interests. Everyone interested in a certain topic is called upon to participate in the computer mediated social group that is also interested in the matter and to contribute not only knowledge but also feelings and emotions, which are the basis for the authenticity of technologically connected communities. For

Rheingold the feasibility of establishing and participating in online communities leads to enormous social and political changes, as their lack of central control increases the efficacy of ordinary citizens.

Rheingold's *Virtual Community* and Licklider and Taylor's conceptualization of the computer as communication device are two examples demonstrating the continuity of pairing a technological infrastructure with values of community in the sense of working together on a certain issue. A later version of this is Tim O'Reilly's outline of the Web 2.0, which called for the development of applications in accordance with the principle of collective intelligence in order to mutualise the knowledge of the people connected by the Internet (O'Reilly 2005). This approach shares its precursors' idea of working together on a more or less defined topic. It also encompasses a high degree of connectivity and easy participation based on technical supply together with a non-hierarchical organization, thus enabling the emergence of a sense of community.

But what at first sounds so similar, reveals differences when we take a closer look. Firstly, whereas Licklider and Taylor presented their idea of prospective online communities, Rheingold described his experience with such communities. Along these distinct lines, Licklider and Taylor asked what is required from the desired connectivity in order to augment the preexistent organization of the scientific group, while Rheingold scrutinized the available technology and its use to achieve the favored social aggregation called community. There is significant difference in purpose: Licklider and Taylor wanted a tool to optimize exchange within the scientific community (Otto 2012: 188), whereas Rheingold sought a new social aggregation through use of the tool. Then, with the advent of the Web 2.0, the relationship reversed and facilities were again in demand.

Necessary to the distinct purposes pursued by Rheingold, on the one hand, and Licklider and Taylor, on the other, is the question, what is meant by 'community'. The scientists of the 1960s referred to their peer group while Rheingold hoped for a change in society. So, unsurprisingly, the extent of the intended community differs significantly with the various implications for its concrete form and organization, as has been pointed out by Felix Stalder. Stalder shows that the delimited group of scientists is composed by equals with a shared routine for solving specific problems. Guiding principles exist in the realm of science, like i.e. publishing research results, which renders them accessible to everyone. Consequently being equal means that everyone is in the same position in respect to gathering the information needed for problem solving. Publishing research results also means that they become disputable: A central part of scientific work includes the open discussion of research questions and their potential answers. The discussion itself is part of the problem solving process, including arguing different approaches in order to archive a rough consensus. This means that the organization of scientific work is inherently collaborative and that the on-line community Licklider and Taylor refer to adds little besides the augmentation of an existing organization (Stalder 2012: 40).

With respect to these principles shared by scientists and their peers, this specific community consists of a group defined by a high degree of homogeneity. Homogeneity is a characteristic that the community described by Rheingold lacks and which, in the best case, could only be achieved through shared interests and emotional investment when participating in online groups. Moreover Rheingold's idea of community is associated with the promise of social and political change; the form of society and democracy is at stake here. The political field operates under a specific logic other than that of science and other than that of economy in which O'Reilly is interested.

Summarized under the buzzword community we find a manifold assemblage of ideas and phenomena dealing with different types of aggregation and social organization. At the same time, their descriptions show a high degree of similarity. They all refer to notions of equality and the absence of hierarchy, of accessibility and participation, connectivity and – most importantly – collaboration. So it might very well be possible that a concept of on-line communities inspired by scholarly work was formulated in the 1960's. But, as it persists beyond its initial sphere, it is conductive even if the context and the conditions have changed: the addressed group has increased, thereby becoming heterogeneous and complex. In other words, the principles ruling early notions of on-line community now encounter realms operating under their own specific logic. Related to the intermingling of the mentioned principles and respective logics, the question of the concrete form of the community arises. Or asked more poignantly: Under which conditions does community-oriented organization take place and how do these conditions give shape to the community? This question refers to objective collaborations like protest movements as well as general relations like democracy in a technological age. In his text "Liquid Demo-cracy and other 'fixes' to the Problem of Democracy" Martin Dege is interested in the latter. He takes a critical view on the attempt to foster democratic values by means of the Internet associated with participation and availability of information. This notion is based on an instrumentalist understanding of technology that is blind to the impact of social development on technology. Collective actions are also the topic of Anne Kaun's paper titled "Crisis and Critique: Histories of Protest Media Participation", which is concerned with changing time regimes and their connection to participation technologies. In Nina Franz's contribution "'Man in the Loop': The Language of Participation and the New Technologies of War" the focus shifts from political participation to military engagement. She questions the consequences of replacing human soldiers with computerized weapon systems and human community with technological collectivity. The section begins, however, with a further perspective on the issue of community and participation in the transformation of sense culture (Sinnkultur). In his text "Other Beginnings of Participative Sense Culture: Wild Media, Speculative Ecologies, Transgressions of the Cybernetic Hypothesis", Erich Hörl argues that participation itself has become our sense and that sense itself is therefore no longer representative but participative.

REFERENCES

Friedewald, Michael (2000): "Konzepte der Mensch-Computer-Kommunikation in den 1960er Jahren: J.C.R. Licklider, Douglas Engelbart und der Computer als Intelligenzverstärker." In: Technikgeschichte 67, pp. 1-24.

Licklider, Joseph Carl Robnett/Taylor, Robert W. (1968): "The Computer as a Communication Device." In: Science and Technology 76. Reprint, http://memex.org/licklider.pdf (August 14, 2015).

O'Reilly, Tim (2005): What is Web 2.0?, www.oreilly.com/pub/a/web2/archive/what-is-web-20.html (August 14, 2015).

Otto, Isabell (2012): "Kollektiv-Visionen. Zu den Möglichkeiten kollektiver Intelligenz." In: Zeitschrift für Medien- und Kulturforschung 2, pp. 185-200.

Rheingold, Howard (1993): The Virtual Community: Homesteading on the Electronic Frontier, Massachusetts: Addison Wesley.

Stalder, Felix (2012): "Autonomie und Kooperation. Der Traum des Internets." In: INDES. Zeitschrift für Politik und Gesellschaft 2, pp. 39-45.

Other Beginnings of Participative Sense-Culture

Wild Media, Speculative Ecologies, Transgressions of the Cybernetic Hypothesis

ERICH HÖRL

> "[...] there is no one that is only One. Until our time, this is what has been the stumbling block of all Western thought."
> JEAN-LUC NANCY (1992: 373)

1 PARTICIPATION IN THE TECHNOLOGICAL SENSE-CULTURE

Participation is nowadays a virulent and virtually omnipresent, political-aesthetic-social-medial phenomenon: the programming industries (Stiegler 2009) and those sciences fascinated with participation celebrate the effectively automatic participation of social media and networks. The recently published *Participatory Cultures Handbook* (Delwiche/Henderson 2012) reconstructs the gradual emergence, since the mid-1980s, of an extensive participatory culture: it appears that the hyper-industrial euphoria for participation has seeped right into the term itself. Today we find ourselves embedded in a new zone of total participation, where participation itself has become a commodity, is tracked and parsed, and forms the basic operation of a new economy not only of data-mining but of reality-mining; the emerging market of behavior and the coming behavioral economy are both

built on participation – a participation cyberneticized and rendered automatic – since it is only through participation that the data traces of behavior
are produced.[1]

But participation is at the same time, still and increasingly, a critical
term, which flourishes alongside of agendas of collaborative digital media
activisms from free software, through open source and commons, to peer-
to-peer-production and post media initiatives; there are debates concerning
the total loss of participation and dis-individuation, symbolic misery, and
even the psychic-collective proletarianisation and algorithmic exploitation
effected through platform industries, social media monopolies, and the new
behavioral economies. Even the most advanced contemporary theories of
the political-aesthetical from Rancière and Nancy to Stiegler are ultimately,
at their core, theories of media and participation, of the shared sense and
"the distribution of the sensible" (Rancière 2009; cf. Stiegler 2014).

Against this background, participation is proving to be a total sense-
cultural fact of the contemporary condition[2]: at least, it is perhaps the center
of the coming governmentality and the heart of the new political economy.
Following Althusser (2014), the subject becomes the subject through partic-

---

1   With the new wave of information and communication technology and the rise
    of what I call third cybernetics, we are witnessing a certain return of the issue of
    behavior and the rise of a new behaviorism that is based on participation. After
    the "fictions" of labor, real estate, and money, on which, as Karl Polanyi de-
    scribed, the market economies of the 19th and 20th century depended, "behav-
    ior", following the analysis of Shoshanna Zuboff, now emerges as "a fourth fic-
    tional commodity" and is apparently becoming "a dominant characteristic of
    market dynamics of the 21st century" (Zuboff 2014). Antoinette Rouvroy coined
    the term "data behaviourism" to describe the "new way of producing knowledge
    about future preferences, attitudes, behaviors or events without considering the
    subject's psychological motivation, speeches or narratives, but rather relying on
    data." This is an integral part of the new "algorithmic governmentality" (Rou-
    vroy 2013: 143-4, original emphasis).
2   The term total sense-cultural fact (totale sinnkulturelle Tatsache) follows Marcel
    Mauss' total social fact, referring to facts that involve the totality of society and
    its institutions (cf. Mauss 1990). Sense-cultural facts are facts that involve the
    totality of a specific sense culture, its basic operations, and its relations as im-
    plemented by its media, technologies, and institutions.

ipation, which is the mode of the interpellation of the subject. "Participate!" is the order, to which critical theories in turn react. The fight for recognition, one could say, is followed by the fight for participation, implying a fundamental rearrangement of sense-culture. And, given that there is a historicity of alienation, as brought to light by Simondon, it may be precisely here that the contemporary problem of alienation is engaged, finding one of its major sites in the question of participation.[3] A pharmacology of participation[4] as an integral part of a technological humanism seems to be urgently needed: a pharmacology that would have the capacity to distinguish between an alienating participation, participation as alienation, and a participation as counter-alienation (an empowering participation).

I am aiming at something different: The ascension of the term participation to the status of a fundamental category of the present, which in itself is already revealed in the great width and complexity of the stratum of phenomena, is in my opinion an indication of a profound transformation of sense-culture – the transformation which I have begun to describe as the technological displacement of sense and which I now want to examine further in regard to how the question of participation appears or reappears at its center. The main thesis of the following reflections is that participation, in the course of the technological displacement of sense, has itself become our sense and that sense itself is no longer representative but participative: Participation has to be considered the new sense of sense, superseding signification, by which the idea of meaning and representational thinking as such ("Vorstellungsdenken" in the sense of Heidegger (1977)) are shattered such that it becomes uncertain "who" or "what" is even participating (cf. Stiegler 1998: 181).[5] It is this essential ambiguity that opens up the ques-

---

3 Simondon (1989: 94-106, particularly 102) suggested that there is a historicity of alienation and of humanisms combating it. Vincent Bontems (2013) has further developed Simondon's concept of alienation.

4 I use the concept "pharmacology" as it has been originally developed by Jacques Derrida (2004) and further fleshed out by Bernard Stiegler (2011; 2013). For Stiegler "positive pharmacology" is the key notion for a rethinking of the technological condition and it is integral part of his general organology.

5 This ambiguity of the "who" and the "what" is no random ambiguity: it marks the technological ruin of the transcendental position of the subject, that always privileges the "who" of meaning-giving and creating subject over the "what". In

tion of participation as such in its whole radicality and which indicates how a new position of the history of sense manifests itself with or in participation. This contribution provides a preliminary sketch of this movement in which we have been living since the beginning of the process of cyberneticization.

The concept of participation may be very old, constitutive of the occidental condition since Plato's teaching of the *méthèxis* and Aristotle's participative theory of the soul and poetics. But the 20th century has seen an unprecedented reconsideration and reassessment of the traditional concept on the basis of profound epistemological, media-historical, and technological-historical changes. The question of participation traverses almost the whole century. Two key theoretical scenes announce this epochal movement: Lucien Lévy-Bruhl's impossible hermeneutics of the affective participation of wild media cultures, which began around 1910 and culminated in the late 1930s, and Gilbert Simondon's speculative ecology of physical, vital, and psycho-collective processes of individuation in the late 1950s and 1960s. In these scenes the term underwent a complete reversal, or rather a radicalisation, towards a thinking of a primary, original, primordial participation as essential relation, which precedes the constitution of its terms, namely the participating individuals. For the first time participation is considered in the strictest possible way. Going far beyond a mere history of the term, I want to illuminate the deep transformation of sense-culture which manifests under the name of participation in the moment of entry into the technological condition and what it brings into question. The precise problem context is the following: We find ourselves in a really important moment in the history of relationality, in a moment of an outstanding transition. Nigel Thrift has characterized our present time as the time of an "augmented relationality" (Thrift 2008: 165). On grounds of newer media technologies, more precisely due to relational technologies and a new algorithmic governmentality that reduces, regulates, controls, and exploits relations, the questions of relation and relationality are being exposed to an unprecedented extent. The exposition of one specific type of relation, the relation of participation, is especially significant for the ongoing transformation. Understanding this relation is essential for understanding both the

---

this sense it is an essential ambiguity. Participatory sense-culture is the ruination of this clear distinction between the "who" and the "what".

contemporary regime of knowledge and power as well as our position within the history of relationality and its inscriptions in our sense-culture.

Contrary to a constantly repeated, fundamentally anti-hermeneutic founding claim of German-speaking media studies, according to which the implementation of symbolic machines heralds the end of all sense or meaning, the general process of cyberneticization (cf. Kittler 1997; Hörl 2013b) and which is currently developing into a third, henceforth termed environmental cyberneticization of distributed if not ubiquitous computing power and the evolution of technical object-cultures, this process eventually leads not only towards the dissolution of objectness as such but also, more recently, towards the entrance into untenable participative process-cultures. This results in the shift from the sense of sense as signification, generated, enforced, and administered by transcendental subjects, towards the new sense of participation which emerges from and as the synergy, the cooperation, involvement, and entanglement of human and non-human forces as the multifarious reality of reference in our new eco-technical medial milieu (cf. Hörl 2011).[6] Another huge problem lies in the question of precisely how this synergy and reference is to be thought and which actors are involved – indeed, a new mythologeme slumbers in this question: the ecological mythologeme of total interconnectivity, which needs to be critically discussed. At its core this also entails a shift from a transcendental sense-culture to one of immanence, a shift with which the avant-garde of the formation of philosophical theory has long struggled, largely oblivious to the technological condition of the shift itself.[7] In the trajectory taken by the term participation we find a strong indicator of this great transformation, where media – and this emerging new sense of media, this historical-ontological turn of the mediality of media, is an effect of this still ongoing transformation as well as one of its causes – are neither substance nor form through which mediated actions or processes happen but simply "an environment of rela-

---

6   Conversely, the struggle for recognition, to return to it once more, belongs to the regime of sense of the working, meaning-forming subject.

7   The shift from a transcendental to an immanence sense-culture does not mean a shift towards an "immanentism", but towards a non-teleological context of reference, in which the relation emerges, without a privileged agent or interpretive ground, without sense, means, and end (transcendental god, transcendental subject, man, state, people etc.) (cf. Lacoue-Labarthe/Nancy 1991: 24-5).

tions in which time, space and agency emerge" (Parikka 2011: 35). Or, one could say: an environment of participations, an environment bursting with participations of every kind.

2 WILD MEDIA: THE REGIME OF AFFECTIVE PARTICIPATION

On March 30th, 1938, after publishing six pertinent books on the modalities of the primitive mentality and a few days before his 81st birthday, Lucien Lévy-Bruhl noted in his diary (carnets) during a stroll at Bois de Boulonge:

"Here is a comment that can reduce the difficulties we find with participations, to which the primitive mentality adapts without any trouble. We do not understand, despite all our efforts, how distinct beings, separated from one another, can nevertheless participate in one other, sometimes to the extent that they become one (bipresence, duality-unity, consubstantiality). But this stems from the differences between their mental habits and ours. For the primitive mentality to be is to participate. [Pour la mentalité primitive être c'est participer.] It does not imagine beings whose existence would be conceivable without putting back into them other elements than those belonging to these same beings. They are what they are by virtue of participation: a member of the human group through participation in the group and in the ancestors; animal or plant by participation in the archetype of the species, etc. If this participation was not given, was not already real, individuals would not exist." (Lévy-Bruhl 1949: 22-23, original emphasis)[8]

These are strong, outrageous allegations, at least to the platonic ear. He who uttered these, at the time fundamentally unsubstantiated, philosophical statements, that primarily concern so-called primitives, has been a professor of the history of modern philosophy at the Sorbonne in Paris since 1904. His lectures on Descartes are legendary. Yet he also has an especially strong bias towards the emerging ethnology, one of those "counter–sciences" as Foucault (1970) called them, which as we know are especially

---

8   Unless otherwise noted, all quotations have been translated from original sources by the translators of this article.

interested in that which will have never been modern. To be precise, he is one of the leading philosophical archaeologists of archaic mindsets who withdraw from any kind of traditional hermeneutics. Lévy-Bruhl is without a doubt famous for his proclamation of a pre-logical mentality of the primitives and that is precisely what ultimately discredited him in the eyes of many intellectuals (cf. Chimisso 1999; Keck 2008: 58-128).[9] At the same time his work – even today – could not be more contemporary, which is why we turn to it again: he makes a rigorous break with all varieties of representation, is interested in everything that shatters representation, he is fascinated by the "bursting of categories", as Lévinas admiringly once encapsulated it. Lévinas went on to say that

"[...] the analyses of Lévy-Bruhl do not describe an experience that could be contained in the categories, that from Aristotle to Kant – despite the nuances – aspired to condition all experience, and to which, with little inconsistency, magic and the miracle also returned. Lévy-Bruhl puts precisely the alleged necessity of these categories for the possibility of experience into question. He describes an experience that plays with causality, substance, reciprocity – as with space and time – with these conditions for 'any possible object'." (Lévinas 1995: 57-58)

It is with precisely this that Lévy-Bruhl places himself at eye-level with the media – and knowledge – historical situation of his day, as characterized by the irruption of unrepresentabilities: in the pre-historic primitive flows of messages between humans, spirits, animals, ancestors, plants, and things, that characterize wild media-cultures on the edge of history and beyond the occidental regime of signification, Lévy-Bruhl rediscovers the facts of transmission in the new electromagnetic media culture and the invisible world of communicating forces of his present that ruined the traditional categories, those of alphabetical sense culture.

The a-representative constitution of the world and experience of the primitives reconstructed by Lévy-Bruhl, in which there is constant communication between all kinds of entities and which is not decipherable by tra-

---

9   I discussed Lévy-Bruhls concept of the prelogical that is not to be confused with something like a *per se* antilogical or alogical attitude in the wider context of the big non-Aristotelian protests and break-ups around and after 1900 (cf. Hörl 2005: 113-229.)

ditional methods, be they Aristotelian, Cartesian, or Kantian, develops the contours of a radical ontology of communication, or more precisely, of the total being-in-communication. In the end this not only maps out the media technological situation around and after 1900, but it still – and that is what matters most – opens the door towards an ontogenetic way of thinking, which potentially belongs to the future. The explosion of technical conditions of communication and transmission, which characterize the then new media culture, is superimposed over the primitive conditions, which then appear as its other scene. Yet in this other scene, the contemporary condition directly finds a breathtakingly original interpretation, which is directly relevant to the description of our own situation, which we can really grasp only today – we, who are confronted again with an explosion of environmental agencies and efficacies by all kinds of ubiquitous computers and media. The point of the matter is this: Lévy-Bruhl's central conceptual creation, with which, deferred onto the scene of wild media and senseless communication, he raises nothing less than the matter of the technological displacement of sense, is nothing less than the concept of participation. This term, in a strange inversion of its platonic application and its dispensing with the Greek modes of being, substances, and accidentals, provides one of the most radical schematizations of the technological condition to date. This is what we must return to once more, especially in contrast to the simplification of the concept of participation with which we are once again burdened.

Even though the question of participation was always present in his work, it only becomes a focal point in Lévy-Bruhl's book of 1931, *Le surnaturel et la nature dans la mentalité primitive*. This is where he speaks of an uncircumventable "affective category", which highlights the mystic experience and the primitive thinking that expresses it. The *Carnets* – a collection of posthumously published notebooks – then establish the main thesis that can be found in varied forms ever since: "What is given first, is participation." (Lévy-Bruhl 1992: 3) There is – and this is the mode of this primordial condition – an "intimate participation" [participation intime], that cannot be "thought" [non pas pensée], but "felt" [mais sentie], enveloped into some kind of "complex", made up of affective and representative elements that are not yet divided as such. According to Lévy-Bruhl "as affective as it is – and it is eminently so – participation has nothing to do with the logical or physical conditions of possibility" (ibid: 7). In other words, participation is an affective regime. As a "feeling *sui generis*" [sentiment *sui generis*], participation is no doubt felt, but it still stays withdrawn from any sensual perception and any representability. It is an a-personal feeling, an impersonal sensation that affects in manifold ways – a dance of relations. "It is felt, so it is real; objectively real" (ibid: 6), he writes, and it therefore stands before or beyond any symbolic representation, which is why participation itself is never represented, even though it schematizes the ways of world-making as well as the production of experience. The world of the primitive is therefore at least twofold, a visible and an invisible world, a world of the senses and a world of participation, with the latter operating as the real. The idea of a detached, divided and separated individual, which seems so simple and natural to us, is, according to Lévy-Bruhl, precisely not primitive (ibid: 19). If the concept stands for the "logical generality", then participation is the "affective generality". It is a matter of "feelings of commonality, solidarity, or communal participation" (ibid: 75), for example among ancestors, totems, configurations of the earth, animals, and plants etc., which are analyzed through the example of the mindset of a "Canaque" (Polynesian, Australasian). All participation is unique and only as real as the respectively felt participation of each individual, which is in turn constituted by participation. This is precisely what makes participation "the general element [...] of an affective order" (ibid: 76). This is thus a generality that is utterly different from the generality of the concept. Participation "is an event that occurs here and now, localized in space and time, or rather, which has its own space and time" (ibid: 76). It is the event of a relation. In it there are no contradictions, but there are "oppositions", "contrasts", and frictions. Even though Lévy-Bruhl first assumed that there might even be a "law of participation", he latter, more cautiously, wrote:

"What remains is the *fact* (not the law) that the 'primitive' frequently has the sentiment of participation between himself and these or those being or surrounding objects, whether in nature or the supernatural, with which he is in or comes into contact" (ibid: 78, original emphasis).

Participation emerges as lying outside of or preceding representation: a "bi-presence", "multi-presence", "consubstantiality", "shared essence", "duality-unity", or a presence split in itself that is never present but remains perpetually approaching. In the constant becoming of participation, the "real

méthèxis" (ibid: 146), the interminable genesis of all beings and things, occurs. Participation is revealed as a process. And if we say, as quoted in the
beginning, that being is participating, then participation is not the key term
of an ontology, but of an ontogenesis.[10] The primitive, the first conceptual
persona of the ontogenetic theory inaugurated here by Lévy-Bruhl, finds
himself at the junction of communicating forces; he is sort of a relay for real communication flows and processes of becoming that traverse him; he is
more-or-less a precarious "site of participation" (Lévy-Bruhl 1996: 251).
To participate means, in this case, to be doomed to take part in the never-
ending flow of information and forces between entities and things, to be
exposed to this participation and to be constituted by it. This isn't just a sur-
real ontology of undefined, a-personal, anonymous forces, but a veritable
cosmo-ontology that not only perfectly corresponds to the tele-
technological facts of the day but also to the transversal tele-technological
assemblages of today.

With this new way of thinking about participation, which Lévy-Bruhl
puts to paper in an unending series of fragments, diary entries, and minor
ecologies of the primitive being, a speculative movement of thought, which
we need in order to decode the technological condition, manifests, that I
want to call a general ecology of participation. But I will return to this later.[11]

---

10 As a counter notion of a non-ontology – against the static understanding of be-
    ing that is symptomatic of standard ontology – the term "ontogenesis" has been
    introduced by Simondon (2005a: 25).

11 This is also the place of today's issue of animism, the site of its incredible actu-
    ality. Our situation is distinguished by a techno-animistic condition that already
    transfers itself onto our thriving neo-animistic theory production. Guattari's de-
    mand for "animist cartographies of subjectivity" (Guattari 2009: 302) in order to
    account for the post-medial condition, which repeats vectors of collective sub-
    jectivation created through what has been called "participation" in "archaic so-
    cieties" (Guattari 1995: 25, 101), directly relates to Lévy-Bruhl's intuition of a
    participative sense-culture. For Guattaris fascination with animist subjectivity
    cf. Melitopoulos/Lazzarato (2012). Lévy-Bruhls revaluation of participation and
    his rethinking of affection respectively affectivity needs a much more careful
    reading than I can offer in this article. I will enfold a more extensive exegesis of
    his position within the history of relationality elsewhere.

3 SPECULATIVE ECOLOGY OF PARTICIPATION

What was beginning to become virulent in Lévy-Bruhl's meticulous minor ecologies of primitive participation turns into a broad speculative program with Gilbert Simondon almost a quarter of a century later. Simondon, a student of Georges Canguilhem and Maurice Merleau-Ponty, stands at the point of convergence of their respective programs – namely Canguilhem's thinking of the living, or rather living individuation, and of technology as an expression of life on the one hand, and Merleau-Ponty's late wild ontology and natural philosophy on the other. He is a philosopher, naturalist, and technologist and creates a general ecology of participation that understands micro-physical, living, and psycho-collective processes of individuation as well as the evolution of technical objects as manifold processes of participation. Man himself, carefully isolated as an entity by traditional anthropology and separated from other entities by the anthropological cut, is embedded back into all-encompassing, multi-scalar communication occurrences of rampant participation(s). Where Lévy-Bruhl attempted to think of participation as a strange ontogenetic figure at the outskirts of history and of the primordial exterior of logical and instrumental reason as having the shape of a wild media-animism, Simondon questions participation within a strictly contemporary frame: as a key issue of the new techno-scientific spirit, which should ultimately only present that which has always – or at least since Greek antiquity – been forgotten. Now participation stems directly from the centers of phenomeno-technical knowledge, the science of field theory, those of thermodynamics and quantum physics, the knowledge of the living (this first and foremost!), and finally cybernetics.[12] The formation of knowledge, as well as the new machine culture, demystifies the inherited idea of the isolated, self-identical individual and instead introduces processes of becoming on all levels of existence. In order to map the diversity of these processes of becoming and the plurivocal experiences that come with them, Simondon creates a new philosophy of nature in the form of a speculative realism of participation. To this end he reanimates and radicalizes the program of a philosophy of the relation, which disregards the substance-oriented model of being of Greek philosophy, in favor of a model

---

12 I have developed the importance of a thinking of the living for Simondon's project more extensively in Hörl (2016).

of a participative becoming. The statement "everything is relational" or "being is relational" (Debaise 2012: 1)[13] – which, according to Didier Debaise, is the keynote of the epochal turn from the paradigm of "being individual" to the paradigm of "being relational" (ibid: 2), and which Simondon embodies like no other – functions as the fundamental principle of a new relational ontology. The relation alone is real – "what is relational is real, and what is real is relational" as Muriel Combes (2013: 18) puts it in her commentary on Simondon. With Simondon the relation as such obtains a new mode of existence, one might say, which in turn directly affects the conceptualization of the different modes of existence. A relational reconsideration of all modes of existence takes place. Relation grows from an inferior category of existence and a simple modality of substantial being, which always precedes any relation that simply connects substantial entities, into "a truly transcendental, genetic, constitutive principle" (Debaise 2002: 54), a principle that therefore always comes before any substantiality, that may even subvert their possibility and that thus motivates a re-inquiry into individuation as such. Relation possesses an immanent genetic, individuating power and ability; it is, as Pierre Montebello (2003: 206) accurately puts it, "the single level of an effervescent productivity in the physical, vital, and mental world". This is the most important part of Simondon's conceptual and theoretical politics.[14] Participation advances to be the relation of the relation *per se*; it is, strictly speaking the relation that instantiates relationality as such and that eventually, as we will see, even carries the whole weight of the real. More to the point: participation is the actuality of

---

13 Both of these statements are in fact quotations from Simondon.

14 Simondon writes: "Being is relation because the relation is the inner resonance of being in relation to itself; the ways, in which it conditions itself inside its own being, splitting and converting it back to unity. [...] The relation can never be understood as a relation between pre-existing terms, but as mutual regime of information exchange and causality in a system that is individuating. Relation exists physically, biologically, psychologically, collectively as inner resonance of the individuated being; the relation expresses individuation, and is at the center of being." (Simondon 2005: 313)

potentiality upon which all becoming is based. Participation is at the very heart of this broad conceptual-theoretical transformation.[15]

As a side note, this does not mean that all relational thinking must eventually lead to a general relationalism as its inevitable consequence or to the statement, to put it simply, that everything is connected to everything, which would be – following Timothy Morton (2010), a pioneer of an "ecology without nature" – the central idea of "ecological thought". Interconnectivity, which Frédéric Neyrat names as the principle of principles of ecology, is what needs to be questioned as such (2014). The predominant euphoria for interconnectivity is an expression of the Californian ideology of a restricted cybernetization, including a certain ecologism and technicism. A critique of what I call the contemporary mytheme of ecology, carried out under the title of a general ecology of media and technology, will need, apart from an ecology of relation, an ecology of separation, without which, and here I follow Neyrat, interconnection is neither possible nor thinkable as the latter is the essential supplement of the former. Separation and separateness are the repressed of ecology. A critical approach to participation will have to keep that in mind. This can also be connected with Nancy's idea of the *partes extra partes*.[16]

---

15 Of course, the focus on relationality, the proclamation of a new age of relational thought as well as the emergence of a relational epistemology, ontology, and even cosmology, are features that are not limited to Simondon. Around and after 1900, Ernst Cassirer, Gaston Bachelard, and Alfred North Whitehead were attentive to the primordiality and originality of relations, though they did not accentuate the relation of participation.

16 Concerning Nancy's expression *partes extra partes,* Derrida writes: "The use Nancy makes of the expression *partes extra partes* seems obsessive at times, and yet it is truly necessary and determining. In addition to an invincible principle of disseminal divisibility, it seems to me to signify a ceaseless desire to mark this break with the immediacy or the continuity of contact, this interval of spacing, this exteriority, at the selfsame moment, furthermore, where there is such insistence on contiguity, touching, contact, and so forth. As if Nancy wanted to mark the interruption of the continuous and challenge the law of intuition at the very heart of contact. And in doing so, his 'intervention' touches and tampers with the philosophic gigantomachy surrounding intuition and intuitionism—no less." (Derrida 2005: 119)

Let's recall that Plato's account of participation, restricted by the philosophy of substance, prioritises a static being over dynamic becoming, thereby depicting participation as directly responsible for the devaluation and secondary status of the relation. As a reminder, for Plato *méthèxis* means a relation of resemblance between intelligible and sensible things, whereby the intelligible things – the ideas – are all that is really true, eternal and self-identical, and are the source of sensible things, which merely participate in the ideas and are therefore afflicted by an ontological loss, hence presenting participation as an asymmetric relation. Bearing all this in mind, Simondon's philosophical and theoretico-political provocation becomes apparent as a genuinely post-platonic operation. Pierre Montebello writes that "Simondon basically invents a new theory of participation after Plato" (2012: 134) and that he does so in order to overcome the previously established inferiority of everything relational: "Nothing appears more disconcerting to Simondon," writes Montebello,

"than the belief that things are separate from each other and external to one another. On the contrary, everything is generated by and results from dynamic processes, ensuing from prehensive relations [*relations préhensives*], relations of capturing and participation [*relations de captations, de participations*], including those at the level of knowledge." (Ibid: 136, original emphasis)

Simondon's astonishment that anyone had ever considered things to be separated, or believed it possible to isolate an individual from its milieu, in a certain sense inverts – while at the same time being at the other end of the evolution of technological object cultures – Lévy-Bruhl's incomprehension of the primitive mentality's operations, which he described so eloquently. Simondon dismisses the "ontological privilege" of the already "constituted individual" (Simondon 2005a: 23); this dominant characteristic of the occidental tradition has lost its long-enduring status: the stable, autonomous, separated individual, that one thought to find in every experience, appears to him as one single irritating abstraction, or – as Whitehead would have it – as a kind of "fallacy of misplaced concreteness" (Whitehead 1997: 51).

Behind this loss of status stands, pretty much as it already did for Lévy-Bruhl, the technological condition, which shifts towards the formalization and operationalization of relations – a move that Cassirer has described as epistemological turn from the notion of substance to that of function – and

that for Simondon counteracts first and foremost the forgetting of operations of either the substantialistic or hylomorphistic hypothesis. Processes
are now of more interest than states and this also and above all applies to
the question of the individual and the process of individuation. Simondon,
the theorist of the evolution of the technical object, points this out more
sharply than anyone else by disclosing the technical primal scene of the
idea of individuation and its lacunae: as the clay pressed into the mold acquires its brick-shape, the hylomorphistic model, which is based on the ancient method of brick production, imagines individuation as operation of an
active form (morphe) that coins, engraves, and informs passive matter
(hyle).[17] But Simondon points out that this representation hides precisely
the concrete, intense, and immanent process of coming-into-shape/in-
formation that happens when material forces are modulated.[18] There are
stringent reasons for this reference to the technical origin of the hylomorphistic scheme even though the human subject as a living individual in Simondon's terms – here he shows himself once again to be a student of
Canguilhem – always already has an "implicit notion" (Simondon 2005a:
50) of the process of vital individuation which must be considered the central "theatre of individuation" (ibid: 27). That is, it still has to refer to "the
technical sphere" (ibid: 50) in order to clarify, explicate, and yes, objectify
this conceptual intuition – it must always pass through the technical experience. It is from this passage on the technical experience that the scheme of
individuation ultimately stems – the scheme which, as I want to formulate
it, dominates each sense-culture, stands at its center, constitutes its unques-
tionable element, and is always and undeniably a technical representation.
This means that if the technical experience changes significantly, then a different scheme of individuation is called for which reveals the limits of the
former scheme: for Simondon this will be the scheme individual/milieu,
which perhaps exposes the relation in all its radicality for the first time and
which corresponds to the transformed technical experience under the tech-

---

17 There are also other narratives concerning the origins of hylomorphism, e.g. Alfred Sohn-Rethel (1976), who suggests that hylomorphism becomes a dominant
ontological paradigm as a consequence of the Greek invention of coinage.

18 Simondon should be regarded as a key figure of a new thinking of modulation.
This is also the scene of origin of Deleuze's conceptualization of the arts as the
"capturing of forces" (cf. Sauvagnargues 2006: 103-105).

nological condition. This is also why Simondon re-evaluates the problem of individuation and promotes it to a position at the front and center of his speculative re-description, rendering it the key issue of his philosophical quest because the inherited scheme has been destabilized, even broken, by the radically different nature of this new technical experience.

If the machine – the already-evolved technical individual succeeding the tool and the instrument – is per se already a "relational reality" (Chateau 2008: 11) and if the technological as a network of open machines and objects becomes the condition, or the associated milieu, of our individuation, then the so called relational technologies and contemporary media technologies that we know to be the epitome of the third cybernetics, as I call it, are today completing the shift into the era of relational reality. They are – and it is a result of cybernetization that we are only now coming to recognize these changes – no longer media or machines of expression: They are not attributes, extensions, supplements or prostheses of the body, the mind or anything, but they have become "prehensive machines" (Parisi/Hörl 2013: 35-51).[19] They appear as assemblages of contraction or rather intensification of forces (Parrika 2010: xxvi), as modulation machines, new associated milieus of sensation etc. More recent approaches of media theory, especially the neo-materialist, media-ecological ones, are all born from this hyper-relationalistic movement and are to be programmatically situated here (cf. Hörl 2013a).[20]

---

19 Media are "prehensive machines of the un-articulatable, un-representable", as Parisi precisely puts it.

20 The third cybernetics is the term I coined for the current level of the cybernetization of all modes-of-being under the condition of environmental media cultures, which must be described in terms of the explosion of environmental agencies through media technologies. The first cybernetics, that accreted around the question of *adaptive behavior*, was mostly concerned with adaptation, while the second, organized around the question of manipulative behavior, was mostly concerned with learning. In both cybernetics, the environment was trivial: it was either a matter of a cybernetic system adapting to an environment or learning to manipulate an environment, transforming it from a non-trivial to a trivial entity. In his *Thèse principle*, defended in 1958, Simondon wrote: "But if it were true that the principle of adaptation does not express the vital functions in depth and cannot account for ontogenesis, it would be necessary to reform all the intellec-

On the basis of the epochal technicity which he exposes – and this is the salient point – Simondon founds a philosophy of nature, which constructs the general sense of nature in the participation of each individual in the pre-individual real. Participative nature, in which communication is everywhere and participation swarms, and this is my thesis, corresponds with the new cybernetic state of nature (Moscovici 1968). It is from here that the question of participation reaches us – it is from here that it befalls us as *our* question. Put differently, this is where our technological epoch of nature finds its theory: the general ecology.[21]

At the heart of what I will from now on call Simondon's general ecology of participation, lies the speculative construction of a level of pre-individual reality. This is the source and the matrix of all existence and every individual or rather every system of individuation, whether physical, living, or psycho-collective, will always be connected to it *qua* participation. It is the storage of potentiality, the origin of every becoming, in which every process of participation as such takes part. This level of pre-individual reality is for Simondon a pre-physical, pre-living nature, understood completely unromantically in the sense of the *physis* of the presocratics. This nature is "a pure *construction*" (Debaise 2012: 4), an unnatural nature as it were, nothing that we could ever encounter or return to; not the entirety of everything that exists, but a layer of reality, which precedes all things and individuals, the source of their creation. Simondon writes – and I emphasize this point to make clear that Simondon's ecology of participation not only is non-natural ecology but also changes the very notion of nature as such:

"We could call this pre-individual reality which the individual carries with him, *nature*, in an attempt to rediscover the meaning in the word nature that the presocratic philosophers put into it: the Ionian physiologists found in it the origin of all species of being, preceding individuation; nature is the *reality of the possible*, [...] Nature is

---

tual systems founded on the concept of adaptation" (Simondon 2005a: 210). I presume that Simondon's speculative ecology is exactly this: an interruption of the fascination with adaptation. His conception of individual-milieu is completely beyond any restricted cybernetics based on adaptation as well as beyond any adaptive concept of the environment.

21 For a first description of the general ecology cf. Hörl 2013a.

not the opposite of man, but the first phase of being; the second being the opposition of the individual and the environment, complementing the individual in relation to the whole." (2005a: 305, original emphasis)[22]

Simondon's pre-individual reality is – and this is important, regardless of whether it may in fact be a Pre-Socratic dream, of which there were others around at the time – contrary to any theory of lack and default, characterized by the abundance and the variety of being. Being is always more-than-one, more than an unity, more than an identity, it is a going-beyond, an excessive power of the mutation, of the excess, the overflow, the transformation.

I cannot go into Simondon's general ecology of participation in greater depth here. In particular, still to be developed are the consequences of integrating its second supporting column, the notion of the milieu and the "pair individual-milieu" (Simondon 2005a: 25), into this participative theoretical structure and how it can fruitfully be put to use in a description of the environmental media cultures of the 21st century, which I have described under the heading of the third cybernetics. In particular, a more precise situating of the concept of the milieu in the history of thought and an account of its theoretical-political force, as offered by Simondon's radicalization of Canguilhem's program, must be left open for now.[23]

Allow me – in passing – to touch on Simondon's theoretical architecture: the characteristic conceptual feature of Simondon's speculative ecology is the double linkage of individual and milieu. On the one hand there is the inseparable "pair individual-milieu" (ibid: 25), Simondon's meta-stable system of individuation, in which the individual always remains connected to its associated milieu, which is simultaneously of the same origin and with which it becomes. On the other hand, this system is itself linked to the

---

22 For Simondon's presocratic notion of nature cf. Duhem 2012. The construction of nature has to be thought of – in Whitehead's sense – in the context of speculative philosophy. It is "the endeavor to frame a coherent, logical, necessary system of general ideas of which every element of our experience can be interpreted" (Whitehead 1985: 3).

23 For a first approach to Simondon's term of the milieu, cf. Petit 2013; on the problem of the reading of Simondon's environmental media condition, cf. Hansen 2012.

so-called pre-individual, from which it emerges *as* a system – the pair individual-milieu is the first dephasement of pre-individual being: the starting point of differentiation, the opening up of differing, a differing and differentiation *before* any difference if the difference of inside and outside can be called the first difference, *différance* in Derrida's sense, a division before any division, not an opposition but rather a tension. The pair individual-milieu always remains bound to this pre-individual as the source of potentiality, into which it inscribes as well as maintains the process of dividing and differing, as long as it keeps individuating and as long as it is phased from one meta-stable state into another.[24] This double linkage is something like the conceptual fundament of Simondon's theory of individuation, which shapes this whole redesign. It is the double linkage of individual and milieu which Simondon tries to grasp with his term of participation.

And that is my main point here: if sense-culture is shifting towards participation, this concerns more than collaborative practices of various kinds; it inscribes itself into our image of thought and calls forth a new image of thought; it becomes an issue in the reconceptualization of knowledge; it requires a speculative construction of nature and a rethinking of the collective and of the political etc. This means that participation is to be explored as nothing less than *a total sense-cultural fact of the technological condition.* Simondon grasped the totality of this problem early on, and sought to respond to it with his speculative ecology of participation.

It is revealing that even Simondon's theory of participation still recognises a magical-animistic scene which shines its light onto the strange neo-animism of our own eco-technological reality and recent reconstructions of animistic subjectivities and ontologies from Guattari through Tim Ingold to Eduardo Viveiros de Castro. Simondon could not have guessed to what extent the cybernetic structuring of earth and world, perception, and thinking and experience would be grasped and realized, by ubiquitous computing, algorithmic environments, multi-scalar networks, and sensory environments. However, the technological networks of his time that heralded the approaching associated technological milieus struck him, nevertheless, as the displaced return of a first pre-subjective and pre-objective – i.e. magical – structuring, which – as we have known since Lévy-Bruhl at the latest –

---

24 On this new idea of becoming as not merely a continued alteration but a linkage of meta-stable states, see Simondon (2005a: 326).

has no immediacy but is always already completely mediated and participatively constituted:

"In adopting the characteristics of networks, the technical reality returns at the end of evolution to the milieu, which it changes and structures (or rather *textures*) in taking account of its general contours; the technical reality rejoins the world, as at the starting point, before the tool and the instrument." (Simondon 2005: 101, original emphasis)

Not only do we glimpse here, at least implicitly, the idea that the whole reconsideration of the problem of the milieu and the development of a radical thinking of the milieu – as Simondon himself first performs – is ostensibly made necessary by technical evolution and its conceptual-political effect. Furthermore this is where a whole program emerges: a contemporary *hermeneia*, adequate to the technological sense-culture, must first of all account for the textures of the modes of being which supersede the modern structuring of subjecthood and objecthood. We need maps of the new media-technological textures, cartographies of the participations that occur on all levels and layers of the cybernetic state of nature, which has been upending the relations between human and non-human actors since at least 1950.

It is precisely these texturalizations of the milieu that occur under the technological condition that must stand at the heart of today's media theory and media philosophy, which follows Simondon in his pursuit of the problem of participation (but which of course is not necessarily only a repetition of Simondon). This is especially valid on the level of the psycho-collective processes of individuation that intersect today with technical processes at the highest intensity. I can only indicate here the direction in which I want to go, following Simondon and at the same time beyond him, by reconsidering and intensifying a very interesting concept that he has coined; namely, the concept of the "second individuation" (Simondon 2005a: 301). The "second genesis" of the human being, which according to Simondon resembles an incomplete being, occurs after its first individuation as a living being, which does not exhaust all forces and potentials, is complete and the individual enters a second career of incompleteness and indeterminacy in its search for a second individuation (cf. ibid: 301). The second individuation, which has been put to work within the long reign of the paradigm of work, under an instrumentalist conception of technique and the stipulations of functionalist sociality, is no genuine individuation, but remains at the level of biological individuation and produces simple, determined and always predetermined individuals, or else nothing (cf. ibid: 302). Somewhere here is where the *transindividual* emerges, as the name for the entire potential of a different second individuation and a different second genesis of individuals as well as where the "collective", as he says, not only appears simply as the milieu to an individual but also as "an ensemble of participation, into which it enters by this second individuation" (ibid: 310). This is where the further perspective of the whole undertaking lies: "There may be other infrastructures," writes Simondon, "than the exploitation of nature by humans in society, other modes of relation to the milieu than those of the relation of elaboration, of work" and which, we might add, have reshaped all other relations, and even the hitherto accepted sense of relation as such. "Even the concept of infrastructure," he says to conclude this thought, "can be criticized [...]" (ibid: 301-2.) Those other, simultaneously inoperative, workless (orig. *désœuvrées*) relations to the milieu are without a doubt modes of participation which together amount to the configuration of a new ecology: Simondon at most only hinted at this new ecology of transindividuation, which could be at the core of the participatory sense-culture, but it is still the grand finale of his work, towards which everything has been leading, even if it is only today that it has become readable and even if it still has to be spelled out.[25] The search for the processes and scenes of the "new individuation", as he also called it, that rearranges other kinds of relations to the milieu, is among the main purposes of a general ecology.

4 POSTSCRIPT ON THE GENERAL ECOLOGY

"Between modernizing and ecologizing, one has to choose", writes Bruno Latour (2012: 20) in his *Inquiry into Modes of Existence*. But the question remains: what does "ecologizing" mean – especially as a counter-term to "modernizing"? Is it merely the overarching name for all operations that push the modern era beyond itself, although these do not necessarily have

---

25 For Simondon's critique of the paradigm of work and his thinking of the worklessness of technology cf. Hörl (2013c).

to be counter- or anti-modern, even if such is and remains the temptation of various ecologisms? (A certain counter- or anti-modern enthusiasm always marks the restricted ecology, as I call it.) Or is it perhaps more than that: the highlighting of the line of flight of our contemporary modes of being and a still-to-come formation?

Working through these questions seems in any case to be urgent, especially as a multifaceted ecological semantics has been descending on us for quite some time, in the broadest diversity of areas, and is about to congeal, within the newly discovered horizon of the Anthropocene and a spectacular reawakening of Gaia, into a new mythology in Barthes' sense, or even become *the* contemporary mythologeme. There is talk of ecologies of sensation, of perception, of cognition, desire and attention, an ecology of infection, an ecology of powers, of information, of media, mind, knowledge, practices, of organization and of the social – to name some central examples which show how the re-description of the modes of being under the technological condition coalesces around the term ecology – of course taking leave of the original biological meaning of the term. This proliferation almost suggests the formation of an ecological unconscious of the episteme and may hint at what can be called "the ecological principle": according to Dirk Baecker (2007: 225) this is the ecological paradigm of the next, computer-shaped society and its overthrowing of the assemblages of experience, enunciation, and knowledge. This proliferation needs to be discussed at its base as a potential expression of our new fundamental position, which of course still lacks a specific structure. A critical approach is necessary here, one that seeks to illuminate the manifold geneses and scenes, as well as the precise conceptual stakes and innovations and the theoretical-political challenges of this *ecologization of the diverse modes-of-being* – for this is what is in question – its non-mythological potential in all its scope. We do not need to raise a new grand narrative under the name of ecology, a new habitation, or an even bigger metaphysical machine than the modern, as Latour suggested (ibid: 34). Just such a critique and elaboration is the purpose of what I have named the general ecology.

Under this title what is to be negotiated is essentially the new eco-technological sense which has emerged during the process of cyberneticization over more than a half (or even a whole) century, and it did so despite various restricting, closing, and nihilistic tendencies and even "monstrosities of the 'cybernetic hypothesis'", which Dieter Mersch (2013: 94) recently discussed in reference to Tiqqun and which brings modernization to its high point and its completion. The term ecologization encapsulates how human and non-human material forces reorganize themselves in the cybernetic state of nature to the extent that the term supersedes the last possibility of what has gone before, surpasses the epistemological and ontological guarantees of the modern age, and questions its basic orientation. Ecologization is therefore the historic final word of the process of cyberneticization as such, the name for an opening: the general ecology focuses precisely on that which has been emanating from cyberneticization as the approaching core content of the new cybernetic state of nature. That, within which opens up its own outside, where it begins – which changes thinking itself and forces it to abjure its modern guiding differences. It is – following Deleuze – what happens to us as the glamour and magnificence of the cybernetic event, whose sense we can affirm and counter-actualize despite and against all the adversity of the phantasms of governance and control of an undeniably expanding technocapitalism and ever more extensive and seamless cybernetic governmentality, in which only these aims may be fulfilled, which Heidegger called the "Gestell" (Heidegger 1994: 24-45). The aim is to analyze the exact content of the technological displacement of sense which has been emerging as the progressive eruption of the historical horizon of technicization and formalization since the late 19th century or at least since 1950. The latter brings forth a fundamental transformation of sense, that first of all inverts the sense of the technical from techniques to technology and then, as a consequence, overturns the sense of the political, the social, the aesthetic, and of knowledge and thinking as such and thereby – and this is the key point – thoroughly "ecologizes" all these spheres, to take up Latour's wording. It is for this reason, and precisely because of the extent to which technology and media are the central actors in this ecologization of the modes of being, that the general ecology is first and foremost a matter of a media- and techno-ecology, which surpasses the cybernetic hypothesis.

In sum: the general ecology thus decisively turns against the claim that "the beginning, the opening [...]" have "no correlate in the technical" (Mersch 2013: 51), as Dieter Mersch recently suggested with great emphasis in reference to the uncircumventable "'fascistic' of cybernetics" (ibid: 87). According to Mersch and others the technical is thus only leading us ever further into the modern cage of servitude. Instead of cyberneticization and computerization; instead of constantly calling on the unavailable, the unthinkable, the uncodeable, uncalculable, uncontrollable, and even the fundamentally anarchic as their other – as a negativistic if not negativity-fixated media theory, although an abstraction-critiquing cultural studies seems to be unable to stop doing this; instead of continually placing trust in the all too simple terminological operations and strategies of a counter-technical, counter-mathematical, counter-logical existentialism that would reveal, in contrast to the various techno-fetishists of media theory, the un-circumventable madness of cybernetic reason; instead of repeatedly falling back into what Nick Land polemically called "transcendental Miserablism" (Land 2013: 16-20); instead of all this, it is a matter of exposing oneself to the new sense that springs forth under the technological condition. This is the only plausible – or should I say neo-critical? – option. I say neocritical because even the sense of the critical might have changed. The other beginning does not in any case lie in Greece – Heidegger already noted in one of his black booklets in 1945/1946 that Greece is no longer the point of refer-ence, before appealing once again to poetry. The other beginning might be the sense of participation, and we will have to describe the scenes of this beginning in all their breadth in order to grasp the genesis of our current situation.

If one thing has become clear, it is that the new sense of sense – and here I follow Nancy's sense-historical reflections (1997) – has lost its sense, its end, its goal and its purpose; thus, it is no longer teleological and, as well as no longer being constituted as modern, it no longer forms part of the traditional sense-culture. Instead, it involves a radically different expe-rience and therefore a renegotiation of the meaning of relation and refer-ence as such; it is a redetermination of the meaning of conjoining and (re)assembling, the emergence of unimagined complicities that have for the first time been uncovered and emphasized, in fact made thinkable, by the technological condition. Here the participative sense reconfigures itself in the time of eco-technology. And just here is the systematic place of the question of participation: where it shows its entire urgency. Hence if I ad-here firmly to the concept of sense, even though it has been transformed in its very foundation, it is because I refute the hyper-nihilistic alliance of technology and capitalism, because I want to radically affirm the sense of technology's nothingness that is still to be grasped, and because I want to show what is opened up within it (cf. Hörl/Tatari 2014). Technology's radical nothingness, the radical no-thing of technology, the absolute opening of technology towards a new thingness through its no-thing-ness: this is what is to be thought of by the general ecology. And one of – if not *the* – core term of the general ecology is participation. Participation may be – in reference to Edgar Morin (2008) – the name for the "ecological relation".

Translated from German by Anne Ganzert and James Burton.

REFERENCES

Althusser, Louis (2014): On the reproduction of Capitalism. Ideology and Ideological State Apparatuses, translated by G. M. Goshgarian, London and New York, NY: Verso.

Baecker, Dirk (2007): Studien zur nächsten Gesellschaft, Frankfurt/Main: Suhrkamp.

Bontems, Vincent (2013): "Esclaves et machines, même combat! L'alienation selon Marx et Simondon." In: Cahiers Simondon, 5, pp. 9-24.

Chateau, Jean-Yves (2008): Le vocabulaire de Simondon, Paris: Ellipses.

Chimisso, Cristina (1999): "Der Geist und die Fakultäten." In: Michael Hagner (ed.), Ecce Cortex. Beiträge zur Geschichte des modernen Gehirns, Göttingen: Wallstein, pp. 224-253.

Combes, Muriel (2013): Gilbert Simondon and the Philosophy of the Transindividual, translated by Thomas LaMarre, Cambridge, MA: The MIT Press.

Debaise, Didier (2002): "Les conditions d'une pensée de la relation selon Simondon." In: Pascal Chabot (ed.), Simondon, Paris: Vrin, pp. 53-68.

Debaise, Didier (2012): "What is relational thinking?" In: Inflexions 5, pp. 1-11.

Delwiche, Aaron/Henderson, Jennifer (eds.) (2012): The Participatory Cultures Handbook, New York, NY and Abingdon: Routledge.

Derrida, Jacques (2004): "Plato's Pharmacy." In: Idem., Dissemination, translated by Barbara Johnson, London and New York, NY: Continuum, pp. 67-186.

Derrida, Jacques (2005): On Touching – Jean-Luc Nancy, translated by Christine Irizarry, Stanford, CA: Stanford University Press.

Duhem, Ludovic (2012): "Apeiron et physis: Simondon transducteur des présocratiques." In: Cahiers Simondon 4, pp. 33-67.

Foucault, Michel (1970): The Order of Things: An Archaeology of the Human Sciences, New York, NY: Pantheon Books.

Guattari, Félix (1995): Chaosmosis, translated by Paul Bains and Julian Pefanis, Bloomington and Indianapolis, IN: Indiana University Press.

Guattari, Félix (2009): "Entering the Post-Media Era". In: Idem, Soft Subversions. Texts and Interviews 1977-1985, Los Angeles, CA: Semiotext(e), pp. 301-306.

Hansen, Mark B. N. (2012): "Engineering Preindividual Potentiality: Technics, Transindividuation, and 21st-Century Media." In: SubStance #129 41/3, pp. 32-59.

Heidegger, Martin (1977): "Die Zeit des Weltbildes." In: Idem, Holzwege, Frankfurt/Main: Klostermann, pp. 75-113.

Heidegger, Martin (1994): Bremer und Freiburger Vorträge, GA Bd. 79, Frankfurt/Main: Klostermann.

Hörl, Erich (ed.) (2011): Die technologische Bedingung, Berlin: Suhrkamp.

Hörl, Erich (2013a): "A Thousand Ecologies: The Process of Cyberneticization and General Ecology". In: Diedrich Diederichsen/Anselm Franke (eds.), The Whole Earth. California and the Disappearance of the Outside, Berlin: Sternberg Press, pp. 121-130.

Hörl, Erich (2013b): "The Artificial Intelligence of Sense: The History of Sense and Technology after Jean-Luc Nancy (by way of Gilbert Simondon." In: Parrhesia 17, pp. 11-24.

Hörl, Erich (2013c): "Das Arbeitslose der Technik. Zur Kritik der Ergontologie". In: Claus Leggewie/Ursula Renner-Henke/Peter Risthaus (eds.), Prometheus, München: Fink, pp. 111-136.

Hörl, Erich/Tatari, Marita (2014): "Die technologische Sinnverschiebung. Orte des Unermesslichen." In: Marita Tatari (ed.), Orte des Unermesslichen. Theater nach der Geschichtsteleologie, Zurich and Berlin: Diaphanes, pp. 43-63.

Hörl, Erich (2016): "'Technisches Leben'. Simondons Denken des Lebendigen und die allgemeine Ökologie". In: Maria Muhle/Christiane Voss (eds.), Black Box Leben, Berlin: August Verlag (forthcoming).

Keck, Frédéric (2008): Lévy-Bruhl. Entre philosophie et anthropologie, Paris: CNRS Éditions.

Kittler, Friedrich A. (1997): "The World of the Symbolic – A World of the Machine." In: John Johnston (ed.), Literature, Media, Information Systems: Essays, Amsterdam: G+B Arts International, pp. 130-146.

Lacoue-Labarthe, Philipp/Nancy, Jean-Luc (1991): Le mythe nazi, Marseille: Editions de l'Aube.

Land, Nick (2013): "Kritik am transzendentalen Miserabilismus." In: Armen Avanessian (ed.), #Akzeleration, Berlin: Merve Verlag, p. 16-20.

Latour, Bruno (2012): Enquêtes sur les modes d'existences. Une anthropologie des Modernes, Paris: La Découverte.

Lévinas, Emmanuel (1995 [1957]): "Lévy-Bruhl und die zeitgenössische Philosophie." In: Idem, Zwischen uns. Versuche über das Denken an den Anderen, München: Hanser, pp. 56-72.

Lévy-Bruhl, Lucien (1992 [1949]): Carnets, Paris: PUF.

Lévy-Bruhl, Lucien (1996 [1927]): L'Âme primitive, Paris.

Mauss, Marcel (1990 [1925]): The Gift. The Form and Reason of Exchange in Archaic Societies, London: Routledge.

Melitopoulos, Angela/Lazzarato, Maurizio (2012): "Machinic Animism". In: Gary Genosko (ed.), Félix Guattari in the Age of Semiocapitalism, Edinburgh: Edinburgh University Press (Deleuze Studies 6/2012), pp. 240-249.

Mersch, Dieter (2013): Ordo ab chao – Order from Noise, Zurich: Diaphanes.

Montebello, Pierre (2003): "La question de l'individuation chez Deleuze et Simondon." In: Jean-Marie Vaysse (ed.), Vie, monde, individuation, Zurich: Georg Olms, pp. 203-214.

Montebello, Pierre (2012): "Gilbert Simondon: Une métaphysique de la participation." In: Didier Debaise (ed.), Philosophie des Possessions, Paris: Les Presses du Réel, pp. 107-141.

Morin, Edgar (2008 [1977]): La Nature de la Nature. In: Idem, La Méthode I, Paris: Seuil, pp. 51-539, here pp. 282-285.

Morton, Timothy (2010): The Ecological Thought, Cambridge, MA, and London: Harvard University Press.

Moscovici, Serge (1968): Essai sur l'histoire humaine de la nature, Paris: Flammarion.

Nancy, Jean-Luc (1992): "La Comparution/The Compearance: From the Existence of 'Communism' to the Community of 'Existence'." In: Political Theory 20, pp. 371-398.

Nancy, Jean-Luc (1997 [1986]): "The Forgetting of Philosophy." In: Idem, The Gravity of Thought, translated by François Raffoul and Gregory Recco, Amherst, NY: Humanity Books.

Neyrat, Frédéric (2015): "Elements for an Ecology of Separation." In: Erich Hörl (ed.), On General Ecology: The New Ecological Paradigm in the Neocybernetic Era (forthcoming).

Parisi, Luciana/Hörl, Erich (2013): "Was heißt Medienästhetik? Ein Gespräch über algorithmische Ästhetik, automatisches Denken und die postkybernetische Logik der Komputation." In: Zeitschrift für Medienwissenschaft 8, pp. 35-51.

Parrika, Jussi (2010): Insect Media. An Archaeology of Animals and Technology, Minneapolis, MN: University of Minnesota Press.

Parrika, Jussi (2011): "Media Ecologies and Imaginary Media: Transversal Expansions, Contractions, and Foldings." In: The Fibreculture Journal 17, pp. 34-50.

Petit, Victor (2013): "Le concept de milieu en amont et en aval de Simondon." In: Cahiers Simondon 5, pp. 45-58.

Rancière, Jacques (2009): The Politics of Aesthetics. The Distribution of the Sensible, translated by Gabriel Rockhill, London: Continuum.

Rouvroy, Antoinette (2013): "The end(s) of critique. Data behaviourism versus due process". In: Mireille Hildebrandt/Katja de Vries (eds.), Privacy, due process and the computational turn. The philosophy of law meets the philosophy of technology, Abingdon and New York, NY: Routledge, pp. 143-167.

Sauvagnargues, Anne (2006): Deleuze et l'Art, Paris: PUF.

Simondon, Gilbert (1989 [1958]): Du mode d'existence des objets techniques, Paris: Editions Aubier.

Simondon, Gilbert (2005a): L'Individuation à la lumière des notions de forme et d'information, Grenoble: Éditions Jérôme Millon.

Simondon, Gilbert (2005b): L'Invention dans les Techniques. Cours et Conférences, ed. by Jean-Yves Chateau, Paris: Seuil.

Sohn-Rethel, Alfred (1976): "Das Geld, die bare Münze des Apriori." In: Paul Mattick/Alfred Sohn-Rethel/Hellmut G. Haasis (eds.), Beiträge zur Kritik des Geldes, Frankfurt/Main: Suhrkamp, pp. 35-117.

Stiegler, Bernard (1998): Technics and Time, 1: The Fault of Epimetheus, translated by Richard Beardsworth and George Collins, Stanford, CA: Stanford University Press.

Stiegler, Bernard (2009): Technics and Time, 2: Disorientation, translated by Stephen Barker, Stanford, CA: Stanford University Press.

Stiegler, Bernard (2011): "Allgemeine Organologie und positive Pharmakologie (*Theorie und 'praxis'*)." In: Erich Hörl (ed.), Die technologische Bedingung. Beiträge zur Beschreibung der technischen Welt, Berlin: Suhrkamp, pp. 110-146.

Stiegler, Bernard (2013): What Makes Life Worth Living. On Pharmakology, translated by Daniel Ross, Cambridge and Malden, MA: Polity.

Stiegler, Bernard (2014): Symbolic Misery, 1: The Hyperindustrial Epoch, translated by Barnaby Norman, Cambridge and Malden, MA: Polity.

Thrift, Nigel (2008): Non-Representational Theory. Space, Politics, Affect, Abingdon and New York, NY: Routledge.

Whitehead, Alfred North (1985): Process and Reality. An Essay in Cosmology, New York, NY: The Free Press.

Whitehead, Alfred North (1997 [1925]): Science and the Modern World, New York, NY: The Free Press.

Zuboff, Shoshanna (2014): "Dark Google." In: Frankfurter Allgemeine Zeitung, April 30, http://www.faz.net/aktuell/feuilleton/debatten/the-digital-debate/shoshanna-zuboff-dark-google-12916679.html (August 14, 2015).

Partial Visibilities, Affective Affinities:
On (Not) Taking Sides

ARNOLDAS STRAMSKAS

"Discipline makes possible the operation of a relational power that sustains itself by its own mechanism and which, for the spectacle of public events, substitutes the uninterrupted play of calculated gazes. Thanks to the techniques of surveillance, the 'physics' of power, the hold over the body, operate according to the laws of optics and mechanics, according to a whole play of spaces, lines, screens, beams, degrees and without recourse, in principle at least, to excess, force or violence. It is a power that seems all the less 'corporal' in that it is more subtly 'physical'."
MICHEL FOUCAULT (1976: 177)

"If we see a succession of movements hurrying one after the other, without leaving anything visible behind them, it must nonetheless be admitted that something persists. A powder trail links what in each event has not let itself be captured by the absurd temporality of the withdrawal of a

> new law, or some other pretext. In fits and
> starts, and in its own rhythm, we are seeing
> something like a force take shape. A force
> that does not serve its time but imposes it,
> silently."
>
> THE INVISIBLE COMMITTEE (2009: 18)

If, according to Gilles Deleuze, Michel Foucault's post WWII model of "disciplinary societies" was replaced by "control societies" (1990), Foucault's insights into the regime of discipline remain both relevant and determinate, and the epochal break cannot be identified. If, as Foucault claimed, a pyramidal structure of power remains, the physics of power are dispersed and operate vertically and horizontally alike. We can locate Foucault's "disciplinary society", with its "surveillance", "supervision", and "gazes" (Foucault, 1976: 177) invested in maintenance of order, as another stage that picks unprecedented speed and intensity in the mediatized, networked, so called participatory era of the societies of spectacle. The major formula of the "society of spectacle", as articulated by Guy Debord, states that since "[e]verything that appears is good; whatever is good will appear" (1994: 15). A few decades later, Deleuze proclaimed that "compared with the approaching forms of ceaseless control in open sites, we may come to see the harshest confinement as part of a wonderful happy past" (1990). Margarida Carvalho, however, describes it as "Monitored, assessed, controlled, divided and owned: such is the complex condition of contemporary space" (2009: 17).

If we would accept that publicness, which today centers around forms of visibility and took new forms and dimensions in the digital era, is an 'open space' of appearance where unprecedented confinement and control takes place, we would not only be forced to rethink normative ideals of the public sphere but would also have to rethink some basic categories of political theory as it is largely based in these ideals. This normalizing imperative of publicness, which paradoxically presents itself as the realm of freedom, indeed becomes a site of technique of life – to use Georg Simmel's formulation (2002: 11). It is not, as Foucault states, that "the spectacle of public events" is "substituted by uninterrupted play of calculated gazes"; rather, they become indistinguishable, and voluntary participation in the spectacle of publicness becomes constitutive of the very notion of public. As counterintuitive and untimely as it may sound, the political question needs to be asked: What is at stake in non-participatory, invisible 'unmediated' presence?

Tiqqun, in their *Cybernetic Hypothesis*, make a claim that within the conditions of cybernetic capitalism analytical importance should be equally placed upon circulation rather than mere production when analzying the basics of political economy (2001: 17). Circulation becomes a distinct category of valorization within the broader process of capitalist production. The banal example of this today could be the phenomenon of Facebook, which extracts economic value through the sheer volume and scope of its network, additionally providing intelligence for security and surveillance services. Questioning this apparatus of "centralized system of panoptical visibility" (Tiqqun 2001: 24) and practicing forms of invisibility, non-circulation, and disappearance seem to be important issues in any conception of affective micropolitics. It also should be pointed out that – to quote Levinas – "invisibility does not denote an absence of relation; it implies relations with what is not given" (1979: 34).

Micropolitics, however, does not present an alternative or totalizing challenge, but should be seen as a crucial element in attempts to think/move beyond the present state of affairs. If publicness comes to mean a mediated, simulated, and pacified zone of post-political reality, then micropolitics, arguably, come to signify a different quality of sociality – if not outside than at least in the shadows of discipline and protocoled, in/formal rules of conduct. But to think micropolitics through, it is useful to conceive of it as more than a mere behind-the-closed-door ethnographic account of the political. The micropolitical approach emphasizes inventiveness, incompleteness, and becoming: "What is usually constituted as *the real thing* – Politics with a capital P – is far less rigorously inventive, precisely because it operates in the sphere of representation where pre-composed bodies are already circulating" (Himada/Manning 2009: 5).

Precautions, no doubt, need to be taken not to espouse a simple binary juxtaposition of macro and micro-levels. Following Massumi and McKim, Micropolitics "seeks the degrees of openness of any situation, in hopes of priming an alter-accomplishment. Just modulating a situation in a way that amplifies a previously un-felt potential to the point of perceptibility is an alter-accomplishment" (2009: 7).

However, the potentiality of micropolitics is precisely what is at stake. No matter how grand any given social architecture of discipline and control is, there is always potential inscribed within the practices of daily life which resist in numerous paths, encodings, and inscriptions. Macro, or – according to Deleuze and Guattari – "molar aggregates" (2005: 40) are powerful only to a certain extent, and their efficiency is co-dependent on micro, or molecular, interventions and "infiltrations". They argue that "Lines of flight", a molecular mode of operation,

"never consist in running away from the world but rather in causing runoffs, as when you drill a hole in a pipe; there is no social system that does not leak from all directions, even if it makes its segments increasingly rigid in order to seal the lines of flight" (Deleuze and Guattari 2005: 204).

The relevant term here, also drawn from Deleuze and Guattari's work, is minor politics. According to Nicholas Thoburn, "minor politics is not a re-signed turn to the local or particular as such. Rather, it is a politics oriented towards *social relations* and their possibilities for becoming beyond identity" (2003: 44).

In this context, the role of 'minor spaces' comes to constitute an essential element in the micropolitical, minoritarian politics of exodus from politics-as-we-know it. In the environment of hyper-mediation and publicness, Ha-kim Bey claims, that "simply to meet together face-to-face is already an action against the forces which oppress us by isolation, by loneliness, by the trance of media" (1994: 16). Bey, however, does not suggest that an 'unqualified' face-to-face meeting – as stated above –is sufficient in itself. Instead, he proposes cell-like proliferation of secret societies, affinity groups, and nomadic bands that flee mechanisms of representation and invent playfulness in everyday (political) life. A Chinese proverb quoted by Bey, that "the mandarins draw their power from the law; the people from the secret societies", is exemplary of such rationale (Bey 1994: 13). However, minor spaces do not need to be secretive per se, nor are they automatically liberatory. Liberty, as Foucault insisted, is a practice and not a stale space or arrangement to be found and used (2000: 354). Minor space is a different modality in relation to dominant configurations of public space and parameters of political engagement. Minor space, tentatively, should first of all be about relationality and the affective dimension of micropolitics that the spaces outside or partially overlapping with publicness exhibit. It could be described as deterritorializing *spacing* or *space making*, and if the space absolutely outside publicness is unavailable, minor spaces could be described as *partial visibilities* which obstruct the field of vision and gaze of surveillance. This space making allows for the expansion of "affective territory" – to use Brian Holmes' term (2009: 75) – not its circumvention.

One such example, which partially represents the theoretical contours outlined above, is the infoshop/social space called Taškas in Vilnius, Lithuania. Taškas literally means point, spot, or dot as well as being a slang word for a place selling alcohol illegally. The idea for Taškas – with some initial disagreement on its necessity – came from two people (Agnė and Noah). The impetus for establishing the space arose after a week-long seminar/discussion in rural Lithuania under the banner of "Don't believe you have rights", which was entitled "Feminist critique of the contract".[1] The goal was to investigate the limits of the legal framework prevalent in feminist and LGBT politics from the ultra-left position. The group consisted mainly of activist and activist-scholars from the UK and Lithuania. However, no strategic elaborations for future actions were conceived. The aim of opening the space in Vilnius was in part an attempt to further these critiques within the existing groups, but over time it became apparent that anti-capitalist trajectory did not resonate with those involved in LGBT, queer, and feminist politics.

The thematic scope within the space was broadened. A Facebook account was created to replace the website. One participant who came to Taškas was encouraging the use of "soft politics" via open social space and "dropping hard lines of ideological standpoint and work of forming radical politics on a level of thought." (Noah, interview) Cooking was also made a regular feature of the space, bringing in people who would not have come

---

1   The following quotes are extractions of an interview I conducted with Agnė and
     Noah on April 5, 2014 in Vilnius.

otherwise. This move made one of the organizers, who in his earlier in-
volvements in similar spaces in the US had often critiqued them as "intro-
verted and apolitical", rethink his previous position on these micropractices. The concentrated, thematic presentation format was also re-
thought since it appeared ineffective. People had come, listened to the pre-
senter(s), and left without serious engagement. Thus, more open-ended
discussions around certain topics were being tried out instead.

Taškas could be seen as a minor space, since it didn't have a protocol
to draw upon and was constantly rethinking its purpose and tactics. It does
resemble and somewhat follow the tradition of infoshops and social centers, but it came about as a space of experimentation and research questions: What kind of organizing exists? Would there be a need for a space
like this? What could this kind of space become? (Agnė, interview) Compared to other countries which have numerous social spaces, opening
Taškas had a singular objective:

"The space didn't form out of reaction, it wasn't positing at exactly something else
or coherence, realization of ideological principles against another existing political
groups but more of an opening inquiry. It is kind of a beginning point. You are going to explore, you have some kind of interest in exploring something, some kind of
horizon." (Noah, interview)

Rancière's insistence against the binary of organization versus spontaneity
seems relevant here:

"All those who deafen us with their old refrain about the critique of spontaneity and
the necessity of organization forget precisely that an organization is only political if
it is 'spontaneous' in the strict sense of the word, that is to say if it functions as a
continuous origin of an autonomous perception, thought or action." (2001: 19)

Noah's take on this:

"[T]here was a lot of discussion in New York and that I saw in London and other
places, whether having dinners once a week was really a first step in autonomously
reproducing ourselves outside of capitalism and I was really frustrated with some of
these discussions because they often folded back on the group dynamic where it was
all about starting a social club and not about directing it towards a political antago-

nism. It took on an extroverted mentality. But [...] it kind of shifted through experiences here where I began to think how we can reconcile these two tendencies. And I think meeting a lot of different people here with vastly different social backgrounds and ideological affinities has been pretty important. But it's always still a question of reconciling that, between having eclectic social affinities and social forms that can actually oppose more direct and violent attacks of capitalism, the state, nationalist movements and these kinds of things." (Noah, interview)

The importance of this political space-time could not be overestimated. It seems that in less than a year of its existence, Taškas was able to bring more people together in various configurations and raise important debates in terms of visions, strategies, and practices of anti-capitalist organization than years of online discussions, Free University lectures, and occasional, minuscule street protests. It is not necessarily a problem that a solid platform has not formed (yet). The significant point is that "a lot more productive discussions and solidarities form among people who've gotten together with different perspectives but somehow continued to work out relationships with one another over time" (Noah, interview).

The affective dimension plays a strong part here. It is not about how affinities and friendships develop which then would be channeled properly into (anti)politics, but how spatially embedded relationships transform in a variety of combinations of politics and friendships. The emphasis on relationships and dissemination or the contamination of ideas creates a political context where a collective political potential starts to be felt and a shared direction is formulated. This approach is in stark contrast to an impersonal circulation of ideas and an individualized consumption model of these ideas that is prevalent at the moment in the Lithuanian context of 'politics' on Facebook.

When asked about the utility of Facebook in reaching out to the participants, organizers agreed that it reached new people but overall engagement was disappointing. The problem was that instead of people getting involved in running the space, organizing and participating in the events, it became another something-to-do outlet, a spectacle of sorts managed by someone else. The Facebook presence increases circulation but does not necessarily contribute to effective and affective engagements. It inevitably affects the content of the events and the perceptions of those events when they are communicated in impersonal manner (e.g. one of many events to attend). Facebook "alleviates responsibility and labor that goes into communication of information and in this alleviation process there is kind of a substitution of social efforts that goes into forming a community with this very consumable information; which is a real problem." (Noah, interview)

The question to be posed, paraphrasing Deleuze and Guattari, is not what the physical space means, but what does it do? This question should be asked in the context of the shrinking importance of time and space as primary vectors of the previous era, but in the context of increasing importance of appearance, as suggested by Alexander Galloway:

"Instead of politicization of time or space we are witnessing a rise in the politicization of absence – and presence – oriented themes such as invisibility, opacity, and anonymity, or the relationship between identification and legibility, or the tactics of nonexistence and disappearance, new struggles around prevention, the therapeutics of the body, piracy and contagion, informatics capture and the making-present of data (via data mining)." (2012: 246-247)

In the context of Taškas, the various issues mapped out by Galloway are relevant to attempts to organize the space on a daily basis, which requires some suspension of the visible. The strength of this project/space is that there is an acute awareness and self-reflection – drawing on a larger ultra-left position – not to become an insular sect and not to turn space into an identity which would consequently preoccupy itself with self-reproduction. That is, a 'horizon' to externalize these affective affinities-in-formation to the outside of place:

"All assumed, when political perspectives have traction and establish themselves and grow it is usually because they're embedded in a pretty tangible struggle. I think that that can happen in a space, but I don't think it's something that can spontaneously form through having ten more presentations or dinners or something." (Noah, interview)

It touches upon the crucial question whether spaces such as Taškas emerge (or should emerge) to fill the needs of movements or whether movements could emerge from these spaces. *On not taking sides*, may, arguably, be a combination of both. The ideas and practices may externalize and then return to – or create new – spaces for movements' needs. Surely, there is a trap in developing an 'activist' mentality and becoming too centered on your ability to see through and analyze reality, as if nothing else happens or matters, submerging yourself in certain safe-havens. But there is also a similar danger in denouncing micropolitical practices and their potential as a mere distraction, elitist voluntarism and so on, in the face of great capitalist totality and real subsumption. The questions and discussions at Taškas are, by various means, addressing precisely these questions, attempting to escape politics as an abstraction – 'heads without bodies' – into something embodied and material, affective and political. Therefore it seems that at this stage of cybernetic capitalism, strategic-partial visibility may be among the practices which seek to invent politics-to-come – indeterminate, experimental and as an experiential play with time, space, body, and appearance.

REFERENCES

Bey, Hakim (1994): Immediatism, Edinburgh and San Francisco, CA: AK Press.

Carvalho, Margarida (2009): "Affective Territories." In: Inflexions: A Journal for Research-Creation 3, pp. 1-22.

Debord, Guy (1994): The Society of the Spectacle, New York: Zone Books.

Deleuze, Gilles/Guattari, Felix (2005): A Thousand Plateaus: Capitalism and Schizophrenia, Minneapolis, MN, and London: University of Minnesota Press.

Deleuze, Gilles/Guattari, Felix (1986): Kafka: Toward a Minor Literature, Minneapolis, MN: University of Minnesota Press.

Deleuze, Gilles/Negri, Antonio (1990): "Gilles Deleuze in conversation with Antonio Negri, translated by Martin Joughin", http://www.generation-online.org/p/fpdeleuze3.htm (August 13, 2015).

Foucault, Michel (1976): Discipline and Punish: The Birth of the Prison, New York, NY: Vintage.

Foucault, Michel (2000): "Space, Knowledge, and Power." In: James D. Faubion (ed.), Power. Vol. 3 of Essential Works of Foucault: 1954-1984, New York, NY: The New Press, pp. 349-364.

Galloway, Alexander R. (2012): "Black Box, Black Bloc." In: Benjamin Noys (ed.), Communication and its Discontents: Contestation, Critique, and Contemporary Struggles, Wivenhoe and New York, NY: Minor Compositions, pp. 237-249.

Himada, Nasrin/Manning, Erin (2009): "From Noun to Verb: The Micropolitics of 'Making Collective.'" In: Inflexions: A Journal for Research-Creation 3, pp. 1-17.

Holmes, Brian (2009): "The Affectivist Manifesto: Artistic Critique in the Twenty-First Century." In: New Communities 39, pp. 74-76.

The Invisible Committee (2009): The Coming Insurrection, Los Angeles, CA: Semiotext(e).

Levinas, Emmanuel (1979): Totality and Infinity: An Essay on Exteriority, Boston, MA, and London: Martinus Nijhoff Publishers.

Massumi, Brian/McKim, Joel (2009): "Of Microperception and Micropolitics." In: Inflexions: A Journal for Research-Creation 3, pp. 1-20.

Power, Nina (2014): "Philosophy and the Collective." Presentation at Kingston University, London, March 13, http://backdoorbroadcasting.net/2014/03/nina-power-philosophy-and-the-collective/ (August 13, 2015).

Rancière, Jacques (2011): "Against an Ebbing Tide: An Interview with Jacques Rancière." In: Paul Bowman/Richard Stamp (eds.), Reading Rancière: Critical Dissensus, London: Continuum, https://www.academia.edu/1115969/Ranciere_Interview (August 15, 2015).

Simmel, Georg (2002): "The Metropolis and Mental Life." In: Gary Bridge/Sophie Watson (eds.), The Blackwell City Reader, Oxford and Malden, MA: Wiley-Blackwell, pp. 11-19.

Thoburn, Nicholas (2003). Deleuze, Marx, and Politics, London and New York, NY: Routledge.

Tiqqun (2001): The Cybernetic Hypothesis, http://theanarchistlibrary.org/library/tiqqun-the-cybernetic-hypothesis (August 13, 2015).

"Man in the Loop"

The Language of Participation and the New Technologies of War

Nina Franz

The narration of a community in battle, a community ready to kill and to die, was at the heart of the ideology of war that drove the two world wars and the ensuing catastrophes of the 20th century (Losurdo 1995). The promise of community might still be one of the strong ideological claims that drive young people to join the military, or militant groups, today. However the 'zero-death' policy behind the highly technicized side of to-day's asymmetrical conflicts makes the idea that an ideology of communal death could steer military policy seem significantly out of place. What happens to the 'claims of community' from past campaigns, when the new military discourse is focused on a type of intervention that turns the notion of combat into an issue of 'targeted killing' and 'surgical strikes', carried out by networked machines and largely operated by remote control? Today, a new global 'theatre of war' stretches from control rooms in remote areas in North America and Germany (Bryant/Goetz/Obermaier 2014) to places like Northern Pakistan and Afghanistan. The purpose of this paper is not to un-cover the hidden and often misrepresented realities of the secret operations of unmanned military technology (this important topic has already been addressed by others[1]), but to analyze a specific way of handling the idea of a 'community in battle' that is projected by a certain military culture at work today.

In the new military discourse as presented in documents like the US-military's 'roadmaps' for unmanned aircraft systems, human actors no longer appear as heroic subjects but as potential hazards for the work of networked machines.[2] And yet the "man in the loop", the human factor within the control and decision making processes, is the key-trope in selling "drones", or weaponized unmanned technologies, to the public. But what does it mean to speak of participation within a network that is no longer defined by human subjects? What are the "claims of community" proposed within this discourse and how do they relate to their historical predecessors? Finally, if exclusion has always been one of the defining features of operable communities, do we perhaps now witness the constitution of an 'operable community' under technological conditions ultimately bound to exclude the human subject?

Next to drill and disciplinary training, group experience in battle situations is a crucial factor in motivating a person to kill: The strong bond between combatants in facing death, accountability to one's comrades, mutual surveillance and what military psychologist Dave Grossman has called "group absolution" (Grossman 2009 [1996]: 152) – meaning the psychological process of shifting responsibility from the individual to the anonymous group – all contribute to forming the "community of death" that has been the basis of the experience of war throughout human history. Crew-served weapons – those that are operated by two or more individuals in concert – are therefore much more effective than those operated by an individual.[3]

---

1   See for instance the reports by the Bureau of Investigative Journalism and the Stanford/NYU Report *Living Under Drones*, which both offer well-researched account of the "drone wars" from the perspective of its victims.

2   The consequences for a changed military ethos have been highlighted by Gregoire Chamayou in his *Theorie du drone* (2013) and more recently by Matthias Delori in a study concerning the attitudes of members of the French Air Force and the construction of "meaning" in the military in the context of asymmetrical warfare (2014).

3   This is illustrated by the fact that during WW2, only 15 to 20% of individual riflemen were able to overcome the reluctance to kill, while nearly 100% of crew-

Distance to the enemy is the second most important factor in overcoming that crucial resistance to kill. Grossman, writing in the late 1990s, claims that the chance of an individual refusing to kill at maximum or long range is very low, as is the chance of psychiatric trauma. Today, questions of distance and proximity are very much complicated by technologies of real-time surveillance and satellite communication that turn perception into a matter of highly mediated "situational awareness".

Instead of being situated in a communal experience of imminent danger and affect, drone operators find themselves within partly anonymous communication networks and in global remoteness from the actual so-called "battlefield" (Power 2013; Bryant/Goetz/Obermaier 2014) – a setting that may create its own fatal group-dynamics, as Derek Gregory has recently shown in his re-reading of the tragedy at Khod (Gregory 2014; 2011: 203). Although the term 'unmanned' suggests otherwise, today's remote controlled military systems must be thought of as "crew-served weapons" in Grossman's sense. UAV-pilots and sensor operators always work in teams of two and are embedded within a larger communicative "crew" of analysts, legal consultants and other staff that is mediated in real-time by live-chat and via satellite feeds. Thus, it is nearly impossible that an individual operator will ever find him- or herself alone with the decision to kill. At the same time, there seem to be new *proxemics* of war at work, both on a geo-political scale and within the personal experience of the weapons-operators, who find themselves merely "18 inches" from the action (the distance from eyes to screen), "on the other side of the globe", and, via immersive experience, a few thousand feet above the target in the imagined cockpit of the drone (Martin 2010: 34). A variety of writers have pointed out that the technologies of remote viewing come with new perceptual intimacies (i.e. Gregory 2011: 206, Weber 2013: 35, Suchman 2015: 9-10). Real-time video feeds allow the operators to witness the effects of their killing more clearly and crisply than in any other battle situation before: This is the paradox of long range and high resolution that presents a sort of truism of digital media in the 21st century.

It is conventional knowledge that distance is one of the most basic purposes of technology in war. Older refined tools, like bow-and-arrow, slings,

---

served weapons (such as machine guns that take two people to operate) were fired (Grossman 2009 [1996]: 153).

darts, and fire arms are distance weapons which have undergone an increase in range over time. One often-cited example is the re-introduction of the crossbow in Europe in the 11th century, which raised very similar 'ethical' questions as the drone technologies of today, because of their sheer deadly force and the "cowardly" remoteness from which they are operated. They were subsequently legal for deployment in distant lands only, and, during the crusades, strictly prohibited from being used "against Christians and believers" as proclaimed in a decree by the Second Council of the Lateran in 1139 (Bumke quoted in Ladewig 2007: 26; see also: van Creveld 1991: 71; Delori 2014: 100).

Enormous efforts were necessary to train and drill the armies of the past for the readiness to lose their lives until, in the 20th century, more sophisticated technological weaponry turned warfare into a matter of well-trained technicians rather than drilled, machine-like warriors (Bröckling 1997). In the age of industrial warfare, steel and machinery distanced this new kind of soldier from the 'hands-on' experience of war. Among others, Ernst Jünger lamented the demoralizing effect of the soldier-technician who has his hands on buttons and levers instead of the throat of his enemy[4] and who is alienated from what used to be a tight-knit community of male companions. In his late novella "Glass Bees" from 1957, Jünger undertakes a kind of nostalgic history of warfare from horseback to the drone age. Richard, a former cavalryman who turned tank-operator, complains: "It was nothing like the great days on horseback..., it was hot machine work, invisible, without honor, ...soldiers were not soldiers anymore",[5] only to discover later, that the hot machine work had yet been replaced by a more intricate mechanism, which he encounters in a 'scene of first-contact' with a swarm

---

4 Jünger emphatically describes combat in close range, as a primal urge that drives all war, in spite of technology, which is "blind and without will" (2002: 19).

5 "Das war das Ende der Reiterei. Wir mussten absitzen. In den Panzern war es eng, heiß und lärmend, als ob man in einem Kessel säße, an dem die Schmiede hämmern. ... Das war keiner der großen Reitertage, von denen Monteron uns erzählt hatte. Es war heiße Maschinenarbeit, unsichtbar, ruhmlos, und immer von der Aussicht auf den Feuertod begleitet, die sich nicht abweisen ließ." (Jünger 1978 [1957], 44-45)

of artificial bees that self-organize in a cybernetic paradigm of control, and which Richard suspects to have the capacity to kill (Jünger 1957: 85-93).

But, outside of the realms of fiction and techno-dystopia, it is only more recently that technologies may actually introduce a new degree of distance to essential categories that constitute human action. The period since WW2 is defined by a tendency of replacing human beings through machines. The progressing automatization on one hand, and the enormous increase in destructive potential with the rise of nuclear weapons on the other, have eventually rendered the idea of 'mass-armies' obsolete. Consequently, the soldier as a heroic subject and the traditional idea of a 'community in battle' appears antiquated (Bröckling 1997: 290-328).

Guided missile technology could arguably be seen as a paradigmatic predecessor of the "unmanned" and "remotely piloted weapons system" from the second half of the 20th century, which led the way to the age of electronic warfare (van Creveld 1991: 268; see also Chamayou 2015: 27). The computerization or "cybernetization" of military technology, with its origins in WW2-antiaircraft defense and the deciphering of the ENIGMA code, has pushed human action even further to the periphery of the battlefield, both in terms of spatial distance and by attributing more and more of the analytical and decision-making powers to the silent work of programmed machines and sensors[6]. Eventually the notion of combat became a categorial problem of sensor- and computer-aided warfare, due to the nuclear arms race of the cold war with its logic of strike and counter-strike on one hand, that calculated in minutes if not seconds, and the human capacity to decide and react at a compatible speed and with sufficient reliability on the other. It is within this context of networked, computerized-organizational war and its replacement of the experience of war as a communal event of human actors that I set my focus on the current discourse about the 'human factor', negotiated predominantly within US military affairs.

Peter W. Singer, author of a well-known book on robotic warfare, states that "humans are becoming the weakest link in the defense system" (2009:

---

6   This famously led Friedrich Kittler to conclude that the computer had won WW2 (2013: 242).

64).[7] When looking at the documents in which the US-military publicizes its "roadmaps" for the coming decades, it becomes clear that this is in fact one significant underlying assumption, even if it is increasingly veiled by a way of speaking that seems to be very cautious about its possible ramifications. Human agency is presented as a matter of "participation" in technological systems; thereby, the discourse emphasizes an apparent precarization of the role of the human subject within the "community of war" it describes.

The Unmanned Aircraft Systems Flight Plan of the US Air Force for 2009-2047 states, under the headline "Path to Autonomy": "Today the role of technology is changing from supporting to fully participating with humans in each step of the process" (Donley, Schwartz 2009: 41). Only a few lines down, in the same document, the role of "participant" shifts from technology to the human being:

"[...] [I]ncreasingly humans will no longer be 'in the loop' but rather 'on the loop' – monitoring the execution of certain decisions. Simultaneously, advances in AI will enable systems to make combat decisions and act within legal and policy constraints without necessarily requiring human input." (ibid)

Following this description, full autonomy is not to be seen as a problem of technological feasibility, but only as one of political and legal constraints: "Authorizing a machine to make lethal combat decisions is contingent upon political and military leaders resolving legal and ethical questions." (Ibid)

A LANGUAGE OF AUTOMATION

The same flight plan that dates back to 2009 states that for the "growing UAS community" many of their current "manpower challenges" will be solved as technological development progresses. Perhaps the key expression in this process is "Human Systems Integration" (HIS), which the 2009-plan seeks to implement in the work of the Department of Defense. Accord-

---

7   Lucy Suchman hints at Singer's complicity in the discourse described here, stating that his position "helps to perform the technological and political 'realities' that it purports innocently to announce" (2015: 13).

ing to the mission statement on a website run by the 'Assistant Secretary of Defense for Research and Engineering', "human use" is a central concern, not referring to its use for humans but the effective "usage of humans":

"Human Use: Optimal establishment and execution of policy related to research, through accordance with all applicable directives, statues, and laws leading to the safe and effective usage of humans in DoD sponsored research." (Assistant Secretary of Defense for Research and Engineering 2014)

The mission for the department for 'Human Systems Research & Engineering' describes humans as "elements" and "components" in operating systems.[8] Similar to Manuel DeLanda's famous "robot historian", statements like these seem to be uttered from the perspective of a machine examining its insufficient human elements, "an angle that stresses the effects of technology on the military, understood [...] as being itself a coherent 'higher level' machine: a machine that actually integrates men, tools and weapons as if they were no more than the machine's components." (DeLanda 1994: 4)

Since 2009, there appears to be a shift in the way issues like the autonomy of technological systems are brought to the table. If the cited document from 2009 gave a straightforward account of the way in which full autonomy is regarded a likely development of the near future, comparable documents from 2011 and 2013 use a much more cautious language. Already in the "Unmanned Systems Integrated Roadmap" of 2011, careful consideration goes into the phrasing of ideas on autonomous machines making kill decisions. Focus is now on efficiency and cost-effectiveness as the driving force for reducing the participation of humans in active combat situations:

"Today's iteration of unmanned systems involves a high degree of human interaction. DoD must continue to pursue technologies and policies that introduce a higher degree of autonomy to reduce the manpower burden and reliance on full-time high-

---

8   *Mission*: Develop true synchronization between hardware, software, and human elements of warfighter systems leading to optimized performance across DoD while minimizing harm and cost to the human component." (Assistant Secretary of Defense for Research and Engineering 2014)

speed communications links while also reducing decision loop cycle time." (Winnefeld/Kendall 2011: vi)

The updated roadmap from 2013 also marks a careful distinction between "remote control", "automation", and "autonomy" of weapon systems in stating that "[...] these two conditions could exist (controlled and uncontrolled)" while "current DoD UAS are remotely operated and capitalize on automation in extreme circumstances, such as a lost link condition, to automatically perform a preprogrammed set of instructions" (ibid: 15).

At the same time it is made clear that the development of autonomous machines is no longer considered a technological problem, thus potentially rendering human participation obsolete:

"[...] [D]evelopments in automation are advancing from a state of automatic systems requiring human control toward a state of autonomous systems able to make decisions and react without human interaction" (ibid).

The term "system", as used in these documents, remains ambiguous whether it refers to purely electronic, technical networks and apparatuses or those that involve human as well as technological nodes.

MANNED-UNMANNED TEAMS

The 2013 document – that bristles with grotesque acronyms in the best military-fashion – indicates the kind of anthropomorphous way the new proclaimed "partnership" between humans and intelligent machines should be thought of: not as one of networks or systems but as "teams". "Manned-Unmanned System Teaming (MUM-T)" refers to the "merging" of "[...] unmanned systems from air, ground, and sea domains into teams of unmanned and manned systems" (ibid: 16).

With conspicuous stress on rhetorical figures like the "manned-unmanned-team", "integration", and "interaction" the language is revealing of the fact that, at least within the way of speaking, human agency has already become an ever so precarious "factor" among others as its remaining role within the action and decision loops is perceived as a potential hazard and therefore subject to careful consideration. Its most obvious lineage is to be found in the field of 'Human Factors Studies', which have their own history of warfare dating from WW2. Also important for understanding the figure of the "human in the loop" is an influential model for decision making, the OODA-Loop ("observe – orient – decide – act"), conceived by the former Air Force fighter pilot and military strategist John Boyd. According to this model, the success of military operations depends on the ability to "[stay] ahead in the decision cycle" (Riza 2013: 41): the quicker one completes the loop of "observe – orient – decide – act", the greater the advantage over the enemy. The figure of the "loop" also conjures a phantasmatic idea of cybernetics, which ultimately privileges the self-regulatory work of calculating feedback loops over the participation of the all-to-human actor. In the context of algorithmic warfare and within the logic of an arms race, the 'human factor' would indeed present a war-deciding limitation, and as robotics-expert Noel Sharkey has pointed out, war as an ultra-fast-extreme-event, comparable to potentially hazardous algorithmic trading practices, would be just one possible consequence (Sharkey 2013).

Today, it is in the theoretical removal of the 'human factor' from the danger zones of war, the *loss of human loss*, so to speak, that the asymmetry of contemporary warfare becomes most apparent. Jean Baudrillard expressed a similar thought in the aftermath of 9/11: Under the new condition of the so-called 'War on Terror', the highly technicized militaries and their societal constraints of the 'zero death' policy are confronted with an adversary model of force that does not even attempt to compete on technological or military grounds, but utilizes precisely the symbolic force that is prohibited in modern militaries because it is the only kind it cannot wield: the force of one's own death.[9] For the German military theoretician Herfried Münkler it is precisely the act of self-sacrifice of a small group (community) for the aim of saving the larger group (society), which defines the central element of the "heroic".[10] This leads him to conclude that it is no

---

9   "Terrorakte sind sowohl der maßlose Spiegel seiner eigenen Gewalt als auch das Modell einer symbolischen Gewalt, die ihm selbst untersagt ist, der einzigen Gewalt, die es selbst nicht ausüben kann: die des eigenen Todes." (Baudrillard 2002: 23)

10 It is, as John Keegan has pointed out, only since the advent of the possibility of nuclear war that would erase all human life regardless of military or civilian status, that some societies have entered a state of "post-heroism". Münkler's contribution is in applying the idea of post-heroic societies to the scenario of the

coincidence that drone technology is the "weapon of choice" of what he calls "post-heroic societies" (Münkler 2013). Consequently, the sacrificial role for society is now taken on by the systems that act both as substitute for and representatives of the remote human subjects in today's wars. Yet, even more than a concern for the heroic, the surrounding discourse purports the voluntary obedience of (still rudimentarily) autonomous technologies thought to forego their human participants. It is here that I would propose to locate one 'claim to community' posed by these technological networks and systems: As the "man in the loop" is rendered more and more remote, responsibilities are obfuscated. "Community" may be then rather thought of as a "bioconvergence", in which, as Suchman puts it, "'our' bodies are incorporated into war fighting assemblages as operating agents, at the same time that the locus of agency becomes increasingly ambiguous and diffuse" (2015: 6).

REFERENCES

Assistant Secretary of Defense for Research and Engineering: "Human Systems Research & Engineering", http://www.dtic.mil/biosys/hsre.html (August 14, 2015).

Baudrillard, Jean (2002): Der Geist des Terrorismus, Wien: Passagen.

Bröckling, Ulrich (1997): Disziplin. Soziologie und Geschichte militärischer Gehorsamsproduktion, Fink: München.

Bryant, Brandon/Goetz, John/Obermaier, Frederik (2014): "Immer fließen die Daten über Ramstein". In: Süddeutsche Zeitung, 4. April 2014.

Chamayou, Gregoire (2015): A Theory of the Drone, New York, NY: The New Press.

van Creveld, Martin (1991 [1985]): Command in War, Cambridge, MA: Harvard University Press.

van Creveld, Martin (1991): Technology and War, London: Brassey's.

DeLanda, Manuel (1994): War in the Age of Intelligent Machines, New York, NY: ZoneBooks.

"New Wars" that was originally developed by Mary Kaldor (Münkler 2006: 313-314; Kaldor 1999).

Delori, Mathias (2014): "Was ist aus den 'Rittern der Lüfte' geworden? Asymmetrische Kriege und das Ethos des Militärs." In: Berliner Debatte Initial 25/2, pp. 90-103.

Donley, Michael B./Schwartz, Norton A. (2009): United States Air Force Unmanned Aircraft Systems Flight Plan 2009-2047, Washington, DC: United States Air Force Headquarters.

Gregory, Derek (2011): "From a View to a Kill: Drones and Late Modern War." In: Theory, Culture and Society 28, pp. 188-215.

Gregory, Derek (2014): Angry Eyes. Lecture held at HAU, Berlin, December 11.

Grossman, Dave (2009 [1996]): On Killing. The Psychological Cost of Learning to Kill in War and Society, New York, NY: Back Bay Books.

International Human Rights and Conflict Resolution Clinic at Stanford Law School and Global Justice Clinic at NYU School of Law (2012): Living Under Drones. Death, Injury and Trauma to Civilians From US Drone Practices in Pakistan, http://chrgj.org/wp-content/uploads/2012/10/Living-Under-Drones.pdf (August 14, 2015).

Jünger, Ernst (2002 [1922]): "Der Kampf als inneres Erlebnis." In: Sämtliche Werke, Band 7, Essays I, Stuttgart: Klett-Cotta.

Jünger, Ernst (1978 [1957]): Gläserne Bienen, Stuttgart: Klett-Cotta.

Kaldor, Mary (1999): New and Old Wars. Organized Violence in a Global Era, Cambridge, MA: Polity Press.

Kittler, Friedrich (2013): "Die künstliche Intelligenz des Weltkriegs: Alan Turing." In: Hans-Ulrich Gumbricht (ed.), Die Wahrheit der technischen Welt, Berlin: Suhrkamp, pp. 232-252.

Ladewig, Rebekka (2007): "Über die Geschicke des Pfeils." In: Jörg Ahrens/Stephan Braese (eds.), Im Zauber der Zeichen. Beiträge zur Kulturgeschichte des Mediums, Berlin: Vorwerk 8.

Losurdo, Domenico (1995): Die Gemeinschaft, der Tod, das Abendland. Heidegger und die Kriegsideologie, Stuttgart and Weimar: Metzler.

Martin, Matt/Sasser, Charles (eds.) (2010): Predator. The Remote-Control Air War Over Iraq and Afghanistan: A Pilot's Story, Minneapolis, MN: Zenith Press.

Münkler, Herfried (2006): Der Wandel des Krieges. Von der Symmetrie zur Asymmetrie, Weilerswist: Velbrück Wissenschaft.

Münkler, Herfried (2013): "Neue Kampfsysteme und die Ethik des Krieges." In: High-Tech-Kriege. Heinrich Böll Stiftung, Schriften zur Demokratie Band 36, pp. 9-14.

Power, Matthew (2013): "Confessions of a Drone Warrior." In: GQ Magazine, October 22, http://www.gq.com/story/drone-uav-pilot-assassination (August 14, 2015).

Riza, Shane (2013): Killing Without Heart. Limits on Robotic Warfare in an Age of Persistent Conflict, Washington, DC: Potomac Books.

Singer, P.W. (2009): Wired for War. The Robotics Revolution and Conflict in the Twenty-first Century, New York, NY: Penguin.

Suchman, Lucy (2015): "Situational Awareness: Deadly Bioconvergence at the Boundaries of Bodies and Machines." In: MediaTropes eJournal V (1), pp. 1-24.

Weber, Jutta (2013): "Vorratsbomben am Himmel." In: Heinrich-Böll-Stiftung (ed.), High-Tech-Kriege. Frieden und Sicherheit in Zeiten von Drohnen, Kampfrobotern und digitaler Kriegsführung, Berlin, pp. 31-43.

Winnefeld, James/Kendall, Frank (2011): The Unmanned Systems Integrated Roadmap 2011-2036, Washington, DC: Office of the Undersecretary of Defense for Acquisition, Technology & Logistics.

Temporal Regimes of Protest Movements

Media and the Participatory Condition

ANNE KAUN

Media technologies essentially address the organization, production and experience of time. From this starting point, this chapter engages with the role of changing time regimes and their link to dominant media technologies for participation. The contexts for this investigation are American protest movements that emerged in the aftermaths of large-scale economic crises – the unemployed workers movement in the 1930s and the Occupy Wall Street movement in 2011. Taking their media practices as examples of participation in and through media, the chapter aims to unveil changes in temporal structuring by the employed media technologies. The assumption is that the production and circulation of meaning changes with the general capitalist mode of production. Hence, the aim of this chapter is to trace these changes over time.

THE PARTICIPATORY CONDITION

Paraphrasing the organizers of an international conference on participation at McGill University in November 2013, participation has become a phenomenon of such scale that it can be considered a condition of our time (Carpentier 2011; Miessen 2010).[1] Indeed participation has not only

---

1 The Participatory Condition, conference website, 2013, http://www.pcond.ca (August13, 2015)

spurred academic engagement, but also emerged within discourses of policy, management, urban planning and the public imagination. Although some call it a nightmare (Miessen 2010), the idea of participation in almost every possible sphere has been normalized. It is no longer a question of whether or not to consider or inspire participation, but rather how participation is enabled or constrained in specific contexts or institutions and by particular means.

The Philadelphia Police Department – as an example for the participatory condition – has even requested that residential and commercial property owners participate in a comprehensive surveillance of private and public spaces in Philadelphia by linking their subsidized, private cameras to the central CCTV system in the so called SafeCam project.[2]

Participation can in this context be understood as the process of part-taking and contributing, i.e. providing data for central surveillance and connecting to a centralized surveillance infrastructure, *as well as* sharing ideas or characteristics, i.e. sharing the understanding that CCTV supports crime prevention and sharing the ownership of the technological device through which actual participation is facilitated. The latter part of the definition is of specific interest here, namely the technological device and how it structures participation. The link between technology and participation has been reinvigorated by the emergence and success of social media, which are considered to be re-establishing participation as an essential condition of our time.

Taking this reinvigoration as a starting point, it has been suggested by, for example, Ian Hutchby (2011) that infrastructures and platforms encompass specific technological and institutional affordances for participation. In other words, various technologies constitute, encourage or discourage participation. Furthermore, the enabling or constraining of participation through media technologies occurs on different levels, like the temporal and the spatial. Hence, this chapter assumes that an analysis of temporal and spatial structuring by media technologies will further understanding of the participatory condition.

---

2 Philadelphia Police Safe Cam, 2011, http://safecam.phillypolice.com (August 13, 2015).

THE BIAS OF COMMUNICATION – INNIS AND THE PARTICIPATORY CONDITION

Harold Innis – considering both time and space as central configurations of civilizations – suggests that premodern societies are characterized by a time bias while modern societies are obsessed with space, i.e. expansion over large territories (Innis 2008 [1951]). Innis' observed that "Western history began with temporal bias and was ending with spatial bias" (Carey 1967: 29). Extending the idea of bias, he focuses on dominant media of communication as a concrete expression of the time or space bias in a given society. He distinguishes between media technologies that emphasize time and those that emphasize space (Paine 1992).

"Media that emphasize time are those that are durable in character, such as parchment, clay and stone [...] Media that emphasize space are apt to be less durable and light in character, such as papyrus and paper. The latter are suited to cater to wide areas in administration and trade." (Innis 2008 [1951]: 26)

The emphasis of time or space is hence part of the material character of the medium, rather than the content or meaning as such, which is famously incorporated in McLuhan's notion of *the medium is message*. The material character and structuring of the carrier medium, according to Innis, determines the specific bias: "particularly if the medium is heavy and durable and not suited to transportation, or to the dissemination of knowledge over space than over time, particularly if the medium is light and easily transported" (Innis 2008 [1951]: 33). In his eyes it is therefore crucial that a multiplicity of media exist and be concurrently supported to balance the biases.

What follows from his argument is that changes in media technologies have consequences for communities and democracy. This latter argument on the role of media technologies for cultural change is of particular interest. According to Innis, media technologies alter "the structure of interest (the things thought about) by changing the character of the symbols (the things thought with) and the nature of community (the arena in which thought developed)" (Carey 1989: 180).

In addition to contributing to the logics of change, media technologies help establish monopolies of knowledge. Monopolies of knowledge are based on the distribution and spread of the power of knowledge through media technologies. Innis argues that "a medium of communication has an important influence on the dissemination of knowledge over space and over time and it becomes necessary to study its characteristics in order to appraise its influence in its cultural setting" (Innis 2008 [1951]: 33).

Innis was particularly critical of modern space-biased media that link large territories but are instable and not durable over time. In his eyes, modern media, in the form of the printing press, ignores duration, leading to an obsession with the present and presentness, while pastness and tradition seemed to fall into oblivion. At the same time the obsession with the present leads to a felt loss and search of time, reflected in the current commentary on "hurried lives" (Davis 2013) and "the end of sleeps" (Crary 2013).

In this context it is hardly surprising that participation has been revived as a successful concept and has been recognized as a condition of our time. As Claus Pias (in this volume) points out, participation is about the presence while pointing towards the future. Employing Koselleck, Pias argues that participation binds the realm of experience (present) to the horizon of expectation (future of how things ought to be).

The focus on presentness and newness is amplified by the structuring of digital online media, especially those that are concerned with participatory elements. In this context digital media enhance the obsession with the present through immediacy. Modern media such as the newspaper and radio share a specific kind of speed as well as ephemerality in terms of knowledge distribution. However there is a qualitative difference in the kind of speed. With the emergence of digital online media there has been a shift from mechanical speed towards digital immediacy (Tomlinson 2007). By considering the media practices of movements of the dispossessed this shift is traced in the following.

MECHANICAL SPEED AND THE UNEMPLOYED WORKERS MOVEMENT

Following the crash of the stock exchange in 1929, the number of unemployed people in the USA exploded from 429,000 in October 1929 to 4,065,000 in January 1930, reaching 9 Million in October 1931

(Piven/Cloward 1977). Unemployment and shrinking salaries had devastating effects on the daily lives of the people, which were indicated by growing malnutrition and diseases such as tuberculosis. Although the number of people in need of financial and social support grew, there was no coherent social relief system in place. At the same time, political actors and organizations such as the socialist and communist parties and labor movement associations started to organize the unemployed, aiming to redefine their hardships not as individual misfortune but as collective experiences in the consequences of the political and economic system. In order to organize and mobilize the unemployed workers, these organizations used a sophisticated set of media, ranging, as Harold Lasswell and Dorothy Blumenstock show in their 1939 comprehensive study of communist media in Chicago, from shop papers written by unemployed workers and distributed in the factories to radio talks.

Shop papers and bulletins produced by organizers of the unemployed workers movement typically included information about relief programs and the structure and contact details of unemployed councils as well as block committees. Besides information sharing as resource, the outlets also gathered experiences of unemployment, poverty, and precarious living conditions, contributing to a collective experience rather than leaving the unemployed to suffer alone.

The production of bulletins and shop papers was self-organized by unemployed workers. Lasswell and Blumenstock remark in their study of World Revolutionary Propaganda that "the shop unit was usually responsible for gathering the material, and a special shop-paper committee was usually formed in the unit" (Lasswell/Blumenstock 1939: 60). In this sense, shop papers and bulletins were collective efforts aimed at gathering the shared experiences of the unemployed as well as information on collective organization. During the peak of the movement, there were hundreds of shop papers and bulletins across the country that were produced collectively and distributed in the factories by workers under the threat of losing their job.

Which characteristics of the production process in the era of mechanical speed do the above-mentioned examples illustrate? In order to tackle this question it is useful to return to a contemporary critic, Walter Benjamin, and his notorious essay on *The Work of Art in the Age of Mechanical Reproduction* from 1936. Benjamin points out that art has always been reproducible. However, what has changed is the speed of the reproduction process.

Through the reproduction process, the artwork loses its specific aura, as "even the most perfect reproduction of a work of art is lacking in one element: its presence in time and space, its unique existence at the place where it happens to be" (Benjamin 1970 [1936]: 220). The fact that an artwork and media image no longer has a unique place in time coincides with its increased mobility. Benjamin suggests "[...] technical reproduction can put the copy of the original into situations which would be out of reach for the original itself. Above all, it enables the original to meet the beholder halfway, be it the form of a photograph or a phonograph record" (Benjamin 2007 [1936]: 220).

This argument suggests not only a democratization of the artwork through its reproduction but also the political potential to spread it to the masses to promote resistance against oppression and political change. Benjamin's arguments hence resonate with the experience of the acceleration of speed through the possibilities of mechanical reproduction in the 1930s. At the same time, he remains hopeful of the potential that comes with reproducibility for political mobilization of the masses.

In contrast to the mechanical speed of the industrial era, the Occupy Wall Street movement emerged in an era of digital immediacy and will be briefly introduced in the following.

DIGITAL IMMEDIACY AND OCCUPY WALL STREET

In July 2011, AdBusters, a notorious facilitator of anti-consumerism campaigns, launched a call to occupy New York's famous Wall Street by introducing the hashtag #occupywallstreet on Twitter. After online mobilization, a few dozen people followed the call on September 17, 2011. Since the Wall Street was strongly secured by police forces, the occupiers turned to the close by Zuccotti Park. Initially there was only a handful of activist, but their numbers grew quickly and the encampment developed into a diverse group of occupiers based on what has been characterized as leaderlessness and non-violence (Bolton et al. 2013). At the same time there was a "division over conventional politics, over reform and revolution" (Gitlin 2012: XV).

Many commentators begin the story of Occupy Wall Street (OWS) with the AdBusters call to occupy Wall Street despite other roots of the movement which can be traced to earlier mobilizations, such as Bloomsbergville, which is illustrated in *Occupying Wall Street*, a collectively written book by a group of occupiers (Writers for the 99% 2011). However, beginning the narrative with the hashtag and Twitter mobilization is a powerful illustration of how the movement described itself and has been described, namely as empowered by social media and similar to its predecessors in North Africa and Europe. DeLuca and his co-authors (2012) observed that the first eight days of the occupation were accompanied by a total news black-out in the mainstream outlets. However, social media were quickly filling up with Occupy Wall Street: On the first day of occupation more than 4,300 mentions of OWS were counted on Twitter, exploding to 25,148 by October 2, 2011. After three months 91,400 OWS-related videos had been uploaded to YouTube (DeLuca 2012). DeLuca et al suggest that not mainstream media, but social media provided the occupiers with visibility, which resonates with reflections of one of my informants:

"A lot had to do with technology. [...] They've organized a fucking media center. I don't know what they were doing, if it was all organized through them, but they must have done something right. Because I have never seen something like that before. It was young people organizing it. You know, I have been to like mass protests in DC, in New York and in other places that had press teams, but never like a media team with laptops, and video fucking cameras, fucking everything. That was so decentralized, but organized. [...] They seemed very busy." (Ady 2014)[3]

Early on in the demonstration, the Media Working Group contributed to a constant stream of tweets, blog and Facebook posts. They also created a 24-hour live stream from the camp, with programming elements including scheduled interviews with occupiers and passers-by, talks, music sessions etc. The group and its affiliates produced a constant flow of images, memes, and texts to be circulated.

---

3   Name is changes by the author. As part of my fieldwork, I conducted a number of interviews with activists, who were involved with Occupy Wall Street in New York and Occupy Philly in Philadelphia.

Out of necessity the activists appropriated the logic of social media from the very beginning. Characteristics of the social media logic as suggested by José van Dijck and Thomas Poell (2013) are programmability, popularity, connectivity, and datafication. Aiming for visibility of the movement and its discussions, the occupiers contributed to the production of digital media content being partly constitutive of current capitalism, or what Jodi Dean (2008, 2012) calls 'communicative capitalism'. Communicative capitalism predominantly builds on the logic that the exchange value of the messages dominates, rather than the use value. Dean suggests that network communication technologies, which are based on ideals of discussion and participation, intertwine capitalism and democracy. Communicative capitalism expanding with the growth of global telecommunications hence becomes the single ideological formation (Dean 2012).

Content or the use value of the exchanged messages becomes secondary or even irrelevant. Therefore, any response to them becomes irrelevant as well and any political potential disperses into the perpetual flow of communication (Dean 2009, 2010). One of the major principles of communicative capitalism is furthermore to accelerate the speed of circulation in order to minimize turn-over time and increase the production of surplus value (Manzerolle/Kjøsen 2012). As digital media enhance personalization, they enable new trajectories and pathways between production, exchange, and consumer. In this sense, personalization, as an organizational principle of digital media, enhances the already accelerated speed of exchanges, which is taken to its extreme, namely the suspension of circulation. Manzerolle and Kjøsen identify that "new is how the logic of acceleration is being taken to its logical end in the conditions of ubiquity and immediacy engendered through digital media" (ibid: 217).

However, political projects such as OWS – which also was a micro experiment for social and political organization in a shared space – need time. The need for time is reflected in the numerous stories of endless meetings of the General Assembly to develop group consensus. Accelerated capitalism however does not allow for these time consuming procedures, which is reflected in the constant request for clear demands and goals of the movement in public discourse. In this sense, the dominant logic of current accelerated capitalism and the time consuming practices of participatory democracy came to stand in stark contrast since the movement adopted parts of communicative capitalism so successfully. Following Innis' idea of biases

(2004), digital media that were crucial for OWS could be considered as space biased media as they connect localities over vast distances. This spatial excess results in an annihilation of time towards presentness and immediacy.

CONCLUSION

Drawing theoretically on Innis' notion of bias and empirically on two examples of protest movements of the dispossessed, this chapter aimed to disentangle changing regimes of time; namely, a shift from mechanical speed to digital immediacy in media practices. This shift arguably reflects the general change towards enhanced (finance) capitalism. Hence, with the help of media of communication, the connection between the general mode of production and the mode of knowledge production and distribution becomes tangible.

As Carey (1967) points out, Innis saw the biggest potential for social change in the periphery and margins of society. In this periphery, new media would be designed and used to question given centers and monopolies of knowledge. "Disenfranchised groups in society would lead the search for new forms of technology in seeking to compete for some form of social power" (Carey 1967: 8).

Whereas the monopolies of knowledge could be found in centrally organized commercial newspapers and commercial radio in the 1930s, in 2011/2012 the dominant medium of communication is an increasingly commercialized Internet and its applications. In the context of the protest movements, activists successfully applied already established media technologies to their purposes while simultaneously challenging mainstream society. In this sense the movements of the dispossessed considered here were not in search of new technologies as such, but aimed to carve out new spaces within the dominant media of their time to place their activities.

REFERENCES

Benjamin, Walter (2007 [1936]): "The Work of Art in the Age of Mechanical Reproduction." In: Walter Benjamin, Illuminations. Essays and Reflections, ed. by Hannah Arendt, New York, NY: Schocken Books, pp. 217-252.

Bolton, Matthew/Weltey, Emily/Nayak, Meghana/Malone, Christopher (2013): "We had a front row seat to a Downtown revolution." In: Emily Welty/Matthew Bolton/Meghana Nayak/Christopher Malone (eds.), Occupying Political Science. The Occupy Wall Street Movement from New York to the World, New York, NY: Palgrave Macmillan, pp. 1-24.

Carey, James (1967): "Harold Adams Innis and Marshall McLuhan." In: The Antioch Review 27/1, pp. 5-39.

Carey, James (1989): Communication as Culture. Essays on Media and Society, Boston, MA: Unwin Hyman.

Carpentier, Nico (2011): Media and Participation. A Site of Ideological-Democratic Struggle, Bristol: Intellect.

Crary, Jonathan (2013): 24/7. Late capitalism and the ends of sleep, London: Verso.

Davis, Mark (2013): "Hurried lives: Dialectics of time and technology in liquid modernity." In: Thesis Eleven 118/1, pp. 7-18.

Dean, Jodi (2008): "Communicative Capitalism: Circulation and the Foreclosure of Politics." In: Megan Boler (ed.), Digital Media and Democracy, Cambridge, MA, and London: MIT Press, pp. 101-121.

Dean, Jodi (2009): Democracy and Other Neoliberal Fantasies: Communicative Capitalism and Left Politics, Durham: Duke University Press.

Dean, Jodi (2010): Blog Theory: Feedback and Capture in the Circuits of Drive, Cambridge, MA: Polity Press.

Dean, Jodi (2012): The Communist Horizon, London, New York: Verso.

DeLuca, Kevin M./Lawson, Sean/Sun, Ye (2012); "Occupy Wall Street on the Public Screens of Social Media: The Many Framings of the Birth of a Protest Movement." In: Communication, Culture & Critique 5/4, pp. 483-509.

Gitlin, Todd (2012): Occupy Nation, New York, NY: HarperCollins.

Hutchby, Ian (2011): Technologies, Texts and Affordances. In: Sociology 35/2, pp. 441-456.

Innis, Harold (2008 [1951]): The Bias of Communication, Toronto: University of Toronto Press.

Innis, Harold (2004): Changing Concepts of Time, Lanham, MD: Rowman and Littlefield.

Lasswell, Harold D./Blumenstock, Dorothy (1939): World revolutionary propaganda: a Chicago study, New York, NY: Knopf.

Manzerolle, Vincent/Kjøsen, Atle Mikkola (2012): "The Communication of Capital: Digital Media and the Logic of Acceleration." In: TripleC 10, pp. 214-229.

Miessen, Markus (2010): The Nightmare of Participation, Berlin: Sternberg.

Paine, Robert (1992): "Time-Space Scenarios and the Innisian Theory: A View from Anthropology." In: Time & Society 1/1, pp. 51-63.

Piven, Frances Fox/Cloward, Richard A. (1977): Poor People's Movements. Why They Succeed, How They Fail, New York, NY: Vintage Books.

Tomlinson, John (2007): The Culture of Speed. The Coming of Immediacy, Los Angeles, CA: Sage.

van Dijck, José/Poell, Thomas Poell (2013): "Understanding social media logic." In: Media and Communication 1/1, pp. 2-24.

Writers for the 99% (2011): Occupying Wall Street. The Inside Story of an Action that Changed America, New York, NY, and London: OR Books.

Liquid Democracy

And other Fixes to the Problem of Democracy

MARTIN DEGE

> "The great constitutional corrective in the hands of the people against usurpation of power, or corruption by their agents is the right of suffrage; and this when used with calmness and deliberation will prove strong enough."
>
> ANDREW JACKSON, 7TH PRESIDENT OF THE US/LETTER TO JAMES BUCHANAN, JUNE 25, 1825.

OVERTURE

One of the more famous descriptions of the advantages and flaws of democracy summarized in a quote surely comes from Winston Churchill: "[D]emocracy is the worst form of government, except for all those other forms that have been tried" (Churchill 2008 [1947]: 574). With the rather obvious sarcastic undertone that characterizes so many of Churchill's ever repeated comments about politics and life itself, Churchill quite accurately expresses an ambiguity in various forms of governance. Surely a system that grants large-scale participation and possibly the free development of all individuals of a given society is generally preferred over an autocratic regime. At the same time, democracy and its adjunct body of bureaucracy often appear to be slow, ineffective, and always one step behind a truly just society. This is particularly true for forms of direct democracy, which only seem to be effective on a small-scale level but can hardly be applied on a nation-state level (the prominent exception here is, of course, Switzerland). As Max Weber (1978 [1922]: 241-245) points out, it is in this context that the public often turns to charismatic leaders in the hopes that they might best represent their interests while at the same time lowering the need for individual involvement. As such, the system we (so far) consider ideal still appears to be extremely imperfect. Democracy prevails not because it is a pristine system but because other systems of government have historically not worked out; that is, no one has, as yet, proposed a better system. In this logic we are essentially stuck with the issues that plagued ancient Greece, which, for example, are spelled out in Aristotle's Nicomachean Ethics, Books VIII and IX: having a powerful ruler, democratically elected or not, has its advantages: fast decision making processes, clear hierarchies, and possibly efficient organizational structures of the state apparatus. The disadvantages of such a τυραννίς (*tyranny*) seem equally clear: every citizen is subject to the decisions of the leader or a specific political elite, no matter what their personal options, needs, and preferences may be. To solve this apparent contradiction, the τύραννος (*tyrant*) needs to be replaced by the δῆμος (*demos*). And this is usually where the problems start: The τύραννος as a δῆμος needs an incredibly long time to coordinate its actions and make decisions. And once decisions have been made, there will inevitably be parts of the δῆμος, which are irreconcilable with the proposed solution and will thus lobby against it – which leads to nothing but more debate, postponing the desired solution.

While this is certainly only one way of looking at democracy and certainly not the most sophisticated one, it is exactly the kind of viewpoint taken by an increasingly powerful group of pundits that shape an ever-growing sector in the public domain. Having witnessed an accelerated growth of their own industry which promises solutions and fixes for more and more parts of our everyday life, these self-proclaimed Silicon Valley spokespersons celebrate the apparent computerization and digitization of our society as the beginning of a new epoch and a new overarching logic that leads to one thing and one thing only in all aspects: improvement. Within this logic, in order to improve, democracy needs to be more efficient. And higher efficiency in the age of digitization regularly translates to more transparency, more participation, less debate, and faster compromises that include more participants. Ultimately, the problem can be boiled down to reducing the difficulty of communication and debate, thereby reducing organizational costs to a minimum by means of interconnected computational devices (see for example Shirky 2008; 2011).

The buzzword connected with these thoughts is of course the Internet. In the minds of most of silicon valley CEO's and technology pundits, the Internet is the ideal solution to (almost all of) our problems simply because it is, in their minds, already built upon the same kinds of ideas liberal democracy rests on: it is open, transparent, and embraces equality and the participation of all (see for example Noveck 2009). And on top of that, it also provides the kinds of technological solutions needed to spread these values with ever-increasing efficiency to an ever-increasing number of participants – with the limit being equal to the size of the total world population. The belief is that we should couple technological evolution with the advancement of democracy to carry over the supposedly wonderful world of Wikipedia, Facebook, Twitter – that is our cyber-reality – into the real world.

1   LIQUID DEMOCRACY: WHAT IT IS

The essential problem can thus be formulated as such: True efficiency requires fast decisions and fast actions. These actions moreover must be efficient in themselves. They must exhibit the right kind of interventions. They not only have to provide a certain answer to a particular question, but they have to provide *the right kind of answer*; namely, they have to provide *the solution* to a particular problem. The concept of Liquid Democracy represents in many ways just that: An attempt to transfuse these Internet values to the real world and thereby fix real world problems as they have been fixed on the Internet before: ease of communication, mass participation, openness, sheer endlessness of information, and constant availability – all part of the Internet structure – help to overcome democracy's shortfalls.

Two theoretical underpinnings of this maneuver are usually deployed. The first rests on a purified understanding of the concepts of the founding fathers of the American constitution, in particular James Madison, fourth president of the United States and his contemporary, George Washington's chief of staff Alexander Hamilton. Madison believed in the power and necessity of representation to make democratic government feasible while

Hamilton is often taken as being convinced that "pure democracy, if it were practicable, would be the most perfect government." The Hamilton-Madison dualism, set up to underpin Liquid Democracy debates, unfortunately already falls short of its promise if we read a little further into Hamilton: "Experience has proved that no position in politics is more false than this" (Hamilton 1788), namely that pure democracy would be the perfect form of government.[1] Be that as it may, Liquid Democracy aims for a representational government that nonetheless includes as much direct participation as possible and somehow hopes to have these aims backed up by the American founding fathers (Behrens et al 2014: 13-26; Johnson 2012: 151-176). Thanks to technological advancements that culminated in the digitization of the world in what we call the Internet, or so the ideology makes its transfer to the present, we can create a form of democracy that is *purer* than it ever was.

The second frequently called upon intellectual pillar is the ancient Greek πόλις (*polis*) (Behrens et all 2014: 40; Jochmann 2013). Here the argument goes something like this: The first democracy that ever really worked was the Athenian democracy. It was a pure democracy in Hamilton's sense and it worked because all the citizens could come together to make their decisions. With the growth of societies, coming together became impracticable and we had to switch to Madison's representationalism. Now with the Internet, so the chain of arguments continues, we can finally come together again; not in the real world but in cyberspace as the new global village. The fact that the Constitution of Ἀττική was somewhat more complex is thievishly ignored in this argument – let alone the number of slaves that guaranteed the prosperity of the city-state in the first place. They are maybe as ignored, one might somewhat polemically add, as the modern slaves at Foxcon and their ilk who build the computers, smart phones, tablets, servers, flat-screens, keyboards, and so forth with which we are to become a new global village in the first place.

In praxis, this is how this supposedly new form of democracy entitled "Liquid Democracy" is theorized to work: Every citizen is given the right to make proposals for political agendas as they see fit. Because everyone supposedly is connected, the distribution of these agendas is fast, easy and

---

1   For an example of this kind of misreading of Hamilton see Behrens et. al. (2014: 14).

essentially without cost. If a proposal captures the interest of a specified percentage of the overall population, the proposal enters a stage at which others can submit counterproposals or improvements to the original. At a certain point in time after stage two, there will be a vote on the proposal. And this is where it becomes "liquid". While the one-person-one-vote rule is still in effect, every member is, in principal, free to delegate her vote to another person. So if you happen to have some stake in a particular decision but no time to get adequately informed about the topic, you can simply give your vote to someone else; that is, you can delegate it. The delegate now decides on your behalf and you don't have to worry about the issue in detail; matters are now in the hands of a person you trust. If you are unhappy with the decisions of your delegate, you can revoke her right to act on your behalf at any given point in time (Behrens et al. 2014; Johnson 2012).

1.1 Teething Troubles

Notwithstanding the great potential that is attested to Liquid Democracy and its digital manifestations, it has hardly been applied in actual decision making processes and a communal, let alone national level. Concerns over problems of implementation, data security, and voter adoption rates seem to be too high (Streetdogg 2012).

One could see mere teething problems of an altogether new way of doing politics in this; a revolution in participation and decision making. But then again, the radical transparency of every single meeting might also hinder people from speaking their minds freely – simply because they cannot and should not trust that whatever they say will not leave the room. Instead, every sentence is prone to being taken "out of context" and possibly scandalized. Liquid Democracy also embodies the hope for full transparency. At the same time, digital implementations often leave the choice to sign up with a pseudonym instead of real names, so as to make the argument count instead of the person. But then again: Can we really form a political will without forming groups associated with specific interests? Do we not need to know who speaks for what? That is to say: does politics not need the politician? And, besides all these minor differences, are the *techniques* of Liquid Democracy really new? Polls, surveys, focus groups, and so forth have been in existence to inquire about the needs and wishes of the party base as long as democratic parties have been in existence (Shefter 1994: 19-98).

And the old ways of doing things curiously seem to beat many implementations of Liquid Democracy in a category that was supposed to be one of its major advantages: efficiency. The more or less hierarchical structures of the old parties enable them to act and argue politically, to give out statements for a controversial discussion within as well as outside the party. Liquid Democracy implementations, in contrast, often fail to create the kinds of identification points that people can relate to. The recent downfall of the German branch of the Pirate Party seems to exemplify this point. The German magazine Cicero in one of its recent issues compared them to the pirates of the French Asterix comics: Instead of taking up a fight with their enemies, they are so afraid that they prefer to sink their ship by themselves (Cicero 2014).

1.2 New for the Sake of Being New

But what about the central idea of Liquid Democracy? Wouldn't it be great if I could give my vote on a specific issue to people I trust are more competent? One of the more famous Internet pundits and outspoken advocator of Liquid Democracy, Steve Johnson, sees two funnels that prevent us from more democratic participation. Funnel A is – of course – "information overflow": We simply cannot follow each and every political campaign, let alone vote in it simply because we also seem to have other things to do. He is definitely getting at a problem here; however the idea to argue *for more time* for everyone to engage in political matters does not occur to him. Funnel B is the party option: Yes, I can vote for a party to endow them with the right to make decisions for a certain time period. But that "compress[es] [my] idiosyncratic values down into a legible straight line" (Johnson 2012: 170). For Johnson then, the answer to all this funneling is "liquidity". However, if we have different people running around trying to collect votes with the promise to do the right thing based on the claim that they know better than the regular voter, wouldn't we call those people "politicians"? And if those politicians come together and form a larger group that shares a certain understanding of political action, wouldn't we call that group a "party"? It seems that Johnson's funnels are not that bad after all – quite the contrary, they seem to be intended side effects of a functional democratic system. What is Liquid Democracy then? Well, it is new and it hits us with a new technology. And this technology is, at least in the minds of the technology pundits, based on what they opaquely describe as "the Internet". Hence, it is open, transparent, and so forth. But that is pretty much everything Liquid Democracy advocates are left with: It is better than the old stuff because it is new. A clear instance of what Evgeny Morozov calls "epochalism" (2013: 36).

If this *newism* or *epochalism* really is the last line of defense for Liquid Democracy advocates, there really is not much that speaks for any kind of revolutionary potential. Specifically because the idea behind Liquid Democracy, after all, does not seem to be all that new: Lewis Caroll wrote about what he called "proxy voting" (Carroll 1884), and the idea of implementing direct democracy in large societies by technological means has been around at least since the 1960s with the hopes of the participation of all through the back than revolutionary technology called *television* (cf. Miller III 1969). The problem of these ideas that mostly rest on concepts of rational choice and public choice discourses is largely the same: For them, democracy means voting and the problem of democracy is how to organize that vote. A rather reductionist understanding of the complexities of which deliberation that democratic politics actually consist.

It seems then that Liquid Democracy would not really be able to fix our democracy, and that its technology, the Internet, cannot really provide ready at hand solutions either. So that is it then? Is Liquid Democracy simply a pouring of new wine into old skins? As far as I can see, the provisional answer to these questions is yes. However, we should be careful not to dismiss such attempts of the technological sphere to fix the public too easily. Liquid Democracy may not be a new 'technique' but it certainly brings new technology with it.

2 DEMOCRACY AND TECHNOLOGY

There is one major and inherent flaw in the discussions about Liquid Democracy. It is a flaw that does not apply to this discourse alone but which stems from a greater ambiguity in our understanding of technology. This ambiguity has been a constant companion of modern democracy ever since its birth, which happened to coincide with the beginnings of the age of increased technological development. Ever since the relationship of the fine arts and the applied arts was reversed (as Leo Marx convincingly argues in

Marx 1997) new technologies have always created the expectation that they will fix social issues as well: the birth of the railway system brought with it dreams of an increasingly mobile and thus peaceful world (Garvey 1852). The invention of the telephone and the telegraph also boosted fantasies of a gigantic interconnected network that would lead to more communication and thus more understanding and eventually peace on earth (Gronlund 1898)[2]. Dreams of endless energy resources that turn desserts into Garden Eden – which were originally spawned by the shining lights of the White City (Nye 1990: 29-84) – have been around ever since Fredrick Soddy and Ernest Rutherford discovered radioactivity as part of the process by which atoms changed from one kind to another while releasing energy (Le Bon 1917 [1905]). This list can be extended ever further – think of the automobile[3], the TV (McLuhan 1994 [1964]: 308-337), space travel (Zimmerman 2003). And at least for the last three decades or so it has been the Internet in its endless reincarnations, dubbed 2.0, 3.0, 4.0, that has spawned one utopia of technological salvation after the other.[4]

Alexis de Tocqueville had captured this ambiguity in his reflections on America. He was worried that democracy's promise for equality might have a stronger impression on the people than democracy's imperative for freedom (Tocqueville 2000 [1840]: 192). It appears that his fear is at least partially realized in today's democracy of common possessions. If freedom is realized through possession – the more possessions, the more freedom – then freedom itself is endangered, as we can see today due to an increasingly overstressed biosphere (Winner 1992: 3-18). This overstressed biosphere then in turn is supposed to be fixed by technology. A situation which both Jürgen Habermas and Charles Taylor have described as "Legitimation Crisis"[5], a state at which we cannot abandon certain technologies despite the

---

2   For further elaboration of this point see also John (2010).

3   For example Frank Lloyd Wright's "Broadacre City" introduced in Wright (1932). For a very recent version of this utopia, see Business Insider (2014).

4   To mention but a few: Keen (2007), Thaler/Sunstein (2008), Noveck (2009), Wu (2010), Kelly (2010), Shirky (2011), Brooke (2011), Weinberger (2011), Jarvis (2011), Diamandis/Kotler (2012), Johnson (2012), Khanna/Khanna (2012), Mayer-Schönberger/Cukier (2013), Zuckerman (2013).

5   For Habermas, the term "Legitimation Crisis" identifies contradictions in modern capitalism (Habermas 1988 [1973]). For Taylor, "societies destroy them-

evidence of their inappropriateness. This ambiguity is the product of the emergence of the idea of technology itself: The idea of technology as a product of Enlightenment suggests an instrumental understanding, whereas a Romantic interpretation renders technology as a mode of expression of our being in the world.[6] If we want to democratize technology and thus improve democracy with technological means, we most likely have to overcome this ambiguity.

2.1 Misunderstandings

For my purposes here, the difference between an Enlightenment approach to technology and a Romantic one may be boiled down to their respective understanding of language: Thinkers like Frege, Russell, and the early Wittgenstein would describe language as a ready made set of instruments that we control in order to leave our impression on the world (Taylor 1985b: 217). Herder, Heidegger, or the late Wittgenstein, in contrast would argue that language is inexhaustible, it is always more than our oversight grants us. Even more so, it is always diachronically and synchronically embedded in culture (Taylor 1985b: 231-232). The former group of thinkers in the tradition of Enlightenment sparked one dominant way of thinking about technology: technology provides specific instruments for the purpose of satisfying individual needs. The latter group, thinking in the tradition of Romanticism, developed another point of view: technology is not very different from other forms of expression; it represents a social praxis, a form of being in the world. The first view relies on a Hobbesian/Lockeian tradition that gives priority to the atomic individual over social arrangements that merely help unfolding individual preferences and needs (cf. Macpherson 1962). A romantic understanding in contrast might best be summarized in Marx's dictum: "It is not the consciousness of men that determines their being, but, on the contrary, their social being that determines their con-

---

selves when they violate the conditions of legitimacy which they themselves tend to posit and inculcate" (Taylor 1985a: 248).

6   This argument is reminiscent of Charles Taylor's more general claim that our times are the product of a continuous dialectical relationship between the Romantic Era and thinkers like Rousseau, Humboldt, Marx etc. and the Enlightenment discourse of Descartes, Locke, Hobbes, and so forth (Taylor 1985b).

sciousness" (Marx 1978 [1859]: 4). Rather than understanding society as the servant of the individual, society becomes the birthplace of an inherently social being (Taylor 1985a: 309). In the first view, the self is the source of individual rights, preferences, desires, fears, etc. In the second view, the self becomes an intersection of social relationships. In the first view, philosophy, arts, science, and technology are instruments for a personalized exploration of the world; in the second view they become forms of expression of a social self.

An instrumental understanding thus renders technology as a mirror of human needs. It adds new tools to our world that serves our individual preferences and interests. A lifeworld perspective on the other hand understands technology to shape our needs and our world, thereby providing the basis for our self-understanding. In this light, Tocqueville's claim becomes clearer: An instrumentalist approach to technology renders design decisions morally neutral and independent from political questions about freedom or equality (see for example Bowles/Gintis/Gustafsson 1993). Ever more technological revolutions take place that supposedly offer ever more tools to improve the fulfillment of individual needs, preferences and desires.[7]

3   WHAT NOW?

If we look at Liquid Democracy from this perspective, its problems might become instantly clear. How could we expect that something as undemocratic in its emergence as "the Internet" to fix issues we have with our democratic order? All the stories of technological revolutions as mentioned above keep throwing improvements in the technological sphere at us that supposedly unfold their liberating potential in the social sphere. The question always is: How can and how will technology and technological development improve democracy? The question how technological development could possibly be democratized – given its intrinsic role in the social sphere – does not occur. This might also be the reason why utopias are spawned by

---

7   For an early critique of this revolutionism see for example Winner (1992: 98-117), Morozov (2013:15). For proponents of this ongoing technological revolutionism see for example Diamandis/Kotler (2012), Johnson (2012), Khanna/Khanna (2012), Townsend (2013).

new technologies which are controlled by states or large cooperations. Rather than waiting for technology as a separate and trans-historical process to unfold (and on its way, almost as if it was an accidental side effect, fix democracy) – as the instrumentalist view would have it, we should ask how technology can be democratized. Not 'how does technology fix democracy?,' but 'What is a democracy like in a technological age?' It seems that technology is the student here and democracy the teacher. For that, instead of neutral technological development, we need an agenda setting phase for technological development. Just as it is important to empower citizens to participate in forming legislative agendas in politics, they need to have a say in the decisions on technological design. For that purpose, rather than Liquid Democracy, we might need something like Liquid Technology or Liquid Design.

3.1 Liquid Design – A Normative Task

In order to overcome a purely instrumentalist view of technology that disguises the actual modes of productions and concrete interest behind the introduction of specific technologies, we have to find ways to implement more liquid technologies. What might that be? We have to broaden the participation in design process, which will lead to a larger number of participants and a greater number of applications (as can be witnessed in the open source software and open hardware movements today already). This also means that we need a focus on technologies, which are compatible with democratic values, that is technologies that express our democratic desires. This would also ensure that a larger number of social needs, concerns and experiences could be taken into account. As such, it is maybe not so much democracy that needs to become liquid but technology: Small and decentralized technologies which are designed by the many for their democratic needs.

Now I know that this argument is far from revolutionary – quite the contrary and quite deliberately so. Lewis Mumford introduced the distinction between authoritarian and democratic technics in 1964 (Mumford 1964). A great storyteller, Mumford believed that this distinction between "system-centered, immensely powerful", and "man-centered [...] resourceful, durable" (Mumford 1964: 2) technics has been with us ever since the Neolithic. The story, however, is one of demise – with the democratic pole slowly disappearing under the pressure of large-scale authoritarian networks. Winner goes one step further. For him our technological progress rests on a specific, albeit hidden ideology, which is characterized by the following beliefs:

- power should be centralized,
- the few are given voice and the rest should be silenced,
- there are structural constraints between social classes,
- the world is hierarchically ordered,
- good things are unevenly allocated,
- men and women have different abilities, and
- one's life is always open to surveillance and scrutiny. (Winner 1993: 283-292)

With this in mind, one may ask: Isn't the ideology of the Internet very different from the authoritarian technics Mumford describes and the respective discursive framing Winner insinuates? Is it not absurd to apply those "old" theories to our "new" technologies? Well, yes: Openness, transparency, universal participation is what the Internet supposedly stands for. But at the same time, the answer is no: Who among us really knows what happens to our emails once we hit the *send* button? Why is a US based and highly undemocratic organization controlling the Internet's global domain name system?[8] Who really knew what the NSA is doing (or, for that matter, that something like the GCHQ existed) before Edward Snowden made public what according to the authorities should have been kept secret for all eternity? Or less dramatically: Have you ever heard of DE-CIX? It's the company that runs the world's largest Internet traffic hub located in Frankfurt, Germany, which most likely means that you are using their services on a daily – and if you have a smart phone most likely hourly – basis. And even if you do not use the Internet at all, your life still depends on them: the regulation of the European electricity network runs largely through their servers.

---

8   This organization is called ICANN (Internet Corporation for Assigned Names and Numbers); attempts to democratize ICANN were made in the past (specifically in 2002) but quickly abandoned because they seemed impractical.

I guess what we are dealing with here is – to paraphrase Pierre Bourdieu – the Internet's ability to "hide by showing" (Bourdieu 1998: 19): That
is, it can hide things by showing something other than what would be
shown if it did what it is supposed to do according to its hawked ideology.
But let us turn away from "the Internet", as if it were a magical, thing towards us: Internet ideology relies on the modern Promethein Self, as Günter
Anders calls it: We as Promethein Selves deal with our own powerlessness
in light of technology's power by means of purely instrumental relationships to public things or people. Despite *and* because we know about possible problems that lie behind the usage of a product, we turn the product into
the pure instrument we need in order to function in the modern world as
self-determined beings. Instrumentality in that sense becomes a justification
of our public practices that become more and more emptied of political sig-
nificance and, in the long run, lose democratic control (Anders 1980: 26-
28).

Philosophy of technology has always been marginal and marginalized.
This marginalization is grounded in an instrumentalist understanding of
technology. This technology is tied to epochalism; that is, theorizing does
not seem to be able to keep pace with the new developments technology
blesses us with. According to this line of thought, the best we can do is use
technology, hopefully for the good.

Let us walk another path: We have to understand technology structurally, that is as a consequence of social developments, as a form of social expression. In that way, we do not have to throw away every bit of theorizing
we already have every time a new technology comes around. Instead we
can look at what we already have understood and counter this weird epochalism of ever new wine in old wineskins with a structural understanding of
technological advancement as social expression that will eventually allow
us to democratically control the kinds of technology we want to enframe
ourselves in (Heidegger 1977 [1962]: 16-17).

If we see it as the essence of democracy that people are empowered to
collectively envision, change, and construct their living conditions, and if
we understand technologies as part of the social sphere rather than understanding it as a trans-historical development detached from human life, it
necessarily follows that we should democratize technological design in order to allow citizens to participate in the creation of new technologies as
well as in its application. Despite its radicalism, this argument might also

seem banal. And you are right: it is banal. But to paraphrase Frank A. Meyer: "Democracy is banal. It is the banality of the Good" (Meyer 2014).

REFERENCES

Anders, Günther (1980): Die Antiquiertheit des Menschen: Über die Zerstörung des Lebens im Zeitalter der Dritten Industriellen Revolution. Vol. 2, München: C. H. Beck.

Aristotle (2000 [350 BC]): Nicomachean Ethics, Cambridge: Cambridge University Press.

Behrens, Jan/Kistner, Axel/Nitsche, Andreas/Swierczek, Björn (2014): The Principles of LiquidFeedback, Berlin: Interaktive Demokratie e.V.

Bourdieu, Pierre (1998): On Television, New York, NY: New Press.

Bowles, Samuel/Gintis, Herbert/Gustafsson, Bo (1993): Markets and Democracy: Participation, Accountability, and Efficiency, Cambridge and New York, NY: Cambridge University Press.

Brooke, Heather (2011): The Revolution Will Be Digitised: Dispatches From the Information War, London: William Heinemann.

Carroll, Lewis (1884): The Principles of Parliamentary Representation, London: Harrison and Sons.

Churchill, Winston (2008): Churchill by Himself: The Definitive Collection of Quotations, edited by Richard Langworth, New York, NY: PublicAffairs.

Diamandis, Peter H./Kotler, Steven (2012): Abundance: The Future Is Better Than You Think, New York, NY: Free Press.

Garvey, Michael Angelo (1852): The Silent Revolution, or, the Future Effects of Steam and Electricity Upon the Condition of Mankind, London: William and Frederick G. Cash.

Gronlund, Laurence (1898): The New Economy: A Peaceable Solution of the Social Problem, Chicago, IL: H.S. Stone & Co.

Habermas, Jürgen (1988 [1973]): Legitimation Crisis, translated by Thomas McCarthy, Cambridge: Polity Press.

Hamilton, Alexander (1788): The Debates in the Convention of the State of New York on the Adoption of the Federal Constitution, In: Convention, Poughkeepsie (http://www.constitution.org/rc/rat_ny.htm).

Heidegger, Martin (1977 [1962]): The Question Concerning Technology, and Other Essays, translated by William Lovitt, New York, NY: Garland.

Jackson, Andrew (1825): Letter to James Buchanan, Buchanan Papers, Historical Society of Pennsylvania.

Jarvis, Jeff (2011): What Would Google Do? Reverse Engineering the Fastest Growing Company in the History of the World, New York and Enfield, NY: Harper.

Jochmann, Jakob (2013): Liquid Democracy in Simple Terms, http://vimeo.com/53659332 (August 14, 2015).

John, Richard R. (2010): Network Nation: Inventing American Telecommunications, Cambridge, MA: Belknap Press of Harvard University Press.

Johnson, Steven (2012): Future Perfect: The Case for Progress in a Networked Age, New York, NY: Riverhead Books.

Keen, Andrew (2007): The Cult of the Amateur: How Today's Internet Is Killing Our Culture, New York, NY: Doubleday/Currency.

Kelly, Kevin (2010): What Technology Wants, New York, NY: Viking.

Khanna, Ayesha/Khanna, Parag (2012): Hybrid Reality: Thriving in the Emerging Human-technology Civilization, New York, NY: Ted Conferences.

Le Bon, Gustave (1917 [1905]): L'évolution de la Matière, Paris: E. Flammarion.

Macpherson, Crawford Brough (1962): The Political Theory of Possessive Individualism: Hobbes to Locke, Oxford: Oxford University Press.

Marx, Karl, and Friedrich Engels (1978): The Marx-Engels Reader. 2nd ed., edited by Robert C Tucker, New York, NY: Norton.

Marx, Leo (1997): "'Technology': The Emergence of a Hazardous Concept." In: Social Research 64/3, pp. 965-988.

Mayer-Schönberger, Viktor/Cukier, Kenneth (2013): Big Data: A Revolution That Will Transform How We Live, Work, and Think, Boston, MA: Houghton Mifflin Harcourt.

McLuhan, Marshall (1994 [1964]): Understanding Media: The Extensions of Man, Cambridge, MA: MIT Press.

Meyer, Frank A. (2014): "Demokratie als Antiutopie." Presentation given at the Literaturfestival Eventi Letterari Monte Verità.

Miller III, James C. (1964): "A Program for Direct and Proxy Voting in the Legislative Process." In: Public Choice 7, pp. 107-113.

Morozov, Evgeny (2013): To Save Everything, Click Here: The Folly of Technological Solutionism, New York, NY: Perseus Books.

Mumford, Lewis (1964): "Authoritarian and Democratic Technics." In: Technology and Culture 5/1, pp. 1-8.

Noveck, Beth Simone (2009): Wiki Government: How Technology Can Make Government Better, Democracy Stronger, and Citizens More Powerful, Washington, D.C.: Brookings Institution Press.

Nye, David E. (1990): Electrifying America: Social Meanings of a New Technology, 1880-1940, Cambridge, MA: MIT Press.

Shefter, Martin (1994): Political Parties and the State: The American Historical Experience, Princeton, NJ: Princeton University Press.

Shirky, Clay (2008): Here Comes Everybody: The Power of Organizing Without Organizations, London: Allen Lane.

Shirky, Clay (2011): Cognitive Surplus: How Technology makes Consumers into Collaborators, New York, NY: Penguin Books.

Streetdogg (2012): Senatus Populusque Piratas. StreetBlogg, http://streetdogg.wordpress.com/2012/11/11/spqp/ (August 14, 2015).

Taylor, Charles (1985b): Philosophical Papers. 1, Human Agency and Language, Cambridge: Cambridge University Press.

Taylor, Charles (1985a): Philosophical Papers. 2, Philosophy and the Human Sciences, Cambridge: Cambridge University Press.

Thaler, Richard H./Sunstein Cass R. (2008): Nudge: Improving Decisions About Health, Wealth and Happiness, New Haven, CT: Yale University Press.

Tocqueville, Alexis de (2000 [1840]): Democracy in America, edited by Harvey C. Mansfield/Delba Winthrop, Chicago, IL: University of Chicago Press.

Townsend, Anthony M. (2013): Smart Cities: Big Data, Civic Hackers, and the Quest for a New Utopia, New York, NY: Norton.

Weber, Max (1978 [1922]): Economy and Society, Berkeley, CA: Berkeley University Press.

Weinberger, David (2011): Too Big to Know: Rethinking Knowledge Now That the Facts Aren't the Facts, Experts Are Everywhere, and the Smartest Person in the Room Is the Room, New York, NY: Basic Books.

Winner, Langdon (1993): "Artifacts/Ideas and Political Culture." In: Al
Teich (ed.), Technology and the Future, 6th ed., New York, NY: St.
Martin's Press, pp. 283-292.

Winner, Langdon (1992): The Whale and the Reactor: A Search of Limits
in an Age of High Technology, Chicago, IL: University of Chicago
Press.

Wright, Frank Lloyd (1932): The Disappearing City, New York, NY: W. F.
Payson.

Wu, Tim (2010): The Master Switch: The Rise and Fall of Information
Empires, New York, NY: Alfred A. Knopf.

Zimmerman, Robert (2003): Leaving Earth: Space Stations, Rival Super-
powers, and the Quest for Interplanetary Travel, Washington, D.C.: Joseph Henry.

Zuckerman, Ethan (2013): Rewire: Digital Cosmopolitans in the Age of
Connection, New York, NY: W. W. Norton.

III. Art and Media: Theory
of Partaking

Introduction: Participation and Relation

SAMANTHA SCHRAMM

In 1969, the American artist Allan Kaprow participated in an experimental workshop at the educational public television sender WGBH. His telehappening *Hello* was originally conceived as an extended form of a happening, in which, through the modalities of closed circuit television, different persons could interact with the TV-studio at WGBH in real time from five locations in Boston. Among the people that would answer the calls from the external locations, being connected through 27 television monitors and five cameras, were artists like Kaprow and Nam June Paik as well as the producers of WGBH, David Atwood und Fred Barzyk. A shorter video version of the happening was broadcasted on March 23 together with six other experimental artistic projects under the title *The Medium is the Medium*.

Gene Youngblood argues that *Hello* exemplifies a "global form of *Hello*, interconnecting continents, languages, and cultures in one sociological mix" (Youngblood 1970: 343-344). Likewise, Kaprow suggested that his telehappening places "[o]neself in connection with someone else" (ibid: 344). *Hello* frames television as a mass medium as it subverts the division between sender and receiver, enhancing a more active mode of participation and giving the viewer the ability to shape the content of the program. Therefore, *Hello* constitutes the viewer in an alternative function, promoting a reflexive form of participation in which they not only perform on television but also react to the interpellation of others as well as interact with their own image which is sometimes displayed on the monitors. The persons in the studio are able to switch between the different audio and video channels, restricting communication by controlling the monitors at the different external sites. However, the participants are at the same time constructed as "participating public" (Kaprow 1993 [1974]: 150) and become subordinated to the visual and auditory modalities of the experimental arrangement of the piece. Furthermore, the modalities of participation are also shaped by the technical objects themselves, with which the audience interacts and which channel and stabilize the communication.

The example of Allan Kaprow's *Hello* relates to experimental forms of participation in arts and media, which are the topic of this section and which serve as a point of departure to address a few thoughts on participation and media, also referring to the claims and irritations of participation as well as the relationship of human and technical agents that are at hand. I will briefly sketch the range of current notions on involvement in the context of arts and media under the terms participation and relation.

PARTICIPATION

Recent notions of participation in art refer to works that are produced by several persons, also leading to shifts in the understanding of the function of the artist as author of the art and the role of the viewer (cf. Bishop 2006, 2012, Billing 2007, Frieling 2008). Projects of participatory art appear as relational entities, insisting not in a final product but in the processes of communication they activate and by which they are surrounded. Not only the understanding of the artwork changes in the context of participatory art, but also the relation between the viewer and his environment, which should be perceived from a new vantage point. The artist thus aims to stimulate projects, that "can ultimately be realized only by the involvement of many" and in which the "social milieu" is also activated (Groys 2008: 1).[1]

Participatory projects like Allan Kaprows *Hello* can be understood as media based forms of shared production and thus precede practices in contemporary media art, which Sara Diamond describes as a process of collaboration between different individuals, which not only negotiates authorship

---

1   However, the notion of the milieu in which participation can take place is challenged by notions of meaning, which is already produced in the relation of beings with-one-another. According to Jean-Luc Nancy, being-with-one-another does not need a space in which it resides, instead is already in circulation "in all the directions of all the space-times" (Nancy 2000: 3).

but can also "create new forms of identification and cohesion." (Diamond 2008: 136) Therefore, the shift from an independent work to a "process-driven" and "multivocal" activity and the way in which media enables and also shapes the outcome is equally significant (ibid).

The term "produsage" emphasizes that in collaborative creations and expansions of knowledge, the distinctions between producers and consumers become insignificant (Bruns 2008: 3). User-lead productions and content-creations, for example visible in the communal extension of knowledge in *Wikipedia* or the collaborative buildings of *Second Life*, show mainly decentralized and distributed models of creativity. In reference to artistic practices, Gregory Sporton describes the possibilities of the web, deepened with Web 2.0, as breaking with the "distinctions between producer and consumer", presenting "new challenges for creative practice" (Sporton 2009: 61). The network itself becomes what he calls a "new performance space", in which "[t]he artist becomes a collaborator in the formulation and re-formulation of work that has no final form." (Ibid: 70) It is instead constantly shifting, being altered and redefined by different actors. However, Sporton does not escape the dichotomy between passivity and activity as forms of participation: "To extract the potential of web 2.0 as a creative experience, the formerly passive spectators of the broadcast age are replaced by the technologically skilled creative partners." (Ibid: 71)

In contrast to rather euphoric descriptions of participation as creation of a "participatory culture" in the context of web 2.0 or as formations of a "collective intelligence" (Jenkins 2006: 2), the aim of the section is to examine specific processes of participation in which participation appears as a "contested site" (Frieling 2008), claimed and defined by different actors, and where notions and possibilities of participation are constantly negotiated. Furthermore, those forms of participation are defined by a relational thinking, which relates to the interrelations of beings as well as to the entanglements of both human and technical agents.

RELATION

In the 1990s, Nicolas Bourriaud established the term "relational aesthetics" to draw attention to an art that addresses the "sphere of human interactions and its social context, rather than the assertion of an autonomous and private public space." (Bourriaud 2002 [1998]: 14) From a Marxist perspective, art is seen as a social "interstice" (ibid: 16), an encounter, unfolding in its own time separate from the necessities of everyday life. Bourriaud refers to artworks as "moments of sociability" in which the notion of a work is constituted by encounters and "objects producing sociability." (Ibid: 33) However, the notion of a relational practice also draws attention to the ambivalent role of the artist and the object, with both conceptualizing their actions to a becoming and understanding themselves as catalysts for participation fulfilled in social spaces defined by various actors. Within such artistic projects, the participants would develop intersubjective relations, in which meaning is not only produced, but also negotiated. From this perspective, the viewer develops more than relations with the artwork, but also with other persons, thereby sharing and developing an understanding of art.

But even a relational artistic practice does not create spaces of participation without constraints and paradoxes relating to the inclusion of the participants. Claire Bishop addresses the idea that the relations proposed by a relational aesthetic cannot be understood as ultimately an democratic enterprise just because they promote an ideal of subjectivity and a community that is shaped by "immanent togetherness" (Bishop 2004: 67). Instead, political concepts in participatory art rely more on the "creative rewards of participation as a politicized working process" (ibid: 2).

Jacques Rancière has consequently criticized the dichotomy in which positions of viewers are negotiated between seeing/knowing, appearance/reality, and activity/passivity, referring to the fact that viewers are already active and thus can simultaneously be spectators and active interpreters (Rancière 2009). Criticizing attempts to release the viewer from the assumed situation of passivity, Rancière argued instead that the experience of art needs moments of difference and that to be conscious of being a spectator already means being involved and taking an active attitude. Therefore, defining participation in art and media is difficult, regardless of whether excluding the viewer from production entails limited involvement, and, in the case of so called participatory art, it is difficult to evaluate the function of the author and if or under which circumstances we can talk about productive part-taking at all. Furthermore, recent notions about the agency of technical objects make it necessary to understand the objects themselves as mediators in the collective process, which is thus shaped by human and non-human agents. Thus, technical objects can equally participate in the buildings of acting networks and social dispositions, by "inscribing" a vision onto technical content (Akrich 1992: 208).

While notions of participation have become widespread in addressing forms of collective involvement in arts and media, a critical notion of participation also raises questions about the intentionality which frames the act of involvement (cf. Livingston 2005). If participation is not seen from a mere perspective of activation, it becomes apparent that those processes are based on various, sometimes diverging intentions that also relate to various claims on participation. As the example of Kaprow's *Hello* suggests, participation hovers between various claims and establishes itself between diverging visions and intentions that are also inscribed in the technical content of the experimental arrangement.

The essays in the section "Art and Media" further raise the discussion on issues of participation and relation. On the one hand, these essays raise issues of imagination in communal expressions as well as critical notions of participation and collaboration, their utopian claims, and restrictions; on the other hand, they discuss forms of relational understanding as individuation through artistic and media based processes.

The authors address historical perceptions of communal practices and their relevance for contemporary theories of participation. These become apparent in the oral practices of ballads and folksongs, as analyzed by Eva Axer, or in 20th century notions of artistic co-design, as shown by Teresa Cruz. In addition, the contributions by Christine Mitchell and Sascha Simons question issues of collaborative translation and, respectively, the interplay of technological, social and aesthetic modalities in the example of memes, both of which address collaborative entanglements between humans and machines. Furthermore, Erin Manning introduces a new perception of relation, referring to artfulness as a lived manner or mode and approaching modalities of individuation in the context of an artistic practice that fosters intuition and constantly evolves and unfolds itself over time.

REFERENCES

Akrich, Madeleine (1992): "The De-Scription of Technical Objects." In: Wiebe E. Bijker/John Law (eds.), Shaping Technology/Building Society. Studies in Sociotechnical Change, Cambridge, MA, and London: MIT Press, pp. 105-127.

Billing, Johanna/ Maria Lind/Lars Nilsson (eds.): Taking the Matter into Common Hands. On Contemporary Art and Collaborative Practices, London: Black Dog 2007.

Bishop, Claire (2004): "Antagonism and Relational Aesthetics", October 110, pp. 51-79.

Bishop, Claire (2006) (ed.): Participation, London: Whitechapel Gallery, and Cambridge, MA: The MIT Press.

Bishop, Claire (2012): Artificial Hells. Participatory Art and the Politics of Spectatorship, London and New York, NY: Verso.

Bourriaud, Nicolas (2002 [1998]): Relational Aesthetics, Dijon: Les presses du reel.

Bruns, Axel (2008): Blogs, Wikipedia, Second Life and Beyond. From Production to Produsage, New York, NY: Peter Lang.

Diamond, Sara (2008): "Participation, Flow and the Redistribution of Authorship. The Challenges of Collaborative Exchange and New Media Curatorial Practice." In: Christiane Paul (eds.), New Media in the White Cube and Beyond. Curatorial Models in Digital Art, Berkeley and Los Angeles, CA, and London: University of California Press 2008, pp. 135-162.

Frieling, Rudolf (2008): "Towards Participation in Art." In: Frieling, Rudolf/Boris Groys/Robert Atkins (eds.): The Art of Participation 1950 to Now, San Francisco Museum of Modern Art, London: Thames & Hudson, pp. 33-49.

Frieling, Rudolf/Boris Groys/Robert Atkins (eds.) (2008): The Art of Participation. 1950 to now. San Francisco Museum of Modern Art, London: Thames & Hudson.

Fried, Michael (1967), "Art and Objecthood." In: Artforum, pp. 12-23.

Groys, Boris (2008), "A Genealogy of Participatory Art." In: Rudolf Friedling/Boris Groys/Robert Atkins (eds.), The Art of Participation. 1950 to now. San Francisco Museum of Modern Art, London: Thames & Hudson, pp. 18-31.

Jenkins, Henry (2006): Convergence Culture. Where Old and New Media Collide, New York, NY: New York University Press.

Kaprow, Allan (1993 [1974]): "Video Art. Old Wine, New Bottle." In: Allan Kaprow, Jeff Kelley (ed.): Essays on the Blurring of Art and Live. Berkeley and Los Angeles, CA, and London, pp. 148-153.

Livingston, Paisley (2005): Art and Intention. A Philosophical Study, Oxford: Oxford University Press.

Nancy, Jean-Luc (2000): Being Singular Plural, Stanford, CA: Stanford University Press.

Rancière, Jacques (2009): The Emancipated Spectator, London and New York, NY: Verso.

Sporton, Gregory (2009): "The Active Audience. The Network as a Performance Environment." In: Alison Oddey and Christine A. White (ed.), Modes of Spectating, Bristol and Chicago, IL: Intellect 2009, pp. 61-72.

Youngblood, Gene (1970): Expanded Cinema, London: Studio Vista.

Artfulness

Emergent Collectivities and Processes of Individuation

ERIN MANNING

> "Thanks to art, instead of seeing a single world, our own, we see it multiply."
> GILLES DELEUZE (1972: 42)

1 THE ART OF TIME

The word "art" (*die Art*) in German means "manner" or "mode." While it is true to say that "*Kunst*" is the term in German currently used for art, might there be a recuperable trace of this early meaning in contemporary notions of artistic practice? Might there be a way to reclaim the processual that has increasingly become backgrounded in the definition of art as tied to an object?

In Romance languages, where art as a word has been retained, mode or manner is eclipsed by a definition of art that emphasizes "the expression or application of human creative skill and imagination". Art is not only reduced entirely to human expression, it is also synonymous, as the Oxford English Dictionary (2014) would have it, with "visual form [...] appreciated primarily for [its] beauty and emotional power."

This current definition of art signals the way the object continues to play a key role in artistic practice, holding art to a passive-active-organization that segregates maker from beholder. For many, whose practice opens the way toward processual concerns, the OED definition will feel outdated. And yet, there is no question that the object's hold remains strong. I would therefore like to propose a new definition of art-as-practice that begins not with the object, but with *what else* art can do. I want to propose we engage first and foremost with the manner of practice and not the end result. What else can artistic practice become when the object is not the goal, but the activator, the conduit toward new modes of existence?

Art, understood as manner, tunes to its thirteenth century definition as "a skill or craft of learning".[1] Art as *a way* of learning. Art as the bridge toward new processes, new pathways. To speak of a "way" is to dwell on the process itself, on its manner of becoming. It is to emphasize that art is before all else a quality, a difference in kind, an operative process that maps the way toward a certain attunement of world and expression.

Art as *way* is not yet about an object, about a form, or a content. It is still on its way. As such, it is deeply allied to Henri Bergson's definition of intuition as the art – the manner – in which the very conditions of experience are felt.[2] Intuition both gets a process on its way and acts as the decisive turn within experience that activates a productive opening within time's durational folds. Intuition crafts the operative problem.

In its feeling-forth of future potential, intuition draws on time: it touches the sensitive nerve of time. Yet intuition is not time or duration per se. "Intuition is rather the movement by which we emerge from our own duration, by which we make use of our own duration to affirm and immediately to recognize the existence of other durations" (Deleuze 1991: 33). Intuition is the relational movement through which the present begins to coexist with its futurity, with the quality or manner of the not-yet that lurks at the edges of experience.[3] This, I want to propose, is art: the intuitive potential to activate the future, to make the middling of experience felt where futurity and presentness coincide, to invoke the memory not of what was, but of what will be. Art, the memory of the future.

---

1   Today, the word for art in German is *Kunst*, and *die Art* is used only to convey the sense of manner or way described above. In French and English and most Romance and Indo-Germanic languages, the two meanings have become separated, though the sense of "the art of" still seems to carry that earlier definition.

2   See, for instance, Bergson's Time and Free Will (Bergson 2001).

3   I have developed relational movement as a concept in both Politics of Touch (2007) and Relationscapes (2009).

Duration is lived only at its edges, in its commingling with actual experience. In the time of the event, what is known is not outside the event: it is the mobility of experience itself, experience in the making. To actually measure the time of the event, a backgridding activity is necessary. Such a reconstruction "after the fact" tends to deplete the event-time of its middling, deactivating the relational movement that was precisely event-time's force. Backgridded, experience is reconceived in its poorest state: out of movement.

Out of movement is out of act. For Alfred North Whitehead, all experience is in-act, variously commingling with the limits of the not-yet and the will-have-been.[4] Experience is (in) movement. Anything that stands still – an object, a form, a being – is an abstraction (in the most commonsense notion of the term) from experience. Such abstractions are not the image of the past (the past cannot be differentiated from the in-act of the future-presenting), but ahistorical cut-outs from a durational field already on its way. Time cannot be held, and with its movement, everything changes in kind. "Object and objective denote not only what is divided, but what, in dividing, does not change in kind" (Deleuze 1991: 41).

This is the paradox: for there to be a theory of the "object", the "object" has to be conceived as out of time, relegated beyond experience, unchanging. Yet, in experience, what we call an object is always, to some degree not-yet, in process, in movement. In the midst, in the event, we know the object not in its fullness, in its ultimate form, but as an edging into experience. What resolves in experience is not, as Whitehead would argue, first and foremost a chair, but the activity of sitability. It is only after the fact, after the initial entrainment the chair activates, after the movement into the relational field of "sitability", that the chair as such is ascertained, felt in all its "object-like" intensity. But even here, Whitehead would argue, its three-dimensional form cannot be disconnected from its quality of form-taking. Form is less the endpoint than the conduit.[5]

---

4   The concept of the in-act weaves its way through all of Whitehead's writings. For an in-depth reading of his process philosophy, see Whitehead (1978).

5   For an account of perception and experience in Whitehead's work, including his key concepts of 'causal efficacy' and 'presentational immediacy', see "Touch as Technique" in Manning (2009) as well as "Coming Alive in a World of Texture" in Manning and Massumi (2014).

That form is held, to a certain degree, in abeyance, that the chair does not ultimately settle, once and for all in experience, does not mean that the form we know as "chair" is contained in an unreachable elsewhere. The object is the abeyance – the feeling-form (a form felt more than actualized) that cannot be separated out from the milieu, from the field that it co-activates, in this case something like the ecology of comfort, sitability and desire to sit. Whether the desire to sit errs on the edge of sitability or leans towards plushness of comfort, the experience of chair is never a finite one, it is never contained by the dimensions of the object (or the subject) itself. The object, like the subject is never it-self.

Art can make this more-than of the object felt. This happens through art's capacity to bring event-time to expression. This crafting of the art of time involves the activation of time's differential. This activation of the dynamic difference, in the event, between what was and what will be, creates a memory of the future. This memory of the future, activated by the minor gesture, is a feltness, in the event, of a tendency. When art is at its most operational, this tendency does not settle in the object. It moves across it, pushing the now of experience in the making to its limit. Here, in the uneasy opening between now and now, art's manner is felt.

All actualization is in fact differentiation. The in-act is the dephasing of the process toward the coming into itself of an occasion of experience. In this dephasing, the differences in kind between the not-yet and the will-have-been are felt, but only at the edges of experience. They are felt in the moving, in their activation of experience's more-than.

To feel in the moving, to activate the more-than that coincides both with object likeness[6] and relational fielding is to experience the non-linearity of time where nothing is yet, but everything acts. Here, there is no succession in the metric sense. To act is to activate as much as to actualize, to make felt the schism between the virtual folds of duration and the actual openings of the now as quality of passage. On its way.

The emphasis on the ontogenesis of time is important: the quality of the way depends on there not being a notion of time or space that pre-exists the event of expression art creates. This is not to deny the past, but

6   For a more in depth exploration of the concept of likeness see Massumi (2011). I also explore the relationship between likeness and counterpoint in "Another Regard" (Manning 2013).

to say instead that what exists in experience is not a linear time-line but "various levels of contraction" (Deleuze 1991: 74). The manner of existence is how experience contracts, dilates, expands.

The manner of experience is felt qualitatively in its event-time. This qualitative expression of experience in the making is not "objective". There is no perfect standpoint from which to explore it, and its effects are unmeasurable. Event-time is in movement, lived, felt. How it connects to what will come to be is how it becomes what it is. In this sense, it is intuitive. The manner created in the practice of art-making is intuitive chiefly in its way of taking and making time. The art of time is elasticity – not object, not genre, not form, not content. This is not to say that these aspects of artistic practice cannot coincide with part of its process. It is to say that the eventness that is the art of time is before all else an elastic opening onto the qualitative difference intuition activates. In the best case scenario, the manner of art's making creates robust effects that nonetheless are capable of generating infinite intuitive openings for art's more-than.

The art of time is not about definitions so much as about sensations, about the affective force of the making of time where "we are no longer beings but vibrations, effects of resonance, 'tonalities' of different amplitudes" (Lapoujade 2010: 9).[7] Nor is the art of time about economy, about marking the worthiness of a given experience, the usefulness of time spent. "We must become capable of thinking [...] change without anything changing" (ibid: 12). Duration is time felt in the beyond of apparent change, independently of any notion of linear succession.

Intuition never stems from what is already conceived. Wary of false problems, it introduces into experience a rift in knowing, a schism in perception. It forces experience to the limits not only of what it can imagine, but what it has technically achieved. For intuition is never separate from technique. It is a rigorous process that consists in pushing technique to its limit, revealing its technicity. Technicity: the outdoing of technique that makes the more-than of experience felt.[8]

A memory of the future is the direct experience of time's differential. "It is a question here of something which has been present, that has been

---

7   My translations throughout.

8   See the chapter "Dancing the Virtual" in Manning (2013) for a more comprehensive reading of technique and technicity.

felt, but that has not been acted" (ibid: 21-22). A memory not only of and for the human: a memory active in duration itself, a memory inseparable from duration's relational movement. Not only of and for the human because duration is not strictly-speaking of the human – "duration does not attach itself to being – or to beings, it coincides with pure becoming" (ibid: 24).

A memory of the future makes felt the smallest vibrational intervals – human and nonhuman – that lurk at the interstices of experience. Paired with the minor gesture, which assists in making these intervals take expression, a memory of the future intuits them, activating their force of becoming by opening them to the untimeliness of their current rhythms. This is intuition: the captivation, in the event, of the welling forces that activate the dephasing of experience into its more-than. A memory of the future because this more-than cannot quite be captured, cannot be held in the presentness of experience. The memory of the future is an attunement, in the event, to futurity not as succession but as rhythm: the future pulses in experience in-forming. The memory of the future is the recursive experience, in the event, of what is on its way. Déjà-felt.

Bergson calls the mechanism by which this future-feeling arises sympathy.[9] Sympathy not "of" the human but *with* experience in the making. "We call intuition that sympathy by which we are transported to the interior of an object to coincide with what it has that is unique and, consequently, inexpressible" (Lapoujade 2010: 53). Sympathy as the motor of excavation allows the movement to be felt, opens experience to the complexities of its own unfolding.

What is intuited is not matter per se: "There is therefore no intuition of matter, of life, of society *in and of themselves*, that is, as nouns" (ibid: 56, original emphasis). There is intuition of forces, of qualities that escape the superficial interrogation of that which has already taken its place. Intuition is always and only compelled by what is on its way.

Gilles Deleuze sometimes speaks of the art of time as essence. Essence here has nothing to do with a stable quality. In his early work on Proust, Deleuze speaks of essence as the force of the as-yet-unfelt in experience. Essence is here everything it usually isn't: it is not truth, or origin. Essence is the ultimate difference in kind. Linked to art, essence

9   For Bergson's account of sympathy, see Bergson (1998).

for Deleuze speaks of the unquantifiable in experience, of that which exceeds the equivalence between sign and sense. "At the deepest level, the essential is in the signs of art" (1972: 13).

The signs of art do not convey meaning; they make felt its ineffability. The essential, the creative sign that does not represent, is a species of time, a durational fold in experience. Its quality of time cannot be abstracted from its coming-into-formation. The field it creates is analogous to its time, a time not of succession but a time-schism. Time, as Deleuze says, "*le temps*", is plural.

A plurality of time in time multiplies experience in the now. This, Deleuze suggests, is what art can do. Art not as the form an object takes, but as the manner in which time is composed. Time, as the force of the differential, has effects. It creates a compositional matrix that transversalizes the act and the in-act. In time, in the art of time, what is activated is not a subject or an object, but a field of expression through which a different quality of experience is crafted. What art can do is to bypass the object as such and make felt instead the dissonance, the dephasing, the complementarity of the between, of what Deleuze calls the "revelatory" or refracting milieu (1972: 47). It does so when it is capable of making operative its minor gesture. The refraction produces not a third object but a quality of experience that reaches the edgings into form of the material's intuition. When this occurs, matter intuits its relational movement, activating from within its qualitative resonance an event that makes time for that which cannot quite be seen but is felt in all its uncanny difference. Intuition, in its amplification of the technicity of a process, in its capacity to think the more-than as memory of the future, forecasts what Deleuze calls "an original time" which "surmounts its series and its dimensions," a "complicated time [...] deployed and developed," a time devoid of preconceptions, a time that makes its own way (1972: 61).

Tuning into the art of time involves crafting techniques that open art to its minor gestures. It requires an attentiveness to the field in its formation. This attention is ecological, collective, in the event. It is relational, relation here understood as the force that makes felt the how of time as it co-composes with experience in the making. It is out of relation that the solitary is crafted, not the other way around: relation is what an object, a subject is made of.

This is what David Lapoujade means when he writes that "at the heart of the human there is nothing human" (2010: 62). The world is made of relation activated by intuition, felt sympathetically on the edges of experience. Here, at the edges, the more-than, the more-than-human tendencies for experience in the making, are lively. "We must move beyond the limits of human experience, sometimes inferior, sometimes superior, to attain the pure material plane, the vital, social, personal, spiritual planes across which the human is composed" (ibid: 62). What is at stake in the intuiting of the more-than that art requires in order to activate a minor gesture is not the requalification of subject and object, artist and work, but the shedding of all that preexists the occasion in which the event takes place. Only this, Lapoujade suggests, makes the unrealizable realizable.

The memory of the future, the art of time – these are not quantifiable measures. These are speculative propositions, forces within the conceptual web of experience in the crafting that lurk on the edges of the thinkable. The art of time is the proposition art can make to a world in continual composition. It is also the proposition that opens art to its outside, to art as in-act, to practice as the crafting of emergent collectivities. Instead of immediately turning to form for its resolution, the art of time can ask how techniques of relation become a conduit for a relational movement that exceeds the very form-taking art so often strives toward. Instead of stalling at the object, art as manner can explore how the forces of the not-yet co-compose with the milieu of which they are an incipient mode. It can inquire into the collective force that emerges from this co-composition. It can develop techniques for intuiting how art becomes the basis for creating new manners, new modes of collaboration, human and nonhuman, material and immaterial. It can touch on the technicity of the more-than of art's object-based propositions. It can ask how the collective iteration of a process in the making itself thinks, how it activates the limits of research-creation. It can ask what forces it to think, to become. It can inquire into the forces that do violence to the act of making time, and it can create with the unsettling milieu of a time out of joint, intuiting its limits, limits that often have little to do with form. In doing so, it can create a time for thought "that would lead life to the limit of what it can do" complicating the very concept of life by pushing life "beyond the limits that knowledge fixes for it" (Deleuze 1983: 101). Art as technique, as way.

This way is relational. It is of the field, in the milieu. Art: the intuitive process for activating the relational composition that is life-living, for creating a memory of the future that evades, that complicates form. The art of time: making felt the rhythm of the differential, the quality of relation. It is not a question, once again, of slow time, or quick time, of lingering or speeding. It is a question of moving experience beyond the way it has a habit of taking, of discovering how the edges of life-living commingle with the forces of that which cannot yet be perceived, but are nonetheless felt. The art of time involves taking a risk, no doubt, but risk played out differently, at the level not of identity or being: risk of losing our footing, risk of the world losing its footing, on a ground that moves and keeps moving. Here, in the crafting of an undercommons where movement predates form, where expression remains lively at the interstices of the ineffable, the field of relation itself becomes "inventor of new possibilities of life," possibilities of life we can only intuit in the art of time (Nietzsche 1996: 3).

2   THE ART OF PARTICIPATION

If the art of time, or art as manner, invents new possibilities for life-living, it does so because of its continual investment in the question of practice. Practice, as that which moves technique toward technicity, cannot be reduced to an individual. Practice is transversal to the field of experience.

Gilbert Simondon speaks of the individual as the point of inflection of a process of individuation. For Simondon, the individual is emergent, not constitutive. In Simondon's vocabulary, there is an intrinsic relationship between individuation (the process), the preindividual (the force of form), and the individual (the turning point that opens the process toward new individuations). The individual (the singularity of a process) is never the starting point – it is what emerges from the middling of individuation. (Simondon 2005)[10] The individual or the 'superject' in Whiteheadian terms, is how the event expresses itself, never what sets it in motion.

The individual, emergent from the process, cannot be fully abstracted from the force of the preindividual, the virtual excess or more-than that ac-

---

10 My translations throughout.

companies all processes of force taking form. If the more-than of a process's individuality accompanies all comings-to-form, this means that there is no phase of a process that is not actively in excess of the form it takes. A process is by its very nature collective. It is an 'ecology of practices'.[11] Whereas in many readings of collectivity, the multitude refers to the sum of individual parts (thereby subsuming the collective to the individuals within it), for Simondon the collective is the very definition of a process. Individuals do emerge from it, but the process can never be returned to the sum of its parts. Even the individual, when abstracted, cannot simply be reduced to a sum, for it continues to carry its preindividual charge, a charge that "contains potentials and virtuality", which means it is susceptible to continuous changes in kind (Simondon 2005: 248).

Simondon uses the concept of the "transindividual" to describe the collectivity at the heart of all individuations, before and beyond any speciating into individuals. He mobilizes the transindividual to make apparent that any shift in the event is a shift in ecology. The transindividual is the concept that most underscores the fact that all events are collaborative, participatory.

Participation is key to the art of time. In the OED's normative account of art as object, art has two times: the time of making, and the time of the spectator's appreciation of that making. Maker and spectator are the two limits of a process. While this account is complicated in participatory art and in collective artistic processes of all kinds, the question remains: to what degree does art retain this original dichotomy between maker and spectator/public/participant even when acknowledging that it is the participatory aspect of the work that makes the work work? To what degree does the maker continue to see themselves as the central pivot? To what degree do we hold on to the idea of the artist as solitary genius?

When a process is delimited by the belief that there is a pre-existing individual creating at its center, the collective becomes an afterthought. The participatory is left to the end, and with this, a decisive stage of the event is muted. In segregating participation from the work, in making it the afterthought of a practice already underway, what we do is set apart integral aspects of a process. The real work is seen as that which emerges before the event opens to the public. Practice thus separates itself from techniques for

---

11 For Isabelle Stengers' writing on the ecology of practices, see Stengers (2011).

activation. When this happens, the participatory is set up in an uneasy dichotomy between what it considers the inside and the outside of a process. An expectation emerges that places the public in a position of uneasy judgment. On the one hand, the public becomes the judge of the work, and on the other hand, the artist becomes the judge of the public's judgment. Even in the best of situations, a certain prescribed choreography cannot but emerge. Not only does this deaden the force of what a practice can do, it limits participation to a pre-defined definition of a public, a tendency that reorients participation to human intervention. As activator after the event, this human presence now has the task to reanimate, to bring into being this new phase of the practice. While this can be successful in the sense that it can produce new modes of encounter that open the work to a potential not yet inscribed in its process, the effects tend to be limited to an us-them-scenario that judges and delimits participation on the basis of an already imagined outcome. Too often, this leads the artist, the organizer, to lament that the participant has not been able to fully attend to the complexity of the proposition at hand.

This kind of scenario is unraveled through the concept of the transindividual. Here, instead of being the add-on to the event, participation is understood as the more-than at the heart of the event in its formation. Participation is not the way the outside adds itself to a process already underway, but the operational multiplicity of a practice in its unfolding.

Participation understood as immanent to the event raises a completely different set of expectations. Now, practice is considered immanent to the ecologies of an ever shifting process. This radically alters the conditions of the work. Now, the problem is not how the participant can reanimate a process, but how the process itself as emergent practice can make felt its own participatory or transindividual nature. The practice shifts from seeing the object as endpoint to exploring how to prolong the art of time in the event such that new forms of collaboration can be engendered. Whether we are talking about the making of an artwork or the setting into place, through a process artfully in-act, of activist practices of emergent collectivity, what matters here is less how the work defines itself than how it is capable of creating new conduits for expression. Participation thus conceived is a putting into relation of an *agencement*, a mobilizing-toward, in the event, that doesn't begin with the human individual.[12] Simondon writes:

"Couldn't we conceive of individuation as being [...] a process intrinsic to the formation of individuals, never achieved, never fixed, never stable, but always realizing, in their evolution, an individuation that structures them without eliminating the associated charge of the preindividual, constituting the horizon of transindividual Being from which they detach themselves?" (Simondon 2005: 13)

The transindividual, it bears repeating, "is neither raw sociality nor the interindividual; it presupposes a veritable operation of individuation from a preindividual reality" (ibid). Preindividual reality, the charge of the more-than that accompanies all processes of individuation, creates not an individual formed once and for all, but a metastability that expresses "a quantum condition, correlative of a plurality of orders of magnitude" (ibid). It is from the perspective of this metastability that the crafting, in an artistic process, of the art of participation can begin, a crafting that takes the event as participatory at its core, a process always in co-composition across the scales and times of its making.

Limits of Existence

To explore the art of participation, it is necessary to return to a few key issues raised earlier around the notion of the art of time.

1) What is activated by an artwork is not its objecthood (an object in itself is not art). Art is the way, the manner of becoming that is intensified by

---

12 Agencement is a concept I discuss in detail in my forthcoming manuscript The Minor Gesture (Duke UP, forthcoming). Often used by thinkers such as Deleuze and Guattari and Foucault, agencement refers to the way a process moves toward its unfolding. Felix Guattari writes: agencement is a junction that "secretes [its own] coordinates, [that] can certainly impose connections, but [does] not impose a fixed constraint" (2013: 24). I prefer the term to "agency," which tends to foreground both the figure of the individual subject, and the notion of individual intentionality.

the coming-out-of-itself of an object. It is the object's outdoing as form or content.

2) Intuition is the work that sets the process of outdoing on its way.

3) The manner of becoming makes time felt in the complexity of its non-linear duration. This is an activation of the future – the force of making-felt what remains unthinkable (on the edge of feeling).

4) The activation of the manner of becoming is another way of talking about the work's technicity, or its more-than. This more-than is a dephasing of the work from its initial proposition (its material, its conditions of existence).

5) The relational field activated by the work's outdoing of itself is a more-than human ecology of practices. Relationally, ecologically, the work participates in a worlding that potentially redefines the limits of existence.

Limits of existence are always under revision. The art of participation takes the notion of modes of existence as its starting point, asking how techniques of encounter modify or modulate how art can make a difference, opening up the existing fields of relation toward new forms of perception, accountability, experience and collectivity. This aspect of the art of participation cannot be thought separately from the political, despite the fact that its political force is not necessarily in its content. This is not about making the form of art political. It is about asking how the field of relation activated by art can affect the complex ecologies of which it is part.

Sympathy

Sympathy, for Bergson, is not the benevolent act that follows the event. Neither is sympathy the result of or a response to an already-determined action. Sympathy is the vector of intuition without which intuition would never be experienced as such. An event sympathetic to the force of its intuition becomes capable of generating minor gestures that open the process to its technicity. Sympathy is what allows the event to express its more-than. It is what opens the event to the novelty (the inexpressibility) intuition has called forth: "we call intuition that sympathy by which we are transported to the interior of an object to coincide with what it has that is unique, and, consequently, inexpressible" (Lapoujade 2008: 11).

It is impossible to think intuition and sympathy as wholly separate from one another, but neither should we consider them as the same. Intuition touches on the differential of a process, and sympathy holds the contrasts in the differential together, such that, coupled with the minor gesture, the ineffable becomes expressive. Sympathy, allied with the minor gesture, is the conduit for the expression of a certain encounter already held in germ. Where intuition is the force of expression or pre-articulation of an event's welling into itself, sympathy, calling forth the minor gesture, is the way of its articulation.

Sympathy is a strange term for this process, so connected is it in our everyday language with the sense of applying a value-judgment to a preexisting process. It may therefore not hold the power as a concept to make felt the force of what it does, or can do. I use it here as an ally to concepts such as 'concern' and 'self-enjoyment' in Whitehead, concepts that remind us that the event has a concern for its own evolution, and that this concern is key to the event outdoing itself.[13] To make sympathy the driver of expression *in the event* is to bring care into the framework of an event's concrescence, to foreground how intuition is a relational act that plays itself out in an ecology that cannot be abstracted from it. Intuition leads to sympathy – *sympathy for the event in its unfolding*. Without sympathy for the unfolding, the event cannot make felt the complexity of durations of which it is composed. Sympathy tends to the complexity of an intuition that lurks at the very edge of thought where the rhythms that populate the event have not yet moved into their constellatory potential.

The Way of Art

If the art of time is inextricably linked to practice as way, then practice and intuition must always be seen as co-operative: intuition is the fold in experience that allows for the staging of a problem that starts a process on its way, or curbs a process into its difference, creating the germ for a practice.

This raises the question of where intuition is situated in relation to practice's inherent double: participation. Is participation also intuitive? I would

---

13 For Whitehead's writing on 'concern' (which only comes up sporadically throughout his work), see, for instance, Whitehead (1967). 'Self-enjoyment' appears throughout, but is most developed in Whitehead (1978).

say that where art as event is mobilized through an intuitive process that crafts and vectorizes the problem that will continue to activate it throughout its life, participation is the sympathy for this process. Participation is the yield in what Raymond Ruyer calls the "aesthetic yield."[14] It is the yield both in the sense that it gives direction to a process already underway and that it opens that process to the more-than of its form or content. A minor gesture is always participatory.

Aesthetic yield expands beyond any object occasioned by the process to include the vista of expression generated by practice as event. This, I want to call artfulness. Artfulness, the aesthetic yield, is about how a set of conditions coalesce to favor the opening of a process to its inherent collectivity, to the more-than of its potential. The art of participation is the capacity, in the event, to activate its artfulness, to tap into its yield. Artfulness is the force of a becoming that is singularly attendant to an ecology in the making, an ecology that can never be subsumed to the artist or to the individual participant. Artfulness: the momentary capture of an aesthetic yield in an evolving ecology.

All ecologies are more-than human. They are as much the breath of a movement as they are the flicker of a light and the sound of a stilling. They are earth and texture, air and wind, color and saturation. And they are the interstitial differentials that populate each of these qualities of experience.

In the context of art as manner, artfulness is closer to the differential than to any object. The artful, when it emerges, has been activated through the punctuality of a minor gesture's movement through a process. The complex ecology of a process outdoing itself that is made operational by the minor gesture is felt, in its intensity, in the artful: the artful is palpably transindividual. This is not to suggest that the crafting of operational problems through intuition, the activation of minor gestures through sympathy for the event, the coming-into-expression of artfulness are quickly or easily done: when writing about intuition's role in the crafting of a problem, Bergson speaks of the necessity of a long camaraderie engendered by a relationship of trust that leads toward an engagement with that which goes beyond premature observations and preconceived neutralizing facts (in Lapoujade 2008:12). Intuition is a rigorous process that agitates at the very

---

14 See Ruyer (1958); Massumi also discusses the concept in detail (2014: 10-13).

limits of an encounter with the as-yet unthought. Artfulness is the sympathetic expression of this encounter.

Tapping into the differential, artfulness opens the world to the kind of novelty Whitehead foregrounds – a novelty not concerned with the capitalist sense of the newest new, but novelty as the creation of mixtures that produce new openings, new vistas, new complexions for experience in the making. This novelty can never be reduced to art as object: only the artful is truly capable of activating new mixtures.

Artfulness does not belong to the artist, nor to art as a discipline. If it needs to be attached to something, it could be said to be what the most operational process of research-creation seeks to actualize. Artfulness is the operative expression of worlds in the making, the aesthetic yield that opens experience to the participatory quality of the more-than.

Artfulness emerges most actively in the interstices where the world has not yet settled into objects and subjects. One lively environment for artfulness is the field of direct perception I have defined elsewhere as *autistic perception*. Autistic perception is the opening, in perception, to the uncategorized, to the unclassified. This opening, which is how many autistics describe their experience of the world, makes it initially difficult to parse the field of experience. Rather than seeing the parts abstracted from the whole, autistic perception is alive with tendings that create ecologies before they coalesce into form. There is here as yet no hierarchical differentiation, for instance, between colour, sound, light, between human and nonhuman, between what connects to the body and what connects to the world.[15] When there is artfulness it is because conditions have been created that enable not only the art of time, but also the art of participation. Autistic perception, the direct participation, in the event, of its welling ecologies, is perhaps the most open register for the experience of the artful. For it is only when there is sympathy for the complexity of the welling event that the more-than of an emergent ecology can truly be perceived. When this happens, a shift is felt toward a sense of immanent movement – and the way at the heart of art is felt. It is not the object that stands out here, not the tree or the sunset or a painting. It is the force of immanent movement the event calls forth that is

---

15 For more on autistic perception, see Manning (2012) as well as the forthcoming manuscript The Minor Gesture, which includes a version of this piece (Duke UP).

experienced, a mobility in the making that displaces any discrete notion of subjectivity or objecthood. This does not mean that what is opened up is without a time, a place, a history. Quite the contrary: what emerges at the heart of the artful in the rhythmic time of autistic perception is always singular – *this* process, *this* ecology, *this* feeling. It is how the constellation of emergent factors co-compose, but also how they are felt in their emergence, that make this singular event artful, an artfulness that will then, in retrospect, carry a history, a commitment to a cause, a politics in the making.

Artfulness is an immanent directionality, felt when a work runs itself, or when a process activates its most sensitive fold where it is still rife with intuition. This modality is beyond the human. Certainly, it cuts through, merges with, captures and dances with the human, but it is also and always more-than human, active in an ecology of resonances that are most readily perceived by the neurodiverse. The process now has its own momentum, its own art of time, and this art of time, excised as it is from the limits of subject-centered volition, collaborates to create its own way. The force of art is precisely that it is more-than human.[16]

Rhythm is key to this process that flows through different variations of human-centeredness toward ecologies as yet unnamable. Everywhere in the vectorizations of intuition and sympathy are durations as yet unfolded, expressions of time as yet unlived, rhythms still unlivable. This is what makes an event artful – that it remains on the edge, at the outskirts of a process that does not yet recognize itself, inventing as it does its own way, a way of moving, of flowing, of stilling, of lighting, of coloring, of participating. For this is how artfulness is lived – as a field of flows, of differential speeds and slownesses, in discomfort and awe, distraction and attention. Artfulness is not something to be beheld. It is something to move through, to dance with on the edges of perception where to feel, to see and to become are indistinguishable.

What moves here is not the human per se, but the force of the direction the intuition gave the event in its preliminary unfolding paired with the force of a minor gesture. Techniques are at work, modulating themselves to outdo their boundedness toward a technicity in germ. Thought, intent, organization, consideration, habit, experience – all of these are at work. But with them comes the germ of intuition born of a long and patient process

16 For an account of animality and creativity, see Massumi (2014).

now being activated by a sympathy for difference, a sympathy for the event in its uneasy becoming. To touch on the artful is to touch on the incommensurable more-than that is everywhere active in the ecologies that make us and exceed us.

Tweaked toward the artful in the process of making, art becomes a way toward a collective ethos. From the most apparently stable structure to the most mobile or ephemeral iteration, art that is artful activates the art of participation, making felt the transindividual force of an event-time that catapults the human into our difference. This difference, the more-than at our core, the non-human share that animates our every cell, becomes attentive to the relational field that opens the work to its intensive outside. This relational field must not be spatially understood. It is an intensive mattering, an absolute mobility that inhabits the work durationally. It is the art of time making itself felt.

A fielding of difference has been activated and this must be tended. The art of participation involves creating the conditions for this tending to take place. This tending is first and foremost a tending of the fragile environment of duration generated by the working of the work and activated by the minor gesture. A tending of the work's incipient rhythms. I say fragile because there is so much to be felt in the process of a work's coming to resonance with a world itself in formation.

Sympathy makes felt how the tendency, the way, the direction or incipient mobility, is itself the subject of the work. Sympathy makes tending the subject, undermining the notion that either the work or the human come to experience fully-formed. Sympathy: that which brings the force of the more-than to the surface. That which makes felt how the force of experience always exceeds the object. That which generates the opening for the minor gesture to take the work on its way.

Vectors

The art of participation does not find its conduit solely in the human. The artful also does its work without human intervention, activating fields of relation that are environmental or ecological in scales of intermixings that may include the human but don't depend on it. How to categorize as human or nonhuman the exuberance of an effect of light, the way the air moves through a space, or the way one artwork catches another in its movement of thought? Artfulness is always more-than.

Whitehead's notion of vectors is useful to get a stronger sense of the more-than human quality of experience artfulness holds. The vector, in Whitehead's work, is defined as a force of movement that travels from one occasion of experience to another or within a single occasion. What is particular to Whitehead's definition is the way he connects the vector to feeling. "Feelings are 'vectors'; for they feel what is there and transform it into what is here" (1978: 87). It bears repeating that for Whitehead, feelings are not associated to a preexisting subject. They are the force of the event as it expresses itself. Understood as vectors, feelings have the force of a momentum, an intuition for direction. They are how the event expresses sympathy for its own intuitive becoming.

Whitehead's theory of feeling catapults the notion of human-based participation on its head. *What the feeling has felt* is how the event has come to expression. The subject is its aftermath. The subject is not limited to the human – it is the marker of an individual that, in Simondon's terms, can be located as the culmination of an occasion of experience. An occasion of experience always holds such a marker – once it has come to concrescence, it will always be what it was. This is what Whitehead calls the superject, or the subject of experience. Making the subject the outcome of the event rather than its initiator reminds us that the subject of an event includes its vector quality – in Brian Massumi's terms, its thinking-feeling. The subject can never be abstracted or separated out from the vector quality, the "feeling-tone" which co-composed it.[17]

The artful is the event's capacity to foreground the feeling-tone of the occasion such that it generates an affective tonality that permeates more than this singular occasion. For this to happen, there has to be, within the evolution of an occasion, the capacity for the occasion to become a nexus that continues to have an appetite for its process. This does not mean to imply that the occasion will not perish. It simply emphasizes that in the perishing, there can be a qualitative shading that persists in occasions to come.

As feeling-tone, vectors attune to the field of relation, and tune it to its more-than. In doing so, they activate the collectivity of a given nexus of occasions. What emerges, in the act, is what Whitehead would call a 'socie-

17 See, for instance, Massumi (2011).

ty' a becoming of a wider field of relation that outdoes the atomicity of the occasion's initial coming into being. As Whitehead underscores, this is a rhythmic (and not a linear) process. It swings from the in-itselfness of a given actual occasion, where what is fashioned is simply what it is, to a wider field where the openness to fashioning remains rife with potential not only in the occasion at hand but across the wider expanse of the occasion's nexus. The artful lives at this intersection.

Whitehead talks about this in terms of the creation of worlds – "feeling from a beyond which is determinate and pointing to a beyond which is to be determined" (1978: 163). To be determined here is resolutely to be *in potentia* – for how a feeling-tone vectorizes cannot be mapped in advance, and whether it lands in a way that activates a worlding cannot be predicted. But it can be modulated through the collaborative, participatory work of the minor gesture, and in the mix the artful can emerge.

Contemplation

A feeling-vector contemplates its passage, attending to the dance of an occasion coming into itself. The occasion cannot be abstracted from its feeling-tone. The contemplation of its becoming cannot be separated out from how it comes into itself.

Placing contemplation, intuition, feeling-tone and sympathy together, what emerges is an artfulness that refuses to be instrumental. It has no use-value – it does nothing that can be mapped onto a process already underway. It has no end-point, no pre-ordained limits, no moral codes. But it is conditioned and conditioning.

To say that a process is conditioning is to say that it is born of enabling constraints that facilitate the most propitious engagement with the problem at hand, enabling the passage toward a field that yields. A practice does its work when this yield – already present in germ in the initial problem that activated its process, in the intuition that tapped into how technique might become technicity – is made operational by a minor gesture. Without propitious conditions, the aesthetic does not yield, and the work or event cannot become in excess of the techniques that brought it into being.

Propitious conditions facilitate contemplation. Contemplation, understood as the act of lingering-with, of tending to a process, is a minor form of doing. It attends to the conditions of the work's work. Contemplation is passive only in the sense that this attending provokes a waiting, a stilling, a listening, a sympathy-with. This sympathy is enveloped in the process, sympathetic to the ineffable share of experience emboldened by the minor gesture, attuned to the fragile art of time. Contemplation, operative at the edges of perception where the conscious and the nonconscious overlap, activates times of its own making, sometimes even opens the neurotypical to autistic perception. For contemplation, like intuition and its counterpart, sympathy, activates the differential of an event, and in doing so, become responsive to the subtle nuances of experience crafting itself.

Contemplation makes the artful felt. It does so in the event, in the uneasy balance between seeding a practice and becoming-with a practice. Here, in the midst of life-living, artfulness reminds us that the "I" is not where life begins, and the "you" is not what makes it art. Made up as it is of a thousand contemplations, the art of time reminds us that "we [must] speak of the self only in virtue of these thousands of little witnesses which contemplate within us: it is always a third party who says 'me'" (Deleuze 1978: 75). This is why artfulness is more rare than art. For artfulness depends on so many tendings, so many implicit collaborations between intuition and sympathy. And more than all else, it depends on the human getting out of the way.

Artfulness: the way the art of time makes itself felt, how it lands, and how it always exceeds its landing.

REFERENCES

Bergson, Henri (1998): Creative Evolution, New York, NY: Dover Publications.

Bergson, Henri (2001): Time and Free Will – An Essay on the Immediate Data of Consciousness, New York, NY: Dover Publications.

Deleuze, Gilles (1972): Proust and Signs, New York, NY: George Braziller.

Deleuze, Gilles (1978): Difference and Repetition, New York, NY: Columbia University Press.

Deleuze, Gilles (1983): Nietzsche and Philosophy, New York, NY: Columbia University Press.

Deleuze, Gilles (1991): Bergsonism, New York, NY: Zone Books.

Deleuze, Gilles/Guattari, Felix (1987): A Thousand Plateaus, Minneapolis, MN: University of Minnesota Press.

Guattari, Felix (2013): Schizoanalytic Cartographies, London: Bloomsbury Academic.

Lapoujade, David (2010): Puissances du temps, versions de Bergson, Paris: Editions Minuit.

Manning, Erin (2007): Politics of Touch. Sense, Movement, Sovereignty, Minneapolis, MN: University of Minnesota Press.

Manning, Erin (2009): Relationscapes. Movement, Art, Philosophy, Cambridge, MA: MIT Press.

Manning, Erin (2013): Always More Than One. Individuations Dance, Durham and London: Duke University Press

Manning, Erin/Massumi, Brian (2014): Thought in the Act: Passages in the Ecology of Experience, Minneapolis, MN: University of Minnesota Press.

Massumi, Brian (2011): "The Thinking-Feeling of What Happens." In: Idem, Semblance and Event, Cambridge, MA, and London: MIT Press, pp. 39-86.

Massumi, Brian (2014): What Animals Teach Us About Politics, Durham and London: Duke University Press.

Nietzsche, Friedrich (1996): Philosophy in the Tragic Age of the Greeks, Washington, D.C.: Gateway Editions.

Oxford English Dictionary, http://www.oed.com (August 13, 2015).

Ruyer, Raymond (1948) : La genèse des formes vivantes, Paris: Flammarion.

Simondon, Gilbert (2005): L'individuation à la lumière des notions de forme et d'information, Grenoble: Editions Jérôme Million.

Stengers, Isabelle (2010): Cosmopolitics 1, Minneapolis, MN: University of Minnesota Press.

Stengers, Isabelle (2011): Cosmopolitics 2, Minneapolis: University of Minnesota Press.

Whitehead, Alfred North (1967): Adventures of Ideas, New York, NY: Free Press.

Whitehead, Alfred North (1978): Process and Reality, New York, NY: Free Press.

Art and Design
as Social Collaborative Praxis

Engineering the Utopian Community

or the Implosion of Techno-Aesthetic Reason

MARIA TERESA CRUZ

The turning point of contemporary culture and art in the direction of a participatory claim seems to have come from afar or has been in preparation for quite a long time. It is perhaps for this reason that their arrival and revolutionary appeal have a familiar sound, or are even somewhat overused, like that of an ideology that has finally found conditions for deployment. But in spite of being familiar it seems to answer some of the anxiety and aspirations at the beginning of the 21st century, marked by the crisis of financial capitalism, by the first effects of globalization and by information networks. On the whole, we are living the expectation that the current disarticulation and complexity allow new social re-articulations, along with political and economic alternatives, aided by an empowering and creative potential that would have finally found the means to fully express itself in a strategic way.

The claim of participatory culture (Jenkins/Ford/Green 2013; Castells 2012) does not therefore constitute a revolutionary event, the advent of an entirely new idea, but is rather the observation that perhaps the time has come for some old ideals (expressed by art and also by some political utopias) to make their way as effective views of society at large, alternative to those of late capitalism and its models of economy and governance. Stated this way, the success of such a venture will not, in fact, be less revolutionary than the revolutions that preceded it. However, in this case, it comes out of some structural possibilities of our time, no matter how tense and critical it presents itself today (Stiegler 2009).

These possibilities have indeed expressed themselves in some modern communal utopias, with roots in anarchist ideals or visions of a "moral economy" and also, more recently, in artistic programs committed to social and political engaged art, that is involved, for example, in the organization of community field work or in the construction of habits of sharing and exchange between individuals. These ways of generating value, distinct from the exchange value that has become increasingly abstract in speculative capitalism, returns to an experiential basis of artistic value that, in turn, would be independent of exchange value.

1 Art as Collaborative Praxis

Collaborative art, participatory art, and relational aesthetics, are some of the names of these proposals, which have arisen especially in the second half of the 20th century (Thompson 2012; Bishop 2006; Bourriaud 1998). It is possible to say that they stem from the DADA movement (1916-1920), the Bauhaus Theatre (1919-1933), at the beginning of the century, and from later movements such as the Black Mountain College or Fluxus (1962-1968), which are understood first and foremost as a kind of experience that is possible to share between producers and beholders.

We may say that there are at least two common aspects in these movements. On the one hand, there is evidence of a crisis of the work of art, favoring the contextual and procedural elements of artistic experience. It is in essence a celebration of the experience of art, instead of a glorification of the work of art as autonomous and immanent presence. The valuing of the reception will come to imply a set of theories about the negotiation of the meaning of the work of art. The enhancement of the role of the recipient will eventually culminate in the negotiation of the space of authorship or authority over the work and in the idea of what we might call a kind of "distributed creativity" (as in "distributed systems" or "distributed capitalism") (AAVV 2011). The other aspect refers to a growing appreciation of the artistic value of action and agency of performance art (performance, happening, actionism, etc.) which will also support favorable participation and interaction of the recipients, namely in the field of plastic and visual arts. The disinvestment in objects, to a large extent replaced by the investment in experience, agency, and processes, namely through "installations" or "site specific objects", have sometimes been criticized as "theatre" (Fried 1998) (because they privilege the experience of the recipients over an immanent and autonomous value of the object of art). These two aspects ultimately culminate in an artistic practice whose participants are increasingly blurred with the work itself, aiming at the ideal of an art of the community and for the community of the recipients.

For a deeper understanding of these trends it is necessary to identify some of the cultural transformations of a longer duration which mark modern experience and art and precede their own movements throughout the 20th century. These transformations can be related to three main aspects. The first is the emergence of eighteenth century aesthetic thinking of an aesthetic vision of art which specifically focus on reception, i.e., sensitive and judicative experience (Agamben 1996). The subjective experience is the territory where art can be understood. In this new paradigm art is defined as "aesthetic art" ("aesthetische Kunst") (Kant 2007 [1790]), entering into a new cultural economy. This aesthetic economy is based on the value of this kind of experience for the construction of a community of taste, as "propaedeutic" (Kant 2007 [1790]: §69) of an ethical and political community. At the same time, aesthetics also recasts the idea of artistic production by including it in the same process of subjectification through the concept of genius and creation. The origin of art thus enters the sphere of subjectivity and so, the foundations are laid for sophisticated theories on the work of art in which author and recipient negotiate the creative act between themselves. The work does not acquire existence before or outside this relation between production and reception. The idea of the "open work", by Umberto Eco (Eco 1989 [1962]), seeks the ultimate consequences of this triumph of aesthetics for modern poetics, and Eco implicitly concludes that this aesthetic view of art will increasingly move towards a relational and performative aesthetics.

The second aspect of this long term transformation of art is therefore the crisis of poiesis. This means the crisis of a conception of art focused on production, know-how, and its result, the work of art. The devaluation of the work of art is the devaluation of the artefact. As Adorno stated in *Aesthetic Theory*, "The concept of an artifact, from which 'artwork' is etymologically derived, does not fully comprise what an artwork is. Knowing that an artwork is something made does not amount to knowing that it is an artwork" (Adorno 2002: 178-79). Duchamp's 1913 question: "Peut-on faire des oeuvres qui ne soient pas 'd'art'?" (cf. Sanouillet/Peterson: 74) is one of the strongest signs of this modern separation between art and fabrication or even art and technique. The answer to this question will be given by his own invention of the readymade as well as by the famous statement produced at the 1957 conference in Houston about "The creative act": "All in all, the creative act is not performed by the artist alone; the spectator brings the work in contact with the external world by deciphering and interpreting its inner qualification and thus adds his contribution to the creative act" (cf. Lebel 1959: 78). The crisis of poiesis, i.e. the crisis of the classic intrinsic relation between art and technique, may be perceived as the specific modern valuing of aesthetic experience and judgment. The "event of art's moving into the purview of aesthetics" (to use yet another famous formula, in this case by Martin Heidegger, 1977: 116) is one of the reverse sides of the crisis of poetics. The long modern process of separation between art and technique required a redefinition of the nature and place of artistic production. The entry of art in an aesthetic economy is part of this redefinition. This process allows for a clear distinction between artists and other producers, but by doing so it will also eventually promote a broader understanding of art as creativity, one that will be shared by other social players which will be invited to participate in the creative act. The role of art in the political economy becomes one of resisting the general proletarianization of craftsmanship, proposing in its place the ideal of a distributive and participatory creative economy (cf. Groys 2010).

When, in the second half of the 20th century, Joseph Beuys seeks to give social and political consistency to these ideals through his art projects as "social sculpture", which call to the participation of everyone as an artist (cf. Beuys 2013), art finds its redefinitions as "extended art" or as praxis. The third fundamental transformation of modern and contemporary art in the direction of a participatory culture is its transformation into practice (praxis). This underlying trend is expressed in artistic activity in general, which means that it finds an end in the activity itself, instead of in its external result, the object of art (cf. Agamben 1996 [1994]: 96-109).

The political implications of the three fundamental aspects should be fully recognized and evaluated. On the one hand, modern criticism, be it around the aestheticization of politics, or around the politicization of art, resulted in mistrust that weighed decisively on the political and artistic promises of those two programs. On the other hand the goal of emancipating the spectator should start, as was shown by Jacques Rancière (2008), by questioning the very opposition between active creative culture and passive culture of spectacle. The fundamental existential tension between agency and spectatorship, and the understanding of the kind of "impassibility" (Lyotard 1988) that is present in the act of receiving is important to understand the specificity of what is already at work at the activity of the spectator. It is therefore important to understand how a political utopian claim of art as a participatory and collaborative activity came to take place as an actual pragmatic, possible to implement into practice.

In a recent essay, Boris Groys describes the mode of production and reception of several circuits of contemporary art as follows:

"Everywhere we witness the emergence of artistic groups in which participants and spectators coincide. These groups make art for themselves – and maybe for the artists of other groups if they are ready to collaborate. This kind of participatory practice means that one can become a spectator only when one has already become an artist – otherwise one simply would not be able to gain access to the corresponding art practices." (Groys 2010, n.p.)

The dissemination of the creative gesture therefore matches the full interchangeability of the roles of producer and recipient and this favors a kind of art practice where "it becomes impossible to distinguish the presentation of the everyday from the everyday itself" (ibid). Developing around common things and common everyday life situations, art becomes a practice in which common people may also more easily take part.

The achievement of this artistic community finds its model, not in a particular mode of production, but rather in an ideal of communication that has become almost fully operable and assisted by several technologies. Throughout the second half of the 20th century, there were many artistic experiments about the activation of audiences. Their ascension to transmitters and producers was ideally tested against the backdrop of a media culture that specifically seemed to prohibit it. The claim made by Brecht in 1932, that radio should be tested and used as a true "apparatus of communication", i.e. "to let the listener speak as well as hear", is a central example of how the communication ideal appealed to art, even if the first media age of broadcasting systems could not allow for its implementation. That "every receiver is a potential sender" (Enzensberger 1970) represented the emancipatory value of media that was soon to be contradicted by further readings of mass media culture such as Jean Baudrillard's "Requiem of the media" (1972). The new media landscape of interactive systems and communication networks, on the other hand, opens the way to an "innovation", that Brecht himself admitted to seem "utopian": art as communication and communication as art.

2 Communication and Design

The emergence of a creative and participatory community has found yet another fundamental path in contemporary culture: that of design. From the Bauhaus avant-garde program up to the dissemination of design in contemporary life (in objects, services, software, interfaces, and lifestyles), the outstanding range of design makes it one of the few art forms that can really claim an enterprise on the social and on the economy. Although it has always been aware of its social function, design also stresses today the specific role that it can play in social innovation and sustainability and the effect it can have on a growing sense of community. The ideas of "social design", "collaborative design" or "co-design" (Manzini 2013; Fuade-Luke 2013) express this kind of ambition, directed to the resolution of practical problems and promoting new forms of social, political, and economic behavior (gift economy and sharing, sustainable lifestyles, smart urban life, etc.). Once again, it is through the double strand of rationalization and stylization that the creative economy makes its way. The alliance between the aestheticization of life and its strategic and technical enframing thus seems to be the key to success of the creative economy. Again, design is the practice and the way of thinking that meets the aesthetic and technological demands of contemporary experience. This techno-aesthetic dimension of design can now respond to new social and political ambitions beyond mass production and mass consumption, to which the artwork offered such a resilient opposition. When approaching the possibility of designing information architectures, software, apps, and interaction, design takes part of the apparatus that engineers new possibilities for producing, editing, and distributing content, which may open the way to "produsers", the term used by Axel Bruns (2008) to refer to the mixed role of consumers and producers that is gaining space in the new cultural economy. This powerful alliance may definitely dissolve the divide between high art and low art, if not the very autonomy of art that was always so strongly questioned by the avant-garde. The institution of art, (namely the museums of contemporary art) are themselves being dismissed on behalf of a new kind of "weak" artistic practice that is taking the place of "great art": "an everyday practice", says Boris Groys, a "weak practice", a "weak gesture" that continuously operates a kind of suspension or "artistic reduction" of the work of art, "resisting strong images", on behalf of this "weak, everyday level of art" (cf. Groys 2010). But can this ambition of an art disseminated in life finally take place outside of the museum and, at the same time, escape the undertaking of cultural industry (Buchloh 2001)?

The utopia of a creative economy as a development of media and cultural industries tends to present knowledge and information, and mostly creativity, as its main asset. This kind of "creative capital" is related to the catalyst role of artistic and aesthetic activity and thinking and their ability to deal with change and innovation (Howkins 2001; Hesmondhalgh 2002). Its success seems to depend on a kind of "cultural political economy of aesthetic production" (Van Heur 2010) as well as on a new generation of media and cultural technologies. Even when it distances itself from them, in practices that are admittedly low-tech, the model of production and distribution of the new creative economy is inspired by the collaborative and participatory paradigm of new media: the relational and contributive model of networks, web 2.0, "Wikipedia", and "open source". Inversely, it could also be said that the model of a community which builds up freely in itself and for itself, based on its creative capital, fed the vision of the web and of its social and cultural experiences of sharing. The current chain of the production of value, however, is not unrelated to the production of capital gains, profit, and some of the investment in large content aggregators profits from the free distribution and appropriation of content by consumers/producers. But there is in fact a noticeable shift towards "user-led forms of collaborative content creation which are proving to have an increasing impact on media, economy, social practices, and democracy itself", as stated by Bruns who coined the term "produsage" to describe this current paradigm shift.[1]

The interchangeability of senders and receivers, producers and consumers, and creators and spectators appears today as the actual stadium of communication design, finally made possible by new information technologies. Communication and design have therefore been the most successful paths for the dissemination of art in life and for the production of a creative aesthetic community. Digital communication media offer aesthetic experience a pragmatic relational model for the transitivity of objects between a sender and a recipient as well as for their ideal exchange of positions. This has allowed the culture of communication and design to become even more influent and ready to ideologically take over the ambitious program that artistic avant-garde had in fact proposed as resistance to media culture and "cultural industries".

The 1960s and 1970s neo-avantgarde that most intensively proclaimed the ideals of "relational aesthetics" and the "open work" as well as performance and participation art are significantly contemporaneous of the first socially important appearance of computers and computer culture. For example, Umberto Eco's text on the "Poetics of the Open Work" (1962), which centered on the case of contemporary music as an art form that demands an active and interpretive recipient, was originally written in the context of one of the first exhibitions of technological art, sponsored by Olivetti. At the same time that algorithms, programming, retroaction, and simulation ensured the establishment of new media as interactive systems designed to predict, inspire, and enframe the recipients' inputs, contemporary art rehearsed various forms of performance and art practice by asking for the participation of the spectator. Very often, a set of suggestions or even instructions were given to the spectator so that he/she may participate in the process of making the work "work" (as in the famous Duchampian verre "A regarder [de l'autre côté du verre] d'un oeil, de près, pendant presque une heure", 1918). As Duguet predicted in 1996, in a few years these kind of instructions would be embedded as algorithms in the interactive installation artwork or "performance-inducing apparatus" (Duguet 1996: 146).

---

1   Cf. Bruns, Axel: "About", http://produsage.org/about (August 15, 2015).

Interactivity thus easily became the official ideology of the creative spectator, code and algorithms took the place of conceptual art, and ICT networks provided the engine of new aesthetic, political, and social strategies. A new art of the masses is in fact taking place every day as millions 'interact' online, 'meet', 'twit', 'blog', and 'share' knowledge, opinions, experiences, worldviews, lifestyles, etc. But active and participative recipients are also the underlying condition on which the new information economy works, and it progresses on the basis of new marketing and business models. "Design thinking" (Brown 2009; Moote 2013) is the strategic mode of reasoning that allows for the implosion of aesthetic, political, and technological utopias. They all need to mobilize the user, the consumer, or the spectator to a new general economy, and this asks for a new critical thinking.

The tendency to "challenge" (Heidegger 1956) and "mobilize" (Jünger 1932) everything and everyone around it was very early pointed out as the defining trait of modern technology. The two major examples of this mobilizing force were industrialization and war. But modern cultural industries were also part of this general mobilization of the masses. The aesthetic and even libidinal investment of capitalist economy risks wearing out the symbolic, imaginary, as well as the libidinal capital of individuals and societies, transformed in masses of mere consumers, burned out to the very last stratus of their desire by marketing strategies. According to Bernard Stiegler we are witnessing the crisis of this economic model based on Fordist mass production and consumerism (Stiegler 2010: 3-7), but we must not expect informational technology societies to escape an industrialized destiny, nor mistake the new forms of mobilization for emancipation. On the contrary, ours will be a hyper-industrialized society, as technology continues the process of transformation of human consciousness, perception an memory, also inevitably transforming social relations in their entirety. This is the reason why in this critical moment of change we should play a conscious role in understanding and shaping the very industrial processes that are forming a new political economy. To acknowledge the present technological and hyper-industrialized forms of experience and to take part at the production of new cultural techniques will be the real mode of contributing to the new creative economy. By acknowledging the inevitability of "ars industrialis" [2] we have to reinvent ourselves both as contributors and as "amateurs" (Stiegler 2008), as Stiegler says, restoring the libido and knowledge invested in the very act of receiving. And this he proposes as a new model of work, which he calls "deproletarianization" (Stiegler 2010).

Information economy points to a contributive mode of production and cultural industry seems to be one of its most accomplished sectors with millions of people daily sharing content, knowledge, and skills. This new economic model has forced record companies, publishers, newspapers, radio and audio-visual broadcasters, and even the movie industry to rethink the way they think about consumers and also to rethink their business models.

Just as the division of labor, proletarianization, consumer society, marketing strategies, and the mass entertainment industry assisted in the design that drove the first age of industrial capitalism, the "economy of contribution" favors contribution and participation under the condition of digital technologies, informational economy, systematic metadata, and networked environments. To engineer the second age of hyper-industrial capitalism, following the model of present cultural technologies and through new design thinking, could be the weak utopia to which art has been pointing at for almost a century.

The kind of design that will boost this new contributive economy is still largely unknown, but it is important to understand that it operates on the vision of a distributed creativity and not on that of Art and its modern institutions. Value will arise out of multiple singular and maybe insignificant acts and images, not out of great works of universal value. It will come out of the experience and making of many and not just of a few: out of sharing and collaborative environments and not of rigid institutions. This new ideal community only emerges in as much as it is anticipated by design thinking and praxis and mediated by information technologies and networks. The appeal to "co-design" (Manzini 2013; Fuade-Luke 2013) represents a challenge to the old ways of modern individualism and mass consumption. It will require a specific ethos and also specific new literacies. In spite of the

---

2   "Ars Industrialis – association internationale pour une politique industrielle des technologies de l'esprit" is an independent cultural association created by Bernard Stiegler in 2005.

challenging proposals of the avant-garde, not everyone has become an artist, but maybe a lot of us will be ready to co-design.

REFERENCES

Agamben, Giorgio (1996 [1994]): L'Homme sans contenu, Paris: Circé (L' uomo senza contenuto, Macerata: Quodlibet).

AAVV (2011): Distributed Systems: Concepts and Design, Boston, MA: Addison-Wesley.

Adorno, Theodor W. (2002 [1977]): Aesthetic Theory, London and New York, NY: Continuum (Ästhetische Theorie, Frankfurt/Main: Suhrkamp).

Baudrillard, Jean (1981 [1972]): "Requiem of the Media", in: For a Critique of the Political Economy of the Sign, translated by Charles Levin, Saint-Louis, MO: Telos Press, pp. 164-184 (Pour une critique de l'economie politique du signe, Paris: Gallimard).

Beuys, Joseph (2013): Every Man Is an Artist. Posters, Multiples and Videos, Milano: Silvana Editoriale.

Bishop, Claire (2006): Participation (Documents of Contemporary Art), Cambridge, MA: MIT Press.

Bourriaud, Nicolas (1998): Relational Aesthetics, Dijon: Les Presses du Réel.

Brecht, Bertold (1964 [1932]): "The Radio as an Apparatus of Communication." In: John Willet (ed.), Brecht on Theatre, New York, NY: Hill and Wang, pp. 51-53 ("Der Rundfunk als Kommunikationsapparat." In: Blätter des Hessischen Landestheaters 16, July 1932).

Buchloh, Benjamin (2001): Neo-avantgarde and Culture Industry: Essays on European and American Art from 1955 to 1975, Cambridge, MA: MIT Press.

Brown, Tim (2009): Change by Design: How Design Thinking Transforms Organizations and Inspires Innovation, London: HarperBusiness.

Bruns, Axel (2008): Blogs, Wikipedia, Second Life, and Beyond: From Production to Produsage, New York, NY: Peter Lang.

Castells, Manuel (2012): Networks of Outrage and Hope: Social Movements in the Internet Age, Cambridge: Polity Press.

Cruz, Teresa M. (2009): "From Participatory Art Forms to Interactive Culture", The International Journal of the Arts in Society 4/3, pp. 243-250.

Duchamp, Marcel (1959 [1957]): "L'act créatif." In: Robert Lebel (ed.), Marcel Duchamp, New York, NY: Paragraphic Books, pp. 77-78.

Duguet, Anne-Marie (1996): "Does Interactivity Lead to New Definitions in Art?" In: Hans Peter Schwarz/Jeffrey Shaw (eds.), Media Art Perspectives, Karlsruhe: Edition ZKM, pp. 146-150.

Eco, Umberto (1989 [1962]): "The Poetics of the Open Work." In: Open Work, Cambridge: Harvard University Press, pp. 24-43.

Enzensberger, Hans Magnus (1970): "Constituents of a Theory of the Media." In: New Left Review 64/Nov.-Dec., pp. 13-36. Reprinted in Enzensberger, Hans Magnus (1974): The Consciousness Industry, translated by Stuart Hood, New York, NY: Seabury Press.

Fried, Michael (1998): Art and Objecthood: Essays and Reviews, Chicago, IL, and London: University of Chicago Press.

Fuade-Luke, Alastair (2013): "Design Activism: Challenging the Paradigm by Dissensus, Consensus and Transitional Practices." In: Stuart Waler/Jacques Giard (eds.), The Handbook of Design for Sustainability, London: Bloomsbury, pp. 465-484.

Groys, Boris (2010): "The week universalism." In: e-Flux April 2010, http://www.e-flux.com/journal/the-weak-universalism/ (August 14, 2015).

Heidegger, Martin (1977): "The Age of World Picture." In: Idem, The Question Concerning Technology and Other Essays, New York, NY, and London: Garland Publishing, pp.115-54.

Hesmondhalgh, David (2002): The Cultural Industries, London: SAGE.

Howkins, John (2001): The Creative Economy, London: Penguin.

Jenkins, Henry/Ford, Sam/Green, Joshua (2013): Spreadable Media: Creating Value and Meaning in a Networked Culture, New York, NY: New York University Press.

Kant, Immanuel (2007 [1790]): Critique of Judgement, translated by James Creed Meredith, Oxford: University Press.

Lyotard, Jean-François (1988): "Quelque chose comme: Communication sans communication." In: L'inhumain. Causeries sur le temps, Paris: Klincksieck, pp. 131-139.

Manzini, Ezio (2013): Making Things Happen: Social Innovation and Design, Cambridge, MA: MIT Press.

Moote, Idris (2013): Design Thinking for Strategic Innovation, Sussex: John Wiley & Sons.

Rancière, Jacques (2008): Le Spectateur émancipé, Paris: La Fabrique.

Sanouillet, Michel/Peterson, Elmer (ed.) (1975): The essential writings of Marcel Duchamp, London: Thames & Hudson, 1975.

Stiegler, Bernard (2008): "Figure de l'amateur et innovation ascendante." Audio recording: Conférence prononcée dans le cadre du colloque organisé par Vivagora le 18 mars 2008, http://arsindustrialis. org/node/1848 (August 14, 2015).

Stiegler, Bernard (2010 [2009]): For a New Critique of Political Economy, translated by Daniel Ross, Cambridge: Polity Press (Pour une nouvelle critique de l'économie politique, Paris: Galilée).

Thompson, Nato (2012): Living as Form: Socially Engaged Art from 1991-2011, Cambridge, MA: MIT Press.

Van Heur, Bas (2010): Creative Networks and the City: Towards a Cultural Political Economy of Aesthetic Production, Bielefeld: transcript.

'Choir of Minds'

Oral Media-Enthusiasm and Theories on Communal Creation (18th-20th Century)

EVA AXER

> "Obviously, conscious effort, cool judgment, and creative intelligence are gifts of men, not of mobs; and it was perhaps too much to expect from a romantic century interest in these qualities."
> LOUISE POUND

I. 'CHOIR OF MINDS' OR 'MOB MIND'?

The 18th century shaped the modern concept of the genius. Ever since, notions of the artist and the work of art have been informed by the idea that the gifted individual can do better than the rest of us. However, in the 18th and 19th centuries a notion of a collective essence also developed – the 'spirit of a people' ('Volksgeist') – in which the individual genius was thought to be embedded (cf. Schmidt 1988: 213-214). This idea of a 'spirit of a people' not only concerned the arts but every aspect of culture, in particular the origins of national language, the development of national law, and the foundations of national community. During the course of almost two centuries, strong opinions evolved on whether 'the people' formed a "choir of minds" (Herder 1779: 34), able to create conjointly, or whether this "mob mind" (Pound 1924: 444) epitomized the very lowest faculties of man, incapable, as Louise Pound argued in the 20th century, of devising something of value. Even though this discourse cannot do justice to our complex societies, the fundamental questions it raises still prevail:

Do we believe that the best achievements come from gifted or informed individuals and that the many are to follow their example or decision? Or do we believe that the many (shall) inform these decisions and achievements? How and why do individuals participate in processes of collaborative creation or decision-making?

There are grave reservations regarding the notion of a 'spirit of a people' and they are indeed justified as the idea can have anti-modernist, anti-liberal, and anti-democratic connotations (cf. Schmid 2005: 157-160). Although not only national concerns but also anthropological curiosity and humanistic values informed the idea of the 'spirit of a people' in the 18th century, a nationalistic and then a racist connotation emerged during the 19th century (cf. Schmidt 1988: 214-215). One can thus trace the development of this notion in Germany from the 18th century to its fatal appropriation by the National Socialists in the 20th century.

With regard to this historical development it is quite understandable that the notions of community, which evolved around the idea of a 'spirit of a people' at first sight appear to be the very opposite of today's concepts. Present-day theories mostly assume that an individual is able to consciously decide whether to partake or not, and groups and communities are thought to be dependent on practices or performances rather than a 'collective being'. Hence, temporary groups and communities come to the fore rather than those reliant on essential and thus enduring features (cf. van Eikels 2013: 12). The idea of a 'spirit of a people', on the contrary, seems to emphasize what we (presumably) are and not what we do – or intend to do – together (cf. Schmid 2005: 158).

However, one can view the discourse from a different angle: From the 18th century onwards the notion of a 'spirit of a people' was linked to a tremendous enthusiasm for oral media such as the ballad and the folksong. These genres were thought to be characterized by their ephemerality and to be dependent on communal practices. Yet questions on collective performance and therefore on the permanence – or volatility – of the community have seldom been raised. The American ballad scholar Francis B. Gummere (1855-1919) was one of the few who were interested in these communal practices. Referring to the works of German scholars, in particular Johann Gottfried Herder, Gummere even aimed at establishing a link between this kind of communal poetry and the foundations of democracy. This paper revisits the discourse which evolved around oral media, communal creation, and the idea of a 'spirit of a people' in Germany in the 18th and 19th century from the viewpoint of this different line of reception in the United States of America at the beginning of the 20th century.

II. SHORT HISTORY OF THE NOTION OF COMMUNAL CREATION IN GERMANY (18TH-19TH CENTURY)

Enthusiasm for the ballad and folksong had its roots in British antiquarianism in the 18th century. When Thomas Percy's influential ballad collection *Reliques of Ancient English Poetry* (1765) was received in Germany towards the end of the 18th century, the genre's potential to serve as foundation of a national literary historiography was soon discovered (cf. Axer 2013). The promotion of native literature in 18th century Germany involved the promotion of German (rather than Latin or French) as the language of scholarly and poetic discourse and writing. This attempt at "democratizing language" (Bendix 1997: 29) had widespread implications regarding the accessibility of cultural goods.

Johann Gottfried Herder criticized that the poetry of his times was elitist as it did not address the whole human being but only the rational faculties of man. In contrast to this tradition of scholarly and neo-classical literature, Herder shaped the idea of an oral and supposedly ancient and primitive poetry. The spoken word in his opinion was spontaneous, sensuous, immediate, and 'alive', which meant for Herder it followed the rules of nature, not those of culture (cf. Herder 1993a: 447-497). Because he saw these qualities epitomized in traditional songs, Herder devised one of the first German collections (*Volkslieder*, 1778/79) and coined the term folksong. He termed the folksong an 'archive of the people' ("Archiv des Volks", Herder 1993b: 558) because in his opinion it secured the vivid remembrance of a people's historic figures and events. Although Herder emphasized the communal purpose, he did not argue that the folksong was a spontaneous creation of an illiterate group, but rather that it was composed by a single but anonymous author. However, Herder considered the text and tune not to be fixed but instead formed by many generations of people singing or reciting it collectively. This can be regarded as an example of communal creation, or at least recreation, as Herder believed the song to be more than the "summation of an infinite series of individual recreative acts" (Barry 1935: 5); he considered it to be changing as a whole. This process is often compared with how the meaning and pronunciation of a word is formed and changed over time. The comparison suggests that there is no common will to change the word; the change is rather an unintentional effect of communal practices. Accordingly, Herder believed that the ongoing transmission and transformation of a song was not dependent on the voluntary decision of the people.

"If a song of good quality should have a few palpable flaws, these flaws will disappear, the poor stanzas won't be sung; yet, the spirit of the song, which affects the soul and inspires the minds to form a choir, this spirit is immortal and will continue to take effect." (Herder 1779: 34, my translation)

The idea of a 'spirit' solved two problems for Herder: First, the ephemerality of the oral medium no longer posed a threat as the song and the community were both based on a supra-individual element. Second, this idea allowed Herder to argue that 'the people' were not just the 'rabble of a nation' like most of his contemporaries thought. An 'immortal spirit' that inspired 'the people' guaranteed a progression rather than a devolution of the cultural good during the adaptive process.

However, in Herder's theories 'the people' are not introduced as a political agent. Still, his concept of folksong promotes a vague political notion that takes shape in a dedication for his collection ("Zueignung der Volkslieder", see Herder 1990: 429-430). It expressed the hope that those who had been without a voice so far would now be heard. Alluding to a phrase in his dedicatory verses (cf. ibid: 429) Herder's collection of folksongs was posthumously republished under the title *Voices of the Peoples* (*Stimmen der Völker*, 1807), which brings its ethnographic dimension to the fore. Herder's dedicatory verses on the other hand highlight that his idea of a 'choir of minds' ultimately transcends the idea of a nation state and envisions humanity as community.

In the 19th century German Romantics adopted Herder's concept. The famous jurist Friedrich Carl von Savigny was among the first to use the term 'Volksgeist' to refer to a common mentality that in his opinion informed the law of a nation. Two of his students, Jacob and Wilhelm

Grimm, then applied Savingy's ideas to poetry. Jacob Grimm believed that as a common mentality had informed folk poetry, surviving specimens enabled the study of the 'spirit of a people'. In 1808 he contrasted early oral poetry ("Naturpoesie", Grimm 1864: 399) with later poetry ("Kunstpoesie", ibid). He considered early oral poetry to be authentic and naïve, meaning not deliberately created or shaped by a people. Modern poetry on the other hand was in his opinion the intentional expression of an individual. Hence Grimm thought that modern poetry ("Kunstpoesie") was not for everyone, while early oral poetry ("Naturpoesie") had been a "common precious good that everyone shared" (ibid: 399, my translation). Because he considered the actual process of communal creation to be set beyond the scope of scientific enquiry and asserted that the poetry of the people 'makes itself' (ibid: 399), his position was often ridiculed as being mysterious (cf. Hustvedt 1930: 7).

The idea of poetry as a common property ("Gemeingut der Menschheit", Uhland 1983: 332) also inspired Ludwig Uhland at around the same time. Uhland was a Romantic poet who authored ballads, a scholar who worked on folk poetry, and a politician who fought for the democratic cause. He advocated the idea of an early stage of culture in which the people still had a poetic mindset, that is to say that they were less rational and more imaginative and emotional (Uhland 1984: 315-317). In Uhland's opinion this mentality, or essence of the people, shaped language, history, religion, law, and more. Like Herder, he suggested that a single individual authored the poems. However, as Uhland thought this individual to be of no different mindset than the other members of its community, he assumed that the poet did not express his individual feelings or opinions but was instead inspired by the common mindset (ibid: 316). He also believed that the "entire people participated in the folksong" (ibid, my translation) because the folksong – being an oral medium – was communally recreated through intergenerational transmission.

This theory was later termed 'hypothesis of reception' ('Rezeptionstheorie') because the folksong was thought to become a common good when the people received the song. Because extant specimens of ancient folksongs and ballads were in many cases inconsistent and of low literary quality, this adaptive process was often perceived as devolution, that is to say scholars assumed that 'the people' leveled (highbrow) cultural goods (cf. Naumann 1921). This process of oral transmission was on the other hand understood as a way of reception that put 'the people' in charge. John Meier, one of the most influential German folksong scholars at the beginning of 20th century, thought 'the people' appropriated songs of miscellaneous origin, thereby neglecting the rights of the individual author and the integrity of his work (cf. Meier 1906: II). In 1929 Roman Jakobson and Petr Bogatyrev proposed that oral transmission gave a community the privilege of 'preventive censorship' (cf. Bogatyrev/Jakobson 1972: 15) and highlighted similarities between the transmission of folklore and the development of language. Their essay is an early example of a structuralistic study of folklore.

III. Debate on Communal Creation in the USA (Early 20th Century)

Francis B. Gummere was a professor for English at Haverford College and part of a group of Anglo-American folk scholars that Louise Pound termed the "Harvard School of communalists" (cf. Wilgus 1959: 6). Pound, a professor at the University of Nebraska and folklorist, attacked the school's notion of a communal origin of poetry and law as well as the idea that property was originally owned commonly (cf. Pound 1924: 448). Pound harshly criticized Gummere because in her opinion he adhered to Romantic notions like the idea of a "common mind" – which she derogatorily termed "mob soul" (Pound 1924: 444). Pound contended on the contrary that the agreement of informed individuals was at the center of the history of government and law as well as being the foundation of the arts.

Gummere's theories are indeed informed by Romantic thought, yet deviate in some regards from Romantic tenets. Gummere aimed at describing the threshold between nature and culture and did not favor a sentimental notion of nature over culture. He did not presuppose a collective essence like the 'spirit of a people' but was interested in collaborative practices which could bring volatile individuals together (cf. Gummere 1911: 218). Gummere envisioned an act of physical and emotional synchronicity that was an expression of social consent. Even though Gummere thought this practice to be enthusiastic rather than deliberate, he implied that it allowed individuals in a group to perceive the power of communal action and communal imagination (cf. Gummere 1896, 1911).

Gummere's favorite example for collaborative creation was the ballad. Even though actual specimens of the genre did not support his theories, he contended that the composing of the ballad depended on practices of communal dancing and singing. He was particularly interested in what he named the principle of "incremental repetition" (Gummere 1901: 194 and passim), which he thought had shaped the particular rhythmic structure of this oral medium. Rhythm is a very important element in Gummere's theory; in a certain regard it stands in lieu of Herder's 'spirit of the song'. Because he was aware that the enthusiastic group's evil twin was the 'violent mob', Gummere was searching for laws that might govern the spontaneous interaction of the group (cf. Gummere 1911: 146). In his opinion rhythm served this purpose. Rhythm for Gummere is no artistic invention (1901: 108) but the physiological foundation of synchronized group movement. In his book on the *Beginnings of Poetry* he summarized: "Rhythm is an affair of instinctive perception transformed into a social act as the expression of social consent." (Ibid: 99) In Gummere's opinion, the 'cohesion' of a group that takes shape in form of spontaneous communal song and dance can be interpreted as the demonstration of an agreement. This is remarkable because the spontaneous 'expression' of feelings or sentiments, in the sense Herder or the Romantics envisioned it, seems to be the very opposite of deliberate decision-making and negotiation. Gummere's notion of 'consent', however, appears to signify not just a harmony of opinions but of sentiments. He hoped that an irrational harmony of sentiments might lead to a deliberate harmony of opinions. This idea of progress also informed Gummere's belief that 'primitive' individuals learned about the power of communal action during their performance and consciously attempted to realize the community that they had glimpsed (cf. ibid: 218). In his book *Democracy and Poetry*, published in 1911, he asserted that rhythm

"timed the first consenting steps of the earliest social groups, taught them in part the secret of coherence and unity and communal life, and will time the steps of poetry so long as poetry shall continue to voice the emotions of social man." (Ibid: 146)

For Gummere rhythm resulted in a "definite order, a scheme" on the large scale (ibid: 119), and hence establishes a whole – be it a poem or a communal dance. Rhythm thus also served as a link between poetry and community in Gummere's theory. In his opinion, this link is not broken when poetry is no longer created communally because poetry is still governed by rhythm, that is to say it still alludes to the power of collective action and "communal imagination" (Gummere 1901: 471).

Gummere did not explicitly address the question of how the spontaneous expressions of collective feelings in an oral and therefore ephemeral medium helped to develop traditions and to establish lasting communities. His theory does not seem to explain how communities evolved from the first "consenting steps" (Gummere 1911: 146), which require the physical presence of each member of the group and rely on the immediacy and apparent authenticity of these practices, to nation states or other forms of communities where one will never meet most of his fellows or compatriots. However, democracy was first of all an "imagined community" for Gummere (cf. ibid: 38-40). While Benedict Anderson later argued that modern societies as "imagined communities" rely on print media to allow the experience of 'national simultaneity' (cf. Anderson 1983), Gummere contended that (oral) poetry was the precedent of "communal imagination" (Gummere 1901: 471) in a synchronic as well as a diachronic dimension (cf. Gummere 1911: 122-123). This possibility of a "communal imagination" was important for Gummere because in his opinion democracy was based on shared ideals, in particular justice, which were not fixed but needed to be achieved "by long processes of cooperative thought" (ibid: 78) and which needed to be kept alive by "civic imagination" (ibid: 39). Yet, poetry did not just serve as the prime example of communal imagination. Gummere believed that poetry could reignite the enthusiasm for democracy, which he found to be damaged in his times. He did thus not avoid the Romantic pitfall of overestimating the (political) influence of the artist and his poetry (cf. ibid: 320). The appropriation of the notion of the 'spirit of a people' in 20th century Germany by charismatic leaders who captured and channeled the imagination of the people (again) revealed the fatal consequences of politics that exploit the enthusiasm of the multitude. If he had still been alive, Gummere might initially have welcomed the National Socialist movement since he was convinced that the Germanic freeman epitomized freedom (cf. Gummere 1911: 50, 54).

Yet, besides these problematic aspects of his theory, it is clear that Gummere was driven by a genuine enthusiasm for democracy. His main concern was to bring one of Herder's key assumptions to the fore – that in order to work towards a just society there needs to be an ideal of community. Rather than assuming this ideal of community to be the essential core of a nation he envisioned it as the result of ongoing processes of "communal imagination". He thus abandoned the German idea of a 'spirit of a people' in favor of a vision of communal practices, which unite volatile individuals.

REFERENCES

Anderson, Benedict (1983): Imagined Communities. Reflections on the Origin and Spread of Nationalism, London: Verso.

Axer, Eva (2013): "'Effusions of Nature' – 'Samenkörner der Nation'. The Politics of Memory in Percy's 'Reliques of Ancient English Poetry' and Herder's 'Volkslieder'". In: German Life and Letters 66/4, pp. 388-401.

Barry, Phillips (1935): "Communal Re-Creation". In: Bulletin of the Folksong Society of the Northeast 5, pp. 4-6.

Bendix, Regina (1997): In Search for Authenticity. The Formation of Folklore Studies, Madison, WI: The University of Wisconsin Press.

Bogatyrev, Petr/Jakobson, Roman (1972): "Die Folklore als eine besondere Art des Schaffens". In: Heinz Blumensath (ed.), Strukturalismus in der Literaturwissenschaft, Köln: Kiepenheuer & Witsch, pp. 13-25.

Eikels, Kai van (2013): Die Kunst des Kollektiven. Performance zwischen Theater, Politik und Sozio-Ökonomie, Paderborn: Fink.

Grimm, Jacob (1864): "Gedanken: Wie sich die Sagen und Poesie zur Geschichte verhalten". In: Kleinere Schriften, vol. 1, Berlin: Dümmler (Harrwitz und Gossman), pp. 399-403.

Gummere, Francis B. (1896): "The Ballad and Communal Poetry". In: Studies and Notes in Philology and Literature 5, pp. 41-56.

Gummere, Francis B. (1901): The Beginnings of Poetry, New York, NY: The Macmillan Company.

Gummere, Francis B. (1911): Democracy and Poetry, Boston, MA, and New York, NY: Houghton Mifflin Company.

Herder, Johann Gottfried (1779): Volkslieder. Vol. 2, Leipzig: Weygandsche Buchhandlung.

Herder, Johann Gottfried (1990): "Zueignung der Volkslieder". In: Ulrich Gaier (ed.), Werke, Volkslieder. Übertragungen. Dichtungen, Frankfurt/Main: Deutscher Klassiker-Verlag, pp. 429-430.

Herder, Johann Gottfried (1993a): "Auszug aus einem Briefwechsel über Ossian und die Lieder alter Völker". In: Gunter E. Grimm (ed.), Werke. Vol. 2, Frankfurt/Main: Deutscher Klassiker-Verlag, pp. 447-497.

Herder, Johann Gottfried (1993b): "Von Ähnlichkeit der mittlern englischen und deutschen Dichtkunst, nebst Verschiednem, das daraus folgt." In: Gunter E. Grimm (ed.), Werke. Vol. 2, Frankfurt/Main: Deutscher Klassiker-Verlag, pp. 550-563.

Hustvedt, Sigurd Bernhard (1930): Ballad Books and Ballad Men. Raids and Rescues in Britain, America and the Scandinavian North since 1800, Cambridge, MA: Harvard University Press.

Meier, John (1906): Kunstlieder im Volksmunde. Materialien und Untersuchungen, Halle (Saale): Max Niemeyer.

Naumann, Hans (1921): Primitive Gemeinschaftskultur. Beiträge zur Volkskunde und Mythologie, Jena: Eugen Diederichs.

Pound, Louise (1924): "The Term. 'Communal'". In: PMLA 39/2, pp. 440-454.

Schmid, Hans Bernhard (2005): "'Volksgeist'. Individuum und Kollektiv bei Moritz Lazarus (1824-1903)." In: Dialektik. Zeitschrift für Kulturphilosophie 16/1, pp. 157-170.

Schmidt, Jochen (1988): Die Geschichte des Genie-Gedankens in der deutschen Literatur, Philosophie und Politik 1750-1945. Vol. 2, Darmstadt: Wissenschaftliche Buchgesellschaft.

Uhland, Ludwig (1983): Werke. Vol. 2, ed. by Hans-Rüdiger Schwab, Frankfurt/Main: Insel.

Uhland, Ludwig (1984): „Über die deutsche Volksdichtung". In: Uhland: Werke. Vol. 4, München: Winkler, pp. 308-321.

Wilgus, Donald K. (1959): Anglo-American Folksong Scholarship since 1898, New Brunswick, NJ: Rutgers University Press.

Mobilizing Memes

The Contagious Socio-Aesthetics of Participation

SASCHA SIMONS

Participation has often been described as the pragmatic backbone of the Web 2.0 (cf. O'Reilly 2005; Jenkins 2006: 3; Schäfer 2011: 31). According to this hypothesis, social media reveal a historically new merging of aesthetic forms and social functions (cf. Münker 2009: 15-18). Contemporary processes of participation hence cannot be separated from media metamorphosis and the analysis of the latter provides insights into the conditions and conventions of related social dynamics.

This dynamic interplay of technology, sociality, and aesthetics will be addressed in the following by focusing on web memes. These memes can be described as transmedia objects; or relatively stable combinations of video footage, images, and text, "which emerge through grass-roots manner through networked media and acquire a viral character" (Goriunova 2013: 71).[1] Hence they undergo processes of spatial dissemination and aesthetic transformation. But they also have to be defined in a pragmatic dimension: Web memes become web memes only if they are detected as such by collaborative aggregating, curating, remixing, sharing, and archiving practices on platforms like *knowyourmeme.com*. Due to this self-referentiality of web based communication, web memes not only short-circuit the production, distribution, and consumption of cultural artefacts in the social web, thereby structuring the immense variety and almost sublime quantity of digital

---

1 All quotes by Goriunova are translated according to an English version of the text, which will be published in the *Nordic Journal for Aesthetics*.

archives, but also display how social entities develop. The morphogenesis of these media forms is inherently linked to the emergence of bottom-up social structures, which seem to be equally associated with common practices as social representations. In a performative sense it is more about *doing symbols* than being represented by them.

Since these collective imaginations produce imaginary collectives, they carry political implications: The question is not whether collectives formed by the production, distribution, and consumption of web memes can become political, but when. This question obviously aims at the tipping point, where participation, in the broad sense of media usage, claims the promise of participation in a more radical sense of disrupting the distribution of the sensible and hence the conditions of "partak[ing] in ruling and being ruled" (Rancière 2001: 2) – as it has been the case with the *99 percent*[2] meme and the Occupy Wallstreet Movement (cf. Shifman 2014: 132-138). From this perspective Olga Goriunova (2013: 83-86) has described the correlation between the bulletin board *4chan.org* and the political hacktivism of Anonymous as political becoming of participation via web memes. Her efforts to grasp the political impact of web memes attest that the explanation of these phenomena also bears a huge theoretical claim. As long as the proliferation of a web meme is not merely retraced but correlated to wider aesthetic, social, and political contexts, it pushes the boundaries of the corresponding theoretical fields and demands a broader perspective.

While Goriunova is drawing upon Gilbert Simondon's concept of individuation to describe meme driven processes of aesthetic, social, and political participation, the following considerations confront and complement her thoughts with Gabriel Tarde's theory of imitation and social monads. They tie in to Tony D. Sampson's (2012: 17-43) work on network virality, which resuscitates Tarde's speculative sociology by taking into account its influence on Gilles Deleuze, Bruno Latour, and Nigel Thrift. Adding Simondon to this list not only enriches the current Tardean renaissance by including a genuine technophilosophical perspective;[3] but Tarde's theory also opens up

---

2 Cf. "We Are the 99 Percent", http://wearethe99percent.tumblr.com (August 16, 2015).

3 Technology does not play a crucial role neither in Tarde's original writings nor their current readings. This could be one reason why he is yet to be discovered as a theorist of (contemporary) media although he was long since rediscovered

a dimension of social contagion by which to describe the virtual politics of web memes. His notion of society as reciprocal possession contributes to the quest for a theoretical vocabulary that adequately approaches the daily routine of social media participation[4] as well as helping revise the biological determinism that forms the genealogical basis of the current revival of the meme discourse in the Web 2.0.

1 WHAT MEMES HAVE BEEN

Talking about popular web memes and the fact that the term meme has become one of the central self-referential formulas of web based communication, one has to keep in mind its particular history. The term meme was coined by Richard Dawkins' controversial bestseller *The Selfish Gene*, which applied the "genes' eye view" (Dawkins 1976: XV) of evolution theory to the cultural sphere. According to Dawkins "all life evolves by the differential survival of replicating entities" (ibid: 191-192). In analogy to the replicating function of the gene for organic nature he introduces the meme as "a unit of cultural transmission" that spreads and prevails in de-

---

in the fields of micro-sociology and micro-politics (cf. Latour 2002; Lazzarato 2004). A media theoretical interpretation can profit from these works but should not just imitate the *Tardomanian* tendency to not only resuscitate but also reinvent a classic, as Klaus Gilgenmann (2010) has argued refering to predominant misunderstandings and possible desiderata of an updated Tarde. In this sense the propositions made here take one step at a time. They orientate themselves closely to Tarde's texts and postpone a fundamental reinterpretation according to today's technological condition to a future occasion.

4   The task here is to develop an infra-language that neither neglects the "elaborate and fully reflexive meta-language" (Latour 2005: 30) of the actors nor takes all of its implied presumptions for granted. This brief article can merely take the first steps in mapping out a theoretical territory, pointing to existing signposts, and identifying possible forks and rallying points along the way. Lists of web memes can be found elsewhere (cf. Shifman 2014: 99-118; erlehmann/plomlompom 2013: 59-199). The same applies to the critique of the economic undercurrent of (web) memetics (cf. Sampson 2011: 64-95; Leeker/Wassermann 2010: 110-114).

pendency of the "survival value[s]" (ibid: 193-194) longevity, fecundity, and copying-fidelity in a competitive socio-cultural environment. This reference to natural selection is not the only parallel to biological evolution. Adopting his differentiation of genes as ruthless principals and organisms as mere vehicles for their proliferation, Dawkins defines memes as the driving force of cultural dynamics. He locates agency clearly and exclusively on the side of the replicating forms, whereas the hosting bodies are reduced to mere "survival machines" (ibid: 200). Although opting for relative cultural autonomy, this claim acknowledges the deterministic logic underlying all processes of replication. In short: Memes are just as selfish as genes (cf. ibid: 197). And cultural evolution obeys the purposes of these living memetic parasites.

Dawkins' examples for this specific culturally replicating form extend from aesthetic artefacts like melodies and literal metaphors to socio-aesthetic dynamics like fashion, from cultural techniques to engineering skills, and last but not least from scientific arguments to the religious idea of God. His speculations – as cursory as they may seem – aim for nothing less than a universal cultural theory. But what kind of glue would bind together such a variety of cultural phenomena?

"Just as genes propagate themselves in the gene pool by leaping from body to body via sperms [sic!] or eggs, so memes propagate themselves in the meme pool by leaping from brain to brain via a process which, in the broad sense, can be called imitation." (Ibid: 192)

However what is imitated does not necessarily stay the same; it blends and mutates more or less as a reaction to the confrontation with or the conglomeration of other memes. But as long as a meme is "sufficiently distinctive and memorable to be abstracted from the context" (ibid: 195), and thus can be identified as such, it serves as a viable unit of replication.

To sum up: For Dawkins memes are the most important agencies of cultural evolution. By spreading out contagiously they aim to saturate their milieus using brains and bodies as instruments of detection and vectors of distribution. They do so in competition or coherence with other memes, which transform their shape and size. The memetic logic of cultural evolution sticks to the Darwinian triad of replication, variation, and selection and hence implies a biological determinism of evolutionary success that forgets about the extinct, and neglects the social and material implications of mediation.

2 WHAT MEMES ARE

Mainly due to this bio-economic reductionism memetic ideas did not add to the intended paradigmatic shift in cultural and media theory and went out of fashion after a rather short academic arousal in the late 1990s (cf. Schmid 2009: 289-290). But around the same time that they vanished from academic publications, they appeared as means to obtain a sense of the immense amount and qualitative variety of content floating the web – euphorically conjured by social media marketers, but also appropriated by the very people generating and distributing this content (cf. Sampson 2012: 64-66; Shifman 2014: 2-4). Right at the peak of the memetic boom the influential Silicon Valley focused magazine *WIRED* (Schrage 1995) and especially Susan Blackmore (1999: 204-225) paved the way for this media-darwinism by highlighting analogies between digital information transmission and memetic inheritance mechanisms while interpreting the internet as sort of a second order meme – constructed by memes with the singular purpose to distribute memes.

And indeed, the digitally enabled possibility to cut, copy, and paste all sorts of texts, images, and sounds; the unleashed compatibility, connectivity, and mobility of soft- and hardware; and the growing coverage and bandwidth of internet infrastructure created an adequate technical environment for the transversal, contagious, and competitive processuality of memetic self-replication (cf. Shifman 2014: 23). Further, one could imagine interpretations of numeric digitization as the missing link "between high-fidelity genes and low-fidelity memes" (Dawkins 1999: X) since memetics has commonly been criticized for missing an equivalent to DNA sequences that could discretely define its "evolutionary algorithm" (Blackmore 1999: 11-14; cf. 53-56; Dennet 1995: 353).

But instead of caring about fundamental philosophical principles, users who invent, copy, alter, and spread web memes seem to be motivated by a rather philological curiosity. In terms of evolutionary theory they are not looking for genotypes but phenotypes – i.e. for a morphology of perceivable forms (cf. Leschke 2010: 12). Web memes are aesthetic rather than cognitive units, which follow a pragmatically reduced, no longer universal-istic approach. Instead of explaining cultural evolution as a whole, memes are used as a curatorial tool to gather and arrange contemporary web phe-nomena. In a situation where established terms for classifying aesthetic ar-tefacts like genre, artwork, and media apparatuses no longer grasp either the aesthetic or the material conditions of media production and distribution (cf. ibid: 181-189) and where their taxonomic boundaries are excessively blurred by the innovative and collaborative experiments enabled and driven by social web applications, the meme provides an adequately flexible con-cept to cluster aesthetic qualities of these hybrid forms and describe their circulation in an economy of networked attention.

For Limor Shifman (2014: 15) it thus "epitomizes the very essence of the so called Web 2.0 era." He defines web memes as a

"[...] group of digital content units sharing common characteristics of content, form, and/or stance. [...] Internet memes are multiparticipant creative expressions through which cultural and political identities are communicated and negotiated." (Ibid: 177)

Shifman's definition highlights the aesthetic nature of web memes, but also emphasizes that they have to be considered as collective phenomena. Web memes are as much forms of media artefacts as they are forms of media practices which have become formulas of social self-reference for those as-sociated with these practices since the appropriation of meme theory by the web has performed a self-referential loop. Unlike Dawkins' interpretation of culture as a neutral and oddly detached "soup" (Dawkins 1976: 192; cf. Fuller 2005: 115-116) digitally networked environments are quite aware of their memetic inhabitants – even to the extent that knowing your memes and how to spread them has become an essential lesson for gaining digital literacy – and of course for detecting and excluding those considered illi-terate. Bottom-up folksonomies like *knowyourmeme.com* serve to reassure the fact that all this generating, remixing, and spreading of images, texts, and sounds actually matters. But how does this *"hypermemetic logic"* (Shifman 2014: 23, original emphasis) shape processes of socio-aesthetic participation?

Thanks to the double logic of repetition and variation mentioned above, users participating as meme vehicles or hubs act as what Harrison Rainie and Barry Wellman have called "networked individuals" (2012: 13). By creating, modifying, and sharing web memes they express their connectivity as well as their uniqueness (cf. Shifman 2014: 33-34). The dialectic relation of individuality and sociality offered by this concept relates to another social dynamic:

"[M]emes may best be understood as pieces of cultural information that pass along from person to person, but gradually scale into a shared social phenomenon. Although they spread on a micro basis, their impact is on the macro level: memes shape the mindsets, forms of behavior, and actions of social groups." (Shifman 2014: 18)

Even though the implicit teleology of Shifman's assumption needs to be superseded in a sense of processual reciprocity, his idea of memetic scaling proves to be highly relevant for the argumentation of the following sections. From the point of view of this continuous social progression, individuals and collectives cannot be conceived of as distinctive units. On the contrary, they share a dynamic common ground and are inherently linked to each other by acts of contagious memetic mediation.

3 WHAT MEMES MIGHT BECOME

These processes of mediation are precisely what Olga Gurionova aims at. In order to discuss web memes as "techno-aesthetic methods of becoming" (Goriunova 2013: 73) she draws upon Gilbert Simondon's ontogenetic concept of individuation. Following Simondon the becoming of life unfolds as process of individuation that divides a metastable state of sheer potentiality into temporal *"stages in the being that are the stages of the being"* (Simondon 1964: 301, original emphasis). Simondon describes non-organic, organic, mental, and collective individuals as such stages of saturation and more or less restricted stability, which unfold in analogical manner. Each of them results from mediating processes in which the energetic spillovers of a preindividual potentiality resonate with the ongoing development of structures and vice versa (ibid: 313). Still, all kinds of individuals remain bound to the same preindividual state they derive from and are exceeded by. However they differ according to the *"forms, modes and degrees of individuation"* (ibid: 311; original emphasis). Sociality for example comes into play because the precarious metastability of the self-contained consciousness does not expend the preindividual reservoirs of being. This insufficiency manifests itself as anxiety, which psychic individuals fail to handle in an affectively resolving manner unless they address it collectively.

"The collective unit provides the resolution of the individual problematic, which means that the basis of the collective reality already forms a part of the individual in the form of the preindividual reality, which remains associated with the individuated reality." (Ibid: 307)

Individuality and sociality are reconsidered as deeply intertwined expressions of an energetic surplus.

Building up on this metaphysical transindividuality, Goriunova describes the aesthetic culture of web memes as the transductive interplay of technical, mental, collective, and, most notably, political individuation. She locates the political potential in the enhanced and decentralized possibility to manipulate and distribute content and form in digital network media. The aesthetic objects circulating in the social web always entail a "promise of social response" (Goriunova 2013: 74) and hence shape an emerging public sphere. However silly or idiosyncratic web memes may appear, they appear publicly and thereby build up new and visible ways for psycho-collective individuations. As an example of how web memes "mediate the becoming of political events" (ibid: 71), Goriunova traces back the origins of the hacktivist collective Anonymous to the image board *4chan.org*, which is one of the most important sources for the emergence and proliferation of web memes. Anonymous, which became popular for supporting Wikileaks, Occupy, and the North-African freedom movements, coordinates cyber-activistic campaigns as well as more traditional mobilizations of physical protest crowds but lacks an institutionalized organizational structure, elaborated political goal, or ethical code apart from the promotion of the so called *lulz*.[5] Facing this discrepancy Goriunova argues, that the political

---

5   For Gabriella Coleman *lulz* marks the dark, more offensive, dangerous, and transgressive side of the so called *lols* – i.e. stories, jokes, images or videos on the web that make users 'laugh out loud'. Similar to the way web memes are treated here she defines the notion *lulz* as an "epistemic object, stabilizing a set of experiences by making them available for reflection" (Coleman 2014: 31).

sensibility of Anonymous is an effect of the collectively habitualized, distributed aesthetic practices of web memes.

"The differentiation or individuation, the open-ended emergence of a political campaign, a sweet meme of a Lolcat, or an attack, mediated through the masterful orchestration of network architecture, software shortfalls, human errors, bespoke code, the dark web, through the enlistment of torrent networks, encryption services and so on, is what unites both memes and Anonymous." (Goriunova 2013: 85)

This highlights the heterogeneity of the involved actions and things, but nonetheless is still rather a list of *what is united* than of *what unites* – unless it is specified by explanations of how the assemblages take place. But since Goriunova refrains from the latter, her Simondonian connection of technological infrastructure, aesthetic artefacts, social association, and political action remains a promise unfulfilled. It seems as if her theoretical toolkit is too broad to get a grip on the route and the vehicles web meme have taken before becoming political articulations. In contrast, the memetic and Shifman's cultural studies approach are more explicit about the actual ways of memetic proliferation, but either neglect any kind of responsibility or lack a conceptual link between technology, aesthetics, sociality, and the political. While Goriunova does not explain how web memes actually disseminate, Shifman and Dawkins cannot or do not want to explain why this dissemination renders political possibilities.

4 A SOCIAL MONADOLOGY OF WEB MEMES

But an understanding of their participative processuality requires an understanding of how web memes are mobilized in order to mobilize political action. Here Tarde's theory of social imitation comes into play. It holds prospects for a precise rendering of the entailed social operating mode of web memes, while sticking to an "infraindividual and infrasocial" description of collectivity similar to the one offered by Simondon (Combes 2013: 52). Hence it may allow combining the advantages of the three portrayed ways to theorize web memes.

Firstly because Tarde (1890: 7) assumes analogies between material, organic, and social realities: For him all three are bound together by a hyperphysical energy of universal repetition that manifests itself as physical waves, biological heredity, and social imitation. Similar to Simondon's concept of transductive individuation, Tarde opens a constitutive tie between the social, cultural, and political spheres and material and organic nature. He even takes one step further by declaring that the very essence of all being is sociality, "that *everything is a society*, that every phenomenon is a social fact" (Tarde 1895: 28, original emphasis). According to Tarde's speculative monadology, all being consists of possibly infinite small monads, which form flows of belief and desire and – in contrast to the windowless microcosmos Leibniz (1714: §7, p. 219) had in mind – are open to mutual diffusion and assembling. Like memes they have the tendency to extend the amplitude of their proliferation towards a universal saturation of their environment but foster more complex ecological relationships with their likewise monadic environments (cf. Tarde 1895: 16-17, 26-27, 60). This implies that every social element cannot be completely assimilated by a higher level of association, but – in analogy to Simondon's argument – always maintains a primordial reservoir of differences that build "the truly substantial side of things" (ibid: 40, cf. 47). Individuals and societies must rather be understood as different bandwidths of resonating, respectively antagonistic interferences of beliefs and desires. They differ in quantity but not necessarily in quality. This argument hits upon the notion of social scaling Shifman was concerned with, only this time it is the other way round, ranging from national or even global societies down towards the irregular variety of infinitely small social particles. Hence Tarde not only offers analogies to the Simondonian concept of transindividuality, but also closes the social circulation that Shifman's description of the sociopolitical logic of web memes could only describe in one direction. On the other hand Tarde's monadology could profit from Simondon's techno-philosophical insights and his understanding of individuation as structure in the making.

The second reason for considering Tarde for the study of web memes is how he describes the actual working mode of social evolution:

"Socially, everything is either invention or imitation. And invention bears the same relation to imitation as a mountain to a river. [...] [I]mitations, like inventions, are seen to be linked together one after the other, in mutual if not in self dependence." (Tarde 1890: 3, cf. 94-95)

Due to the desire of the social monads to expand as far as possible, the alternating succession of innovation and imitation leads to contagious effects, which Tarde compares to cyclones, viral epidemics and – most relevant for this context – political insurrections (cf. ibid: 34-35). The speed and scope of this contagious dissemination depends on its distributional media – as Tarde (1901: 12) has argued for the newspaper of his time and its associated public spheres, which are distributed in a double sense of transmission and reconfiguration – namely a reconfiguration of printing press, telegraphy, and the railroad system. Therein lies a social theory of media *avant la lettre* to use as a springboard for studying the virtual politics of web memes, which spreads by the same rules and contagious dynamics of imitation and variation.

Thirdly, Tarde's vocabulary is quite similar to the memetic one (cf. Marsden 2000, Latour 2002: 121). This becomes obvious when comparing Dawkins' quotes above with Tarde's definition of imitation as a "generation at a distance" (Tarde 1890: 34):

"I have always given it a very precise and characteristic meaning, that of the action at a distance of one mind upon another, and of action which consists of a quasi-photographic reproduction of a cerebral image upon the sensitive plate of another brain." (Ibid: XIV)

So why not simply stick with the memetic vocabulary if the alternative is almost the same? Precisely because it is only almost the same, as Hans Bernhard Schmid (cf. 2009: 299-309) has worked out poignantly with regards to the different concepts of intentionality. Although Tarde may consider imitation as a mainly unconscious process or social somnambulism (cf. Tarde 1890: 76), it nevertheless always aims at either a desire or a belief (cf. ibid: 145). Unlike meme theory, it does not discard or, substitute subjective intentionality as a whole, but qualifies and permeates it with a lateral social dimension. By describing imitation leading from the inner to the outer side, from the signified to the symbol, from the idea to its expression, from the means to its medium (cf. ibid: 109-207), he holds on to the necessity of symbolic reference and introduces a collective form of intentionality which leads beyond the deadends of Dawkins' biological determinism and opens up a space for social and political action.[6]

Fourthly, Tarde's monadology not only bridges the three portrayed theoretical streams in the discourse on web memes. It also offers a unique perspective on memetic participation due to its definition of society "as each individual's reciprocal possession, in many highly varied forms, of every other" (Tarde 1895: 40). This model of social share-holding performs a major ontological shift from the philosophy of *being* to a universal sociology of *having*. It no longer asks for what elements *are* part of the world, but rather how they *take part* in it, assuming that *having* is a prerequisite for *acting*.

"The elements are, certainly, agents as much as they are proprietors; but they can be proprietors without being agents, and they cannot be agents without being proprietors. Moreover, their action can be revealed to us only as a change in the nature of their possession." (Ibid: 54)

Tarde (ibid: 57-58) clearly sees, that taking part most often and most probably intends to transform a situation of mutual possession into a unilateral one: "They transform in order to conquer;" but they necessarily fail in doing so since every spreading "sovereign monad" also disseminates a virtual difference yet to unfold that was induced by the appropriated "vassal monads". In contrary to memetics it is not mainly about competition, but also about collaboration. Each monad's desire to become a "universal milieu" (ibid: 49) finds its limits in other monads' desires and beliefs since its realization depends on being imitated by them (cf. Tarde 1890: 146). Although social hierarchy is anything but neglected (cf. ibid: 78-85; 213-243), every attempt to maximize social shares incorporates variations, which might be too tiny to be noticed, but nevertheless bear a virtual resistance.

In a Tardean perspective on participation any political or any other action is always a collective one: formed by imitation and variation and depending on the propagation and mutual saturation of beliefs and desires. And although these seem to be big words for describing the vaudeville cir-

---

6   In the context of web aesthetics Vito Campanelli's (2010: 74-83) history of memetic ideas misses this opportunity as it ignores Tarde's denial of the social Darwinisms of his time (cf. Tarde 1884: 613-614, 1895: 21, 1896: 422-423).

cus of *LOLcats* and *Harlem Shakes*, they allow discussing web memes in a way that does not reduce them to selfish parasites but treats them as an ongoing invitation to participate.

REFERENCES

Blackmore, Susan (1999): The Meme Machine, Oxford, MA: Oxford University Press.

Campanelli, Vito (2010): Web Aesthetics. How Digital Media Affect Culture and Society, Rotterdam: NAi.

Coleman, Gabriella (2014): Hacker, Hoaxer, Whistleblower, Spy. The Many Faces of Anonymous, London and New York, NY: Verso.

Combes, Muriel (2013): Gilbert Simondon and the Philosophy of the Transindividual, Cambridge, MA and London: MIT Press.

Dawkins, Richard (2006) [1976]: The Selfish Gene. 30th Anniversary Edition, Oxford and New York, NY: Oxford University Press.

Dawkins, Richard (1999) "Foreword." In: Susan Blackmore, The Meme Machine, Oxford and New York, NY: Oxford University Press, pp. VII-XVII.

Dennett, Daniel C. (1995): Darwin's Dangerous Idea. Evolution and the Meaning of Life, London: Penguin Books.

Erlehmann/plomlompom (2013): Internet-Meme, Köln: O'Reilly.

Fuller, Matthew (2005): Media Ecologies. Materialist Energies in Art and Technoculture, Cambridge, MA: MIT Press.

Gilgenmann, Klaus (2010): "Gabriel Tarde oder die Erfindung und Nachahmung eines Klassikers." In: Soziologische Revue 3, pp. 261-286.

Goriunova, Olga (2013) "Die Kraft der digitalen Ästhetik. Über Meme, Hacking und Individuation." In: zfm – Zeitschrift für Medienwissenschaft 8/1, pp. 70-87.

Jenkins, Henry (2006): Convergence Culture. Where Old and New Media Collide, New York, NY: New York University Press.

Latour, Bruno (2002): "Gabriel Tarde and the End of the Social." In: Patrick Joyce (ed.), The Social in Question. New Bearings in History and the Social Sciences, London and New York, NY: Routledge, pp. 117-133.

Latour, Bruno (2005): Reassembling the Social. An Introduction to Actor-Network-Theory, Oxford and New York, NY: Oxford University Press.

Lazzarato, Maurizio (2004): "From Capital-Labour to Capital-Life." In: ephemera – Theory and Politics in Organization 4/3, http://www.ephemerajournal.org/sites/default/files/4-3lazzarato.pdf (August 16, 2015).

Leeker, Martina/Wassermann, Alfred (2010): "Meme, Virals, Vlogs und Mimikry. Zum Scheitern von Theatralität und Performativität im Web 2.0." In: Frank Bonczek (ed.), Theatralität Online! Berlin: Schibri, pp. 89-121.

Leibniz, Gottfried Wilhelm (1898 [1714]): "The Monadology." In: Robert Latta (ed.): The Monadology and other Philosophical Writings, London, Edinburgh and New York, NY: Henry Frowde, pp. 213-271.

Leschke, Rainer (2010): Medien und Formen. Eine Morphologie der Medien, Konstanz: UVK.

Marsden, Paul (2000): "Forefathers of Memetics: Gabriel Tarde and the Laws of Imitation." In: Journal of Memetics – Evolutionary Models of Information Transmission 4, http://cfpm.org/jom-emit/2000/vol4/marsden_p.html (August 16, 2015).

Münker, Stefan (2009): Emergenz digitaler Öffentlichkeiten. Die Sozialen Medien im Web 2.0, Frankfurt/Main: Suhrkamp.

O'Reilly, Tim (2005): "What Is Web 2.0? Design Patterns and Business Models for the Next Generation of Software", September 30, http://oreilly.com/web2/archive/what-is-web-20.html (August 16, 2015).

Rainie, Harrison/Wellman, Barry (2012): Networked. The New Social Operating System, Cambridge, MA, and London: MIT Press.

Rancière, Jacques (2000): "Ten Theses on Politics." In: Theory & Event 5/3, http://muse.jhu.edu/login?auth=0&type=summary&url=/journals/theory_and_event/v005/5.3ranciere.html (August 16, 2015).

Sampson, Tony D. (2012): Virality. Contagion Theory in the Age of Networks, Minneapolis, MN: University of Minnesota Press.

Schäfer, Mirko Tobias (2011): Bastard Culture! How User Participation Transforms Cultural Production, Amsterdam: Amsterdam University Press.

Schmid, Hans Bernhard (2009): "Evolution durch Imitation. Gabriel Tarde und das Ende der Memetik." In: Christian Borch/Urs Stäheli (eds.), Soziologie der Nachahmung und des Begehrens. Materialien zu Gabriel Tarde, Frankfurt/Main: Suhrkamp, pp. 280-310.

Schrage, Michael (1995): "Revolutionary Evolutionist." In: WIRED 3/7, http://archive.wired.com/wired/archive/3.07/dawkins_pr.html (August 16, 2015).

Shifman, Limor (2014): Memes in Digital Culture, Cambridge, MA: MIT Press.

Simondon, Gilbert (1992 [1964]): "The Genesis of the Individual." In: Jonathan Crary/Sanford Kwinter (eds.), Incorporations, New York, NY: Zone Books, pp. 297-319.

Tarde, Gabriel (1884) "Darwinisme Naturel et Darwinisme Social." In : Revue Philosophique 12, pp. 607-637.

Tarde, Gabriel (1896): "L'Idée de 'l'Organisme Social'." In: Archives d'Anthropologie Criminelles 11, pp. 418-428.

Tarde, Gabriel (1901): L'Opinion et la Foule, Paris: Les Presses Universitaires de France (Recherches Politiques).

Tarde, Gabriel (1903 [1890]): The Laws of Imitation, 2nd ed., New York, NY: Henry Holt.

Tarde, Gabriel (2012 [1895]): Monadology and Sociology, Melbourne: re.press.

Who Will Translate the Web?

Machines, Humans, and Reinventing Translation as a Participatory Practice

CHRISTINE MITCHELL

Has translation ever been a participatory activity? That is, while language use and transformation is governed by social relations, translation has tended to be practiced out of sight. The invisibility of translators and translation, in the form of fluent, naturalized text, has long served as a quality guarantee. It helps to mask the so-called treachery of translation, the impossibility of serving two masters (source culture and target audience) (Venuti 1995), and aligns with the familiar strategy of remediation, where transparency and immediacy are sought as a measure of truth and authenticity (Bolter/Grusin 1999). Translation is popularly regarded as an individually realized skill: "brainbound" cultural and technical expertise, to adopt Hayles' term (2009), realized in cognitive and clerical isolation.

But recent years have seen initiatives to make translation a collaborative, public activity suitable for and demanded by the socially realized, text-heavy web. The move responds to desires for informational, social, and commercial seamlessness in digital networks and drives for linguistic and cultural self-representations online. Social networking platforms and content portals, such as Facebook, Twitter, TED, and Coursera tackle translation projects much like translation agencies do: tasks are divided up, assigned to translators and editors, and translations are produced. Unlike agency work, crowdsourced initiatives leverage linguistic participation from translator 'communities' defined not by professional abilities, protocols, and domains of practice, but by their attachment to specific platforms in the delivery of highly variable web content. Most dramatic in this new regime is the suggestion embodied by Duolingo, one of the new initiatives, that bilingualism need not even be a necessary prerequisite to produce translations.

This is not the first time bilingualism has been conceived as an 'optional' route to translational success. The 1950s witnessed an earlier instance, when scientists contemplated how computers might be tasked with translating between languages. Warren Weaver, drawing on WWII exposure to cryptography and information theory, penned a memorandum in 1949 that inaugurated an intensive period of research into machine translation, or "MT". Now a subfield of Natural Language Processing within Artificial Intelligence, MT still holds a sacred and contradictory place in that domain, having been its first major challenge and remaining its most visible failure.

Given this legacy, it is significant that Duolingo and other sites and platforms that thrive on text-oriented sociability and media spreadability position their translation projects as urgent and interim remedies to much desired automated translation capabilities that are *not-yet-there*. Such statements are made, paradoxically, as MT services proliferate in tandem with crowdsourced options that are entirely dependent on a range of machinic affordances. Indeed, translation enters the scene as a transmission protocol, a step in a media production and distribution chain, part of Kittler's discourse networks: "the network of technologies and institutions that allow a given culture to select, store and produce relevant data" (1990: 369).

I contend that participatory translation needs to be seen in light of this longer history of information processing, with attention to the ways *collaborative entanglements between humans and machines* have been conceived and engineered to perform marketable and cost-effective translation in pre-web institutional contexts. In other words, while translation and linguistic practice might more readily be seen as newly social or communitarian in these alternative forms, it can also be viewed as newly instrumental and corporatized: MT reconfigured *to exploit* the social web.[1]

---

1 In the non-egalitarian sense suggested by Galloway and Thacker with respect to networked culture (Galloway/Thacker 2007).

1 TRANSLATING "ALL THE WORLD'S INFORMATION"

"Who will translate the web?" is of course a loaded question that underscores the urgency and anxiety faced by the fact that the Internet, as cultural
storehouse, is still made of language. Screen ubiquity and mobile telephony
have not displaced text, but multiplied it, necessitating image annotation,
speech transcriptions, subtitles, and translation. The question carries the
same assumptions that information-universalists or web-maximalists carry
– that the Internet as communications hub and depot is graspable in its totality and needs to be translated, or multiply 'versioned'. This well-honed
rhetoric is normalized through expressions of desire like Google's, to make
"All the world's information, universally accessible and useful."[2] Here,
translation is equated with web accessibility, and translation initiatives are
responses not only to a linguistically uneven web, but to content distribution and social networking that increasingly happens in real time.

A similar urgency was felt at the dawn of the computer age. Anxieties
around information overload extended to multilingual materials and were
especially high around access to Soviet scientific research; access was hin-
dered first by language, second by the lack of translator capacity. A decade
later, the first issue of *Mechanical Translation* rationalized its mission, declaring: "nearly all of the world's printed output remains untranslated, and a
large portion of the most worthwhile material, by any standard, remains untranslated. The cost of translation is high. But can we afford not to translate?" (Yngve 1954) This was the first research publication in the upstart
field of MT, which, in its earliest incarnations, strove for something called
'FAHQT', or Fully Automatic High Quality Translation.

Today, professor and Duolingo CEO Luis von Ahn pushes ahead with
MT of a very different kind – computationally conceived and situated, but
human performed. Duolingo's slogan – "Free Language" – extends the
cyberlibertarian refrain about the entrapment of information to the linguistic sphere. An economic argument is forwarded around volunteer translation as well; language barriers do not pose a problem for NGOs and under-
served communities, it is that language (localization) services are too
costly.

---

2   Google's "About" page. See https://www.google.ca/about/company/ (August
     15, 2015).

Von Ahn is already well-known as the developer of the CAPTCHA human identification test. His way of making tasks do double duty – what he refers to in his TEDx talk as "Human Computation" (von Ahn: 2011) – was pioneered with ReCAPTCHA, which supplements the verification test with a transcription task, exploiting millions of individual moments of human attention to do text transcriptions, including the *New York Times* archive. Duolingo extends this model to translation by organizing free language lessons that include translation activities, and encouraging users to visit the site's "Immersion" section to translate, edit, and adjudicate other users' work for additional practice. Like his predecessors, von Ahn frames translational need as an access problem divorced from specific cultures, territories, texts, and translation conventions, conceiving of the web as a monolithic, pan-global informational entity that is partitioned by language. Von Ahn's aim is stated simply: "to translate all of the Web, or at least most of the Web, into every major language" (ibid).

While von Ahn acknowledges that MT might have been used for the job, he claims it's not ready: "it makes so many mistakes, you don't know whether to trust it or not." A better option is to make translation "something that millions of people want to do" and something that "helps with the problem of lack of bilinguals" (ibid). Leveraging linguistic philanthropy, along with false urgency and a dubious scarcity, Duolingo has mobilized an army of 12.5 million active language trainees to translate from new languages as they learn them; crowd wisdom is used for quality control – using statistics and a system of up- and down-voting with points awarded and levels achieved.

It is significant that von Ahn justifies his approach with reference to the failings of MT. Discourse around MT tends to polarize around aspirations and disappointments, log-jammed around either-or contemplations of machine vs. human 'sense' and contextual sensibility. But hiding behind these binaries are less fantastic, incremental, and tech-heavy developments that conjoin humans, machines, and language in institutional workflows. What was characterized as AI in the research lab, as researcher Kevin Warwick notes, gets blackboxed inside real applications, losing "the tag of 'AI'", "regarded as just another part of a computer program" (2012: 8). These human-machine entanglements prefigure and help to contextualize the emergence of participatory translation platforms in the social web, including Duolingo, as engineered by design.

2   CONVEYOR BELT TRANSLATION

One of the first noted successes in MT was TAUM-MÉTÉO system, a fully automatic system for the translation of Canadian public weather forecasts from English into French, used from the mid-1970s to 2001. It was successful because it worked within a limited domain, a syntax and lexicon – a 'sublanguage' – particular to meteorological observation. The value of sublanguages was not lost on multinational corporations seeking effective, lower-cost means of translating technical documentation destined for global markets. Text production throughput was engineered to ensure consistency, uniformity, modularity, and reusability – from authoring and translation, to formatting, printing, and binding. Caterpillar, Xerox, IBM, Scania, and Siemens all developed so-called "Controlled Languages" – simplified, bounded languages streamlined for document production, including MT – consisting of simple syntax, limited, one-word-one-definition vocabularies, style and writing rules, and software that checks for compliance. MT protocols and writing protocols were conceived and implemented together, carving out new job designations and duties for pre- and post-editors to prepare text for easier processing by MT systems, and read and correct texts post-MT.

Translation work at institutional centers had always emulated the factory line to some extent, such that Peter J. Arthern, Head of the English Translation Division of the Council of the European Communities, described the EC as a "controlled-translation" situation (1979: 94). The prospect of linking terminals to a single mainframe led institutions to reconceptualize their translation resources and procedures. Texts were highly repetitive and work was already being done using photocopiers and a manual 'cut and stick' method. At this point, Arthern imagined an interlinked text-processing system that would store all texts and translations in a single memory and perform translation by text retrieval. Terminology banks – once held in massive card catalogues – were going online to grant collective access, hardware was getting cheaper, and storage capacity was growing. "Why not go the whole hog", Arthern asked, "and store all the translations we have ever done in the word processor's memory?" (1979: 72)

This kind of "Translation Memory" (TM) that Arthern imagined is now a standard part of the "Translator's Workbench," the software complex now used by a wide swath of translators. Crucially, the workbench concept was articulated in the 1980s amid ongoing debates over the usefulness and applicability of MT in institutional settings. These were the only places that could afford to experiment with MT, but MT was alienating translators, now relegated to editing poor translations they would have preferred to generate from scratch. In a landmark article, computational linguist Martin Kay, then of Xerox PARC, argued that the computer be positioned as assistant to the translator, not as colleague or substitute. This potential device, the "Translator's Amanuensis", would "always be under the tight control of a human translator" (Kay 1980: 18).

Translation would be enhanced "in little steps" (ibid: 11) with split-screen viewing, automatic dictionary look-up, recall, display, as well as MT, albeit in a new form that would allow translators to intervene according to their needs and intuitions. This would be a translator-driven collaboration that took advantage of the software speed, flexibility, and storage capacity. Most intriguing in Kay's proposal is his reference to the machine's "use of history" (ibid: 19) – the computer's build-up of cross-references, terminological notes, and structural relationships – an entire register of the translator's decision-making process. Development should be modest and even paced; "The translator's amanuensis will not run before it can walk", Kay wrote, insisting the device would be summoned only for duties "for which its masters have learned to trust it" (ibid: 20). While the statement asserted the authority of the human translator, it also confessed that their machines were being apprenticed. "Trust" in the technological workplace, after all, is largely a product of procedure, dependency, and daily routine. Even more relevant of Kay's observations on the relocation of translation to the web is the current architectural shift between people and machines; Kay's perception was of a one-to-one relationship between translators and their, or their company's, stored work history; today's social translator operates inside a network that tracks all linguistic operations, making collaboration a network effect whose massified behavioral history is largely opaque due to proprietary algorithms.

Kay's comments were made during the 1980s, when MT systems were still rule-based. IBM introduced statistical MT a decade later. It built a probability model of the translation process on the basis of a bilingual corpus – the French-English proceedings of the Canadian parliament – then estimated the likelihood that a given sentence would 'produce' another variant. Simply stated, the system performed calculations to suggest likely matches between existing terms. The findings were controversial, and those pursuing so called 'rationalist' approaches, bent on discovering purer, theory-driven simulations, questioned whether such empirical 'brute force' approaches really counted as MT.

Two voices called out of the controversy to suggest energies should not be wasted debating the feasibility of approaches, but directed towards finding proper domains for what the various systems were churning out. They advocated finding "Good Applications for Crummy Machine Translation" (Church/Hovy 1993). Decisions to invest, develop, or employ MT, they argued, were always economic. Enchanted by dreams of perfect translations, developers were blind to instances in which 'quick-and-dirty' translations were used, valued, and even preferred by end users who wanted quicker access. But this new product could only be delivered to end-users if one could circumvent the translating professionals: "end-users are more easily convinced than the translators, and therefore, for this approach to fly, it is important that the end-users be in the position to choose between speed and quality" (ibid: 10).

Once the product of MT was made meaningful beyond the production chain, the perfectionist expert could be subverted, reserved for more specialized tasks, and the end-user embedded more intimately and productively into the system. Church and Hovy asked us 20 years ago to entertain a view that translation might be something other than what translators do. The end-user-machine assemblage could be entrusted to make sense of language. Putting student trainees in control of web translation, as Duolingo does, now seems an extension of an earlier process, even mirroring the rule-based learning expected of earlier MT systems, carried out using basic word insertions, dictionary look-up, and simple grammar.

MT services for use by the public first came online in 1994 on CompuServe's "World Discussion Forum" in English, French, German, and Spanish. Google Translate has been available free of charge since 2004 and as a paid service for web developers since 2011. The translation services industry has long replaced the word 'crummy' with the more respectable 'gisting' to refer to raw quality output. While individuals and amateurs play with translation at the push of the button and journalists debate its quality and prospects, Google also invites seasoned translators to use its "Translator Toolkit", a cloud-based text editor (launched June, 2009) much like what Martin Kay envisioned, a translator's helper that supports and stores translation memories for individual or group use, searches databases and provides rough drafts with MT, and also encourages collaborative work. Of course, the aim, as with all of Google's cloud services, is to have its users, now a data corps, expand and finesse its product: the data corpus.

3 LINGUISTIC PARTICIPATION BY DESIGN

Access to free, easily available, and incrementally improving MT intensifies digital linguistic desire, especially as MT is encountered and 'sampled' in contexts that strive for informational and social seamlessness. To test and popularize their services, Google experimented with a "Translate this page" link on search results and Facebook tried offering in-post translation. MT's failure to succeed as an instant translation button reaffirms the drive and urgency on the part of multilingual actors to linguistically self-represent online in culturally meaningful ways. Significantly, popular translation initiatives to date have focused on securing means of communication, rather than content (non-English Facebookers should not have to click "Like"). Linguistic vibrancy, too, is a function of 'network effect', and cultural representation is now measured and secured by online presence and digital reach.

What is interesting about putting translation operations into crowdsourced and algorithmic hands is that it reconceives language in posthuman terms, recognizing it as constituted and sustained throughout the social body and held in place by media systems. However non-intuitive, distributed translation is transformative in making translation newly visible to new constituencies, emphasizing the material constructedness of language at fine grain and addressing broader linguistic variations and differences on the Internet. Duolingo is especially unique in this regard, enrolling anonymous novices in the online process, conferring risk, responsibility, and possibility to the task in ways that could be deemed appropriate to what Lennon has called our "plurilingual condition" (2010: 127).

At the same time, questions of linguistic stewardship as a community endeavor become problematically aligned with economic concerns that relate more directly to the replication and circulation of text documents. This points back to the ways human and machine translation have been positioned vis-à-vis AI in the cultural and technological imaginary. AI's striving for cross-linguistic seamlessness tends to conceive of language as a competency inherent to individual human bodies and replicable by machines (e.g. IBM's Watson supercomputer winning the game show *Jeopardy!* using natural language processing skills), rather than a system created and held together by social and technical apparatuses. When MT is pursued in the spirit of the former, it pursues the dream of making *bodies* multilingual (speak or read any language at the touch of a button); MT in the lab or on the market, on the other hand, renders *text* in different languages.

The history of human-machine entanglements in translation demonstrates that MT is foundational to collaborative translation as it's been applied to the distribution chain and engineered to include translators, writers, pre- and post-editors, programmers, non-translators, editors, and end-users. And, insofar as participatory initiatives now make the replication of existing sets of content or platforms their main objective, management strategy terms may be more appropriate. Such initiatives are better characterized as project-based localizations, which work to secure product penetration into multilingual markets and which follow the concept of "imposed multilingualism", described by political economist Daniel Dor as language variability controlled by the economic center (2004: 98).

Participatory translation sites are, of course, more haphazard. The Duolingo community is able to upload Creative Commons content to its "Immersion" center for translation practice by the crowd. Curiously, while a certain documentary randomness is to be expected, many of the blurbs are "About" pages or Wikipedia articles, documents extracted from equally open, distributed, community-built compendia. But the promise of keeping Duolingo's learning software free comes in exchange for community service, and Duolingo now has content-translation partnerships with Buzzfeed and CNN – sites with rapid turnover of pop culture news, seemingly entrusting the Duolingo community with the provision of multilingual linkbait.

What is more, Duolingo's incubation center invites the community to multiply the product itself by adapting the language curriculum to new language pairs. Thus far, 22 of 42 pairs are English learning modules, significant given that Duolingo's "Immersion" practice only provides articles for translation into one's native tongue. The global power imbalance that makes English skills necessary to secure employment – and which promises to make Duolingo English lessons popular – sits uncomfortably inside a scheme in which one gains skills in English in order to render American articles for one's own language community. Complicating Duolingo's commitments further are its efforts to enter the language certification business, undercutting major providers and deterritorializing the test by offering inexpensive, audiovisually proctored exams (cf. Straumsheim 2014).

The easiest proof that participatory translation is more about method than membership is in the patents. Of its efforts to make social networking linguistically seamless, Facebook now holds a U.S. Patent for "Community translation on a social network" (Wong 2012) which describes a procedure by which source phrases can be selected for translation, translated, viewed, and voted on. Von Ahn has recently applied for a patent for a more general method for "Crowd-Sourcing the Performance of Tasks through Online Education" (von Ahn/Alfonso/Hacker 2012). It describes the method as applicable to translation, image annotation, and descriptive video. The significant point is that "valuable metadata" is produced.

Von Ahn's TEDx talk introduces Duolingo as "The Next Chapter in Human Computation" (2011). Human translation is no longer opposed to MT; the two are finally aligned. It accommodates more people, in context-independent ways, to tasks in support of machine learning. It operates recursively, enfolding humans back into a model inaugurated by FAHQT, individualizing users as machine components and their verbal outputs as entries in an expanding, increasingly autonomous linguistic database. Making up for the failures of MT in the short-term, the normalization of participatory translation capitalizes on these shortfalls as a promise of immaterial labor over the long.

Thus, while participatory translation frames itself as working to strengthen human cultural and linguistic ties while addressing some of the web's linguistic imbalances, it operates inside a vast socio-technical apparatus that relies on linguistic contributions with the objective of developing methods for cost-effectively and automatically mitigating linguistic difference. While such methods are not necessarily opposed to community goals, local control over linguistic decision-making and data becomes lost to a vaster MT engine that runs on human linguistic labor. This has significant implications for perspectives on language and translation that are inclined to bias the sociocultural over the technical, or are concerned about linguistic longevity as a function of linguistic diversity, and not also a product of linguistic standardizations.

REFERENCES

Arthern, Peter J. (1979): "Machine Translation and Computerized Terminology Systems: a Translator's Viewpoint." In: Barbara M. Snell (ed.), Translating and the Computer, Amsterdam: North-Holland Publishing Co.

Bolter, Jay David/Grusin, Richard (1995): Remediation: Understanding New Media, Cambridge, MA: MIT Press.

Church, Kenneth W./Hovy, Eduard H. (1993): "Good Applications for Crummy Machine Translation." In: Machine Translation 8/4, pp. 239-258.

Dor, Daniel (2004): "From Englishization to Imposed Multilingualism: Globalization, the Internet, and the Political Economy of the Linguistic Code." In: Public Culture 16/1, pp. 97-118.

Galloway, Alexander (2004): Protocol: How Control Exists After Decentralization, Cambridge, MA: MIT Press.

Galloway, Alexander/Thacker, Eugene (2007): The Exploit: A Theory of Networks, Minneapolis, MN: Minnesota University Press.

Hayles, Katherine (2009): "Distributing/Disturbing the Chinese Room." In: http://onthehuman.org/2009/05/distributingdisturbing-the-chinese-room (April 15, 2014).

Kay, Martin (1980): The proper place of men and machines in language translation, Palo Alto: Xerox Palo Alto Research Center.

Kittler, Friedrich (1990): Discourse Networks 1800/1900, Stanford, CA: Stanford University Press.

Lennon, Brian (2010): In Babel's Shadow: Multilingual Literatures, Monolingual States, Minneapolis, MN: University of Minnesota Press.

Straumsheim, Carl (2014): "Proficient Enough?" Inside Higher Ed, http://www.insidehighered.com/news/2014/07/29/carnegie-mellon-u-test-duolingo-app-international-admissions (August 17, 2015).

Venuti, Lawrence (1995): The Translator's Invisibility: A History of Translation, New York, NY, and London: Routledge.

Von Ahn Aranello, Luis Alfonso (2011): "Massive-scale online collaboration", https://www.ted.com/talks/luis_von_ahn_massive_scale_online_collaboration/transcript (August 17, 2015).

Von Ahn Arellano, Luis Alfonso/Hacker, Severin Benedict Hans (2012): Crowd-sourcing the performance of tasks through online education,

United States Patent Application: US20120141959, patent published June 7.

Warwick, Kevin (2011): Artificial Intelligence: The Basics. Abingdon, UK: Routledge.

Wong, Yishan et al. (2012): Community translation on a social network, United States Patent: 8271260 B2, patent published September 18.

Yngve, V.H. (1954): "Editorial." In: Mechanical Translation 1/1, p. 2.

Perspectives

Between Demand and Entitlement

Perspectives on Researching Media and Participation

ELKE BIPPUS/BEATE OCHSNER/ISABELL OTTO

As outlined in the introduction, the challenge of "ReClaiming Participation" documented in this book is part of the research initiative "Media and Participation: Between Demand and Entitlement". The initiative was launched at the University of Konstanz, Germany and lead to a research group funded by the German Research Foundation with Beate Ochsner as its speaker. The research group comprises the three authors of this article along with Erich Hörl and Urs Stäheli.[1] Despite being positioned at the end of this book, the following contribution is not intended to summarize or conclude the previous articles. We rather want to outline some perspectives on researching media and participation by drawing upon some of the theoretical concepts and case studies pursued by the research group.

By using "medial participation" as a key concept, the research group proceeds on the supposition that participation is located in media-cultural exchange processes. This reconceptualization is founded on a process-related understanding of media, which allows the description of the relations between demand and entitlement in the assemblages of subjects, technological objects, practices, and communities. The interdisciplinary project combines media-historical, -ethnological, -aesthetic, -sociological, -philosophical as well as artistic and literary case studies. This is necessary in order to fill the unmet need of grasping the relations between media and par-

---

1 For more information on sub-projects and involved researchers see http://media andparticipation.com (August 14, 2015).

ticipation. The research group takes the full scope of its socio-political and cultural implications into consideration and aims to enrich the current, mainly application oriented approaches with a deliberation on participation from a media theoretic perspective.

The research group focuses on historically and culturally different configurations of (tele-)technological participating in which the conditions for in- or exclusion can change and where the specific challenges for participants and non-(or not yet)-participants are posed. These configurations are regarded as socio-technical power structures in which human and non-human actors are generated reciprocally. The research group therefore focuses its analyses on the reciprocal relation of the central parameters 'media configuration' and 'community building', considering 'media participation' as undetermined and unfinished. It assumes that the calling to partake in a community is always connected to the interpellation of subjects, which is fed by the high level of attractiveness that participation offers and which includes demands towards the interpellated subject.

The research questions emerging from this line of questioning can be sorted into three modalities: 'co-existence' (Mitsprechen), promise (Versprechen), and 'dissent' (Widersprechen). Whereas the term 'co-existence' addresses community building or obstructing and other such operations of "sharing" (Jean-Luc Nancy), political imaginations and utopias of participation fall under the heading 'promises' and studies on 'dissent' concentrate on disruptions in participation processes, which can be located in the media configurations themselves. Cooperation between these three modalities not only allows us to address urgent, current, and socially relevant questions as well as form a media theoretic approach to the term participation and the flipsides of media participation but, more importantly, it facilitates the development of a differentiated, media-cultural basis for future scientific analyses and the political facilitation of participatory cultures.

1   CO-EXISTENCE (MITSPRECHEN)

According to the United Nation's *Convention of the Rights of Persons with Disabilities,* persons with disabilities should have the opportunity of active participation in decision-making processes about policies and programs, including those directly concerning them. This promise of equal co-existence between hearing, deaf and hard-of-hearing people implies the possible use of different

"languages, display of text, Braille, tactile communication, large print, accessible multimedia as well as written, audio, plain-language, human-reader and augmentative and alternative modes, means and formats of communication, including accessible information and communication technology."[2]

There are, however, still many socio-cultural situations in which the realization of equal participation remain difficult. The right of equal speech, for example, is almost 'naturally' linked to the capacity of 'normal' hearing and, hence, 'normal' communication. Deaf or hard of hearing people, that do not share these practices, have to adapt or to be adapted to the demands of the(ir) right to enjoy active social participation. Although the neuroprosthetic cochlear implant (CI), a surgically implanted electronic device, does not restore 'normal' hearing, it operates in a "tendentially methexic" (Nancy 2007: 10) sound environment and can potentially provide a deaf or severely hard of hearing individual with a representation of the environmental sounds that can be co-shared with hearing people. The CI-generated production of 'common' acoustic experiences thus enables (and, at the same time, conditions) deaf or hard of hearing people to understand oral language and to 'function' in the hearing world:

"Having the cochlear implants has enriched my life in so many ways. They have provided me with the opportunity to function independently in a hearing world, attend school, excel at academics, attend a college preparatory school, and participate in extra-curricular activities [...]. Without the ability to hear [...] I would not have had this opportunity. I am very thankful that I am able to function at such a high level in a hearing world!"[3]

---

2   *Convention of the Rights of Persons with Disabilities*, http://www. un.org/disabilities/convention/conventionfull.shtml (August 15, 2015). Rather interesting that sign language is not mentioned explicitly.
3   *Cochlear Implant Patient Testimonials - Continued ...*, Taryn Surovik's testimonial on http://www.dallasear.com/cochlear-implant-testimonials.html (August 14, 2015), emphasis by B.O.

This form of participatory co-existence, nevertheless, demands not only a surgical intervention but also entails a (sometimes) long lasting and exhausting process of audiological adaptation in the context of (self-)normalization. So, far from being a simple instrument of transmission, the CI "participates as [an] agent [...] in social interaction" (Pickering 1997: 59). It thus establishes – as the above cited testimonial shows – not only a fundamental dichotomy between the hearing and the deaf worlds, it also insinuates a qualitative asymmetry linking the possibility of co-existence (and, hence, co-determination) to the ability to hear and to speak orally, i.e. 'normally'. This process, however, instead of creating equal co-existence, produces what Jean-Luc Nancy calls a "being-of-togetherness" under the participatory conditions of the hearing world. The becoming of this (singularly hearing) community "necessarily loses the 'in'" of "being-*in*-common [...]. The truth of community, on the contrary, resides in the retreat of such a being" (Nancy 2001: xxxix, original emphasis).

While many theoretical approaches to participation highlight the idea that participation offers a free choice of togetherness in emerging communities, they often neglect the mostly invisible, socio-technical space and the mediatic processes indispensable to its realization. It is, in the following, our aim to analyze so called "activation-scenes" (Kincheloe 2010), i.e. film or video scenes of deaf people hearing for the first time after the activation of their cochlear implant, in order to specify the mediatic modes of addressing that produce future participants (or non-participants) in the hearing world. In our understanding, participation, hence, has to be thought as a chain of operations which are proceeded in and through techniques, objects, and practices. According to medical success stories, the CI seems to enable almost 'normal' hearing and realizes equal rights between deaf and hearing people.[4] It thus functions as a positively locatable and systematically available address, allowing deaf or hard-of-hearing people to participate in social life. What needs to be clarified is *how* this medical instrument mobilizes (discourses of) interactions between humans, practices, and technical objects. Before analyzing our filmic example, we, first of all, have to point out that the chosen scenes are not to be considered as a mere re-presentation of a (autonomously existing) first-time-hearing-event. Instead, this kind of au-

---

4 At the same time, it mobilizes resistant forces, like the *Sourds en colère,* cf. Ochsner 2013.

diovisual production has to be taken seriously as the 'fabrication' of a specific knowledge space within and through which something that is supposed to be *re*presented first comes into being. Relations, perceptions, or reflections that arise from the interaction of the different actors in this space then solidify into images, texts or practices (Engell 2010: 136; cf. Barker 2012). Therefore, rather than analyzing the behavior of hearing, deaf, hard-of-hearing, or CI-hearing people, we focus on the mediality of the participatory space and the translational processes between (hearing/non-hearing) identities and alterities as well as between ability and disability. Or more specifically, the aim is to grasp hearing and deaf practices that are produced in and through the audiovisual arrangement of "activation-scenes", thereby fabricating deaf people as participants in the hearing world.

In the first part of his long-term documentary SOUND AND FURY Josh Aronson explores one family's ongoing struggle for identity and respect in both the hearing and the deaf world.[5] We must note that the Artinian family offers a kind of perfect model structure, presenting two sons of hearing parents, one of them, Chris, hearing, the other one, Peter, deaf, each with their respective families composed of both hearing and deaf wives and children. Primarily through the eyes of Heather Artinian, Peter and his wife Nita's six-year-old daughter, we witness a highly emotional family debate about a controversial medical device, the cochlear implant. The conflict between Peter, outspoken leader of the anti-implant deaf community, and his brother Chris escalates when Chris and his hearing wife Mari, herself a daughter of two deaf parents, learn that one of their new-born twin sons, aptly named Peter, is deaf and decide to implant him. After the surgery, we attend little Peter's activation only a few weeks later.[6] What we get to see is a meanwhile rather well known cinematographic dispositif showing the audiologist together with the child and his (hearing) family in the Cochlear Implant Center in New York (cf. Ochsner/Spöhrer/Stock 2015; cf. Kincheloe 2010). Usually, the audiovisually documented activation and mapping processes of babies or toddlers follow a standard protocol, thereby producing an almost identical audiovisual arrangement. While, in the self-made YouTube-

---

5   Aronson released the second part of Sound and Fury six years later, in 2006.
6   See the clip showing little Peter's first hearing on SOUND AND FURY (2000), www.youtube.com/watch?v=0ki4qo-Dfos, TC 1:11:20-1:14:25 (November 20, 2014).

Videos, the (almost always!) hearing family members are mostly positioned in the background, the CI-wearer is placed in the foreground, often on his or her mother's lap while the father, just as often, is operating the camera. In our example, Peter sits on Mari's lap, while his family is placed in the background. After a significant cut, the camera, in a close-up, directly focuses on him and his CI, which, simultaneously, makes the other actors disappear. This specific constellation between human and non-human actors ensures that most of the children, shortly before the activation act, look directly into the camera in order to register their turning around to the acoustic source.

"Technological objects determine the mode of representation of the scientific object, and sufficiently stabilized scientific objects in their turn become constitutive moments of the experimental arrangement." (Rheinberger 1992: 70, translated by B.O.)

The experimental arrangement of "activation-scenes" thus conditions the questions that can arise in this system. A space for the performance of epistemic things is produced and, through an "on-going" (Weber 1989/90: 981) process, the epistemic things are transformed into technological things. In fact, each stabilization of a technological object only means meta-stabilization, i.e. each scientific object is transformed into a technological one, which can in turn open a new space for the scientific object. It is, however, important to remark, that, as we have pointed out above, representation is to be understood here in terms of production or fabrication, not of depiction. Thus, the audiovisually produced audiological space also serves as a structure and condition for the isolation of a series of (pre-)determined reactions that will be stabilized. Disturbing factors, like family members, a (partially) functioning auditory nerve or, in the case of post lingual deafened CI-wearers or a still existing impression of 'normal' hearing, are to be eliminated and continually overwritten in order to produce clear signals and unambiguous reactions. In and through these practices, hearing, deafness, and CI-hearing are formatted.

As the eventness of mediation that enables something to appear cannot communicate itself, an in-between space becomes necessary. Media processes cannot be conceived of without the practices that shape media and are formatted by them. Hartmut Winkler, a German media theorist, assumes a cyclic inscription of social practices and media technologies that, while reciprocally executed, are mediated, (meta-)stabilized and displaced in order to remain potentially open and ready for redefinitions of social relations and associations (Winkler 1999: 228). From this perspective, the CI is actually not a stabilized, time resistant technical object; like its wearers, it rather continually has to be mapped in terms of hearing. In or through this specific constellation a new understanding of the relations between environment, ear, hearing (non-hearing, CI-hearing) and what is or has to be heard is created in a participatory process during which the CI is transformed from a mere "instrument to a medium" (Vogl 2001: 121) with specific data and knowledge production (cf. Vogl 2012). In the sociotechnical arrangement of discussions, implantations, activations, and mappings the practice of hearing with the CI is completed, or rather replaced, by the reflections on 'normal' hearing and its rules. Thus the CI-wearers, after a while, will not/no longer hear what cannot be heard through the practices of 'normal' hearing.

Back to little Peter: In the next scene, the audiologist explains how she will proceed. Firstly, Peter's implant is connected to an external transmitter, then "*adjustments* to the processor settings [will be made, B.O.], to allow the user *to hear as well as possible*" [emphasis by B.O.]. By imagining possible scenarios, the audiologist is 'adjusting' the parents as well as us, the spectators, in terms of expectations. Either nothing, a defense reaction, or a kind of blinking will happen: "We are going to pay very close attention in terms of watching him, because that is what we really need to see." A series of close-ups on Peter, the audiologist, and the computer screen follows, then the camera pivots between the audiologist and Peter, anticipating the promised reaction. In the same moment, we hear a very low frequency sound, and little Peter, albeit unable to see the acoustic source, is turning around: "His ears were [...] born today." In further tests the audiologist makes Peter hear speech and his mother Mari calls him by his name: "Peter, Peter!" Again the little boy turns around. By inscribing Peter into a symbolic order which is not one of his own but rather an open door into an unknown universe, Peter has finally been made addressable in a manifest way, materialized in and through the CI.

As an identificatory or attributional process, participation essentially focuses on the addressability of future participants (and non-participants alike!) in complex socio-technical arrangements. Social participation hence depends on a system apt to resolving the improbability of addressability by shaping standard protocols and standard architecture or layering of services in order to enroll further (non-)participants. It equally depends on a participatory act of identifying with the fact of being addressed, like Peter's 'responding' to his mother's call. After having implanted the CI, the process of connecting Peter activates the communicational program that will be inscribed through the CI. This process takes place in an audiovisually (re-) configured "transepistemic arena" (Knorr-Cetina 1982), in which, according to a standard operations procedure of adjustment, a new biosocial identity that overcomes 'social deafness' (cf. Vonen 2007) is produced.

In his highly instructive article on addressability as the fundamental notion in sociological system theory, Peter Fuchs uses the example of adults talking to a baby or a toddler. According to the author, this communicational situation is characterized by a "unilateral consciousness in the surrounding of an unconscious address" (Fuchs 1997: 65), and can thus neither ensure whether something has been communicated, nor if it has been understood. However, the author continues, precisely this uncertainty leads to an on-going process during which the baby acquires a means of address(ability) and thus the possibility of developing self-consciousness. The above cited "activation scene" repeats this production of addressability, albeit with the difference that the imaginary identification process seems to be positively materialized in and through the technical object that operates in between. In the process of mapping the CI-equipped Peter, his awakening (self-)consciousness is (re-)produced in a kind of behaviorist performance that, via interpellation, makes the little boy addressable under the conditions of a hearing system. In the same moment, Mari is produced as Peter's mother (another address) and the now concretized CI tends to disappear in the black box of the audiovisual arrangement.

'Switching-on Peter', just like the communication system described by Fuchs, presupposes self-referenceability that – in Peter's case – is performed by different actors such as parents, audiologists, technical objects, a specifically produced audiovisual knowledge space, a low-frequency sound, and the boy's physical reaction. The complex interactions between physical nature, techniques, and practices is also the subject of Jean-Luc Nancy's reflections on bio- or ecotechnological processes. The French philosopher hereby points out that technique not only complements nature but also supplements its ends and means (Nancy 2013: 1). The double logic of the supplement thus derives directly from the relation between nature and technique (Nancy 2013: 2). While ends and means (mediums) constantly exchange their roles, in the process of unfolding nature, technique develops a "general regime of inventing ends that are themselves thought through the perspective of means" (Nancy 2013: 2). In order to clarify the idea that technique actually reveals the purposelessness of nature, Nancy uses the term "struction": a "non-assembled ensemble" (Nancy 2013: 4) that is both beyond con- and deconstruction.[7] Thus, technique should not be confounded with the concrete technical object or device; instead, it refers to *techné* as practice of coming-into-being, something that emerges co-existentially with the body that, in order to produce technique, has to be technicized itself. From this perspective, the participatory element of the CI is based on a general technicity and, hence, potentiality, of the body and its environment, a relation Nancy calls "ecotechnology" (Nancy 2013: 7) or world of separated connections or connected separations.

Nevertheless, one might ask where or when this potentiality ends and the biosocial 'adjustment', which is a deliberate stabilization of the difference between hearing and deaf people, begins. A difference that, after its stabilization, can be (partially) bridged by the medical interface CI. One might also wonder if this effort to connect people maybe produces and thus destroys the openness of the ecotechnological milieu.

According to Peter Fuchs, the fundamental process of addressing is based on the temporality of the supplement in the context of which communication or address points are presupposed to only be realized or become social facts afterwards. The claim of 'switching-on' Peter thus demands a vacancy, a formless but addressable (pre-)consciousness that enables prospective form(ation)s. From this perspective, the processes of participation in both our example and that of Peter Fuchs (1997) need an ever-displaceable topology of relations which, in and for itself, has no place. Georg Christoph Tholen, however, draws attention to a decisive difference between the operational closeness and coherence of system or cybernetic theory and symbolic difference (cf. Tholen 1999). While, according to Tholen, the former simply skips the difference (between human beings and technique) by, for example, bridging or closing it through a CI, symbolic

---

7   Perhaps it can be compared to what Alfred North Whitehead calls a "nexus", "a particular fact of togetherness among actual entities" (Whitehead 1978 [1929]: 20).

difference intervenes to start endless processes of differentiation. The materialization through the CI makes Peter's 'miracle' appear as a pure emergence, a pragmatically performed act of consciousness based on a (pre-) consciousness that has always been there and that now is positively addressable through the CI in its sociotechnical arrangement. The CI thus offers a material location for a placeless symbolic topology. At the same moment and by 'adjusting' further differentiation processes, it leads to the self-exclusion of a deaf or non-hearing as a – in the closed system of the hearing world – non-addressable person. The technical object guarantees the addressability of the deaf person, a selection that entails a fundamental inclusion, because the "subject" is interpellated and produced at the same time that the communication is made possible. However, simultaneously, it brings up exclusion on a very elementary level because it anticipates and separates what can/cannot be an eventual address in the future.

So, once again, far from being a simple instrument or tool, in its experimental sociotechnical arrangement the CI reveals a nature of "combination, interaction and, later, feedback, [...] a quasi-organicity" (Nancy 2013: 7). From this perspective, it is technical matter or materiality "that proves itself more and more thanks to exploratory technologies that are increasingly precise, but which are themselves becoming intricately connected to their objects" (Nancy 2013: 7) and their sociotechnical arrangements. The adjustment process of the CI and/in its environment, however, seems to reduce the potential openness by becoming more and more concrete under the medical, economic, and cultural conditions of the hearing world – unless the wearers obtain the source code of the device in order to program themselves and their own 'hearing', a claim the CI-(Cy)borg community tries to enforce (cf. Ochsner/Stock 2014).

2 PROMISE (VERSPRECHEN)

Current debates about participatory media as well as claims for more political and social participation are often accompanied by the staging, even spectacles (Debord 1999 [1967]), of an all-including media society. These spectacles can, for instance, be observed at artistic performances, public gatherings summoned 'ad hoc' by smart phone messages, or at media effective TV appearances of disabled people: Those who decry insufficient participation, those who request more participation or those who want to illustrate felicitous inclusion depend on strategies of visualization. These strategies are often criticized as being superficial exhibitions or the exploitation of people who seem to be unable to decide for themselves (cf. Bergermann 2009). Yet it would be rash to dismiss these scenarios of participation as mere illusions or 'false promises'. Our research perspective counters that idea that only through the different forms of staging participation can the 'co-appearance' of community, in Nancy's terms its "comparution" or "compearance" (Nancy 1992: 371), be enabled and, above all, be visible and describable – not only in promises and utopias, but also in denials and lapses.

In our understanding of 'medial participation' an entirely including participation is a utopian project vectored towards the future. In this sense it is necessarily a promise that has to be repeated again and again. Promises of participation are not only spectacularly staged and celebrated. As temporary stabilized sociotechnical relations (cf. Latour 1991) they are also inscribed into technological processes. On the one hand, this relates to technologically conditioned potentials, i.e. certain options for action in an 'online democracy' (cf. Coleman/Shane 2011). On the other hand, this concerns the production of cultural attributions, i.e. the discursive formation of the Social Web as a participatory re-formation of the Internet (Mandiberg 2012).

Promises of participation have thus to be understood both as procedures of community building and as formations of human and technical actors, who are meant to take part. Promises of participation limit the possibilities of partaking and determine the criteria of inclusion and exclusion; they act as demands and impositions for potential participants. A cellphone app, for instance, may keep its promise to transform the device into a mediator of a social network. But by this very promise it also defines the conditions and affordances, that a phone and/or a user have to fulfill in order to synchronize with an emerging community. This process can be described in more detail by scenarios connected with the text-message broadcast system "TXTmob", an early example for "Mobile Social Software" for cellphones (Thom-Santelli 2007; cf. Goggin 2011) which is often referred to as a forerunner of Twitter (Sifry 2012).

TXTmob was created in 2004 by developers from the *American Institute for Applied Autonomy*, a group of artists, activists, and programmers that described its mission as "to study the forces and structures which affect self-determination and to provide technologies which extend the autonomy of human activists."[8] The messaging service is one of several products the institute offered to autonomy seeking Internet and mobile phone users. One of them was the application "i-See", which allowed its users to walk around urban environments without being surveilled by locating routes that avoided CCTV-cameras.[9] In the case of TXTmob, which was developed by an institute member with the pseudonym "John Henry" and the MIT doctoral candidate Tad Hirsch, a strong connection to the issue of political participation is crucial, as the programmers argue:

"TXTmob was developed specifically for, and in collaboration with protest organizers, and was enabled both by the widespread adoption of SMS-enabled cell phones among activists and by evolutions in protest tactics. In turn, TXTmob facilitated new social formations and modes of participation." (Hirsch/Henry 2005: 1455)

First deployed during the protests at the 2004 Democratic and Republican National Conventions in Boston and New York, the free service was later used by activists during the Ukrainian Orange Revolution and in protests against George W. Bush.[10]

TXTmob works like a web-based mailing list. Prospective users are asked to sign up online with their phone numbers on the webpage www.txtmob.com. They are then able to create closed (private) or open (public) groups, which are connected before and during the protests by the sending and receiving of text messages. These groups can be further specified by regulating whether any member can send messages (unmoderated) or only selected users are able to send messages (moderated). The developers state that four major types of groups can be configured by these technological conditions: Closed and open forums (unmoderated, private, and unmoderated, public groups); closed groups with a few operators monitoring the protests and sending warning information, e.g. about clashes be-

---

8   Institute for Applied Autonomy: "Mission", http://www.appliedautonomy.com/ mission.html (August 14, 2015).

9   Institute for Applied Autonomy: "i-See", http://www.appliedautonomy.com/ isee.html (August 14, 2015).

10 Tad Hirsch: TXTmob (2004) (with the Institute for Applied Autonomy), http://web.media.mit.edu/~tad/htm/txtmob.html (December 17, 2014).

tween protesters and polices from a safe and distant place (moderated, private group); and 'comms' networks or transitory flashmobs which deliver "semi-spontaneous public performances involving dozens of strangers in coordinated acts that resembled absurdist theater." (Hirsch/Henry 2005: 1456)

It is this latter type of possible group formation, which is entangled with the most spectacular scenarios of re-enacted political participation by disapproval. A *New York Times'* article quotes Hirsch describing the protests against the Republican National Convention in New York in August of 2004: "'We wanted to transform areas around the entire city into theaters of dissent'" (Moynihan 2008). The same article reports on "transmitted messages detailing the action, often while scenes on the street were still unfolding"; it states that open TXTmob groups may also contain useful information for news coverage about spectacular rackets: "Reporters began monitoring the messages too, looking for word of breaking news and rushing to spots where mass arrests were said to be taking place." (Ibid) The TXTmob based performances within the New York protests also included a Critical Mass bicycle ride through Manhattan with participants communicating with each other about route changes or traffic snarls via cellphones (cf. Di Justo 2004). This riding flashmob, constituted and re-formatted by text messages, spectacularly made visible what participation by TXTmob could achieve.

But, as mentioned above, no staging of successful participation goes without promises that anticipate a desirable future. The TXTmob developers and the activists planning the protests in New York tried, in a way, to re-enact prior uprisings in which the sending and forwarding of messages played a crucial role, especially the protests against Joseph Estrada, President of the Philippines, in Manila 2001, which were believed to have emerged from circulating cellphone messages (Hirsch/Henry 2005: 1455; cf. Rafael 2003). Anticipating a 'theater of dissent' is only possible with discursively fabricated promises of participation. Central to this fabrication is Howard Rheingold's book *Smart Mobs. The Next Social Revolution*, first published in 2002, which closely based its definition of 'smart mobs' on the concept of "mobile ad hoc social networks" (Kortuem et al. 2001):

"The *mobile aspect* is already self-evident to urbanites who see the early effects of mobile phones and SMS. *Ad hoc* means that the organizing among people and their

devices is done informally and on the fly, the way texting youth everywhere coordinate meetings after school." (Rheingold 2002: 170, original emphasis)

In an interview Hirsch denies that Rheingold was an inspiration for the
TXTmob protests, arguing that people have used text messaging in protests
since long before the publication of *Smart Mobs* (OpenSource.net 2004).
But in naming their broadcasting service 'TXT*mob*' they drew intensively
upon a discourse surrounding 'protests by text messaging', which combines
these protests with a supposed formation of community. Rheingold's book
is a very influential part of this discourse: "On January 20, 2001",
Rheingold comments on the Manila protests, "President Joseph Estrada of
the Philippines became the first head of state in history to lose power to a
smart mob." (Rheingold 2002: 157)

Promises of participation were discursively attributed and technologically inscribed into the code of the SMS service TXTmob. The visible
flashmobs in the streets of New York were repeating a scenario that was as-
sured to happen. But it would be a misunderstanding to state that the whole
community building process within the New York protests in 2004 was determined in advance. In interplay with discursive attribution and technological inscription, user practices play a crucial role in the process of participation. Hirsch and Henry failed to anticipate one thing in their description of
the four different group formation possibilities that were intended to organize protests in an urban environment: people joining the protests who were
not on-site in New York but took part tele-presently by sending and receiving text messages; "'it's like I can be there, because I can know what's going on directly from the people who are there in the streets'", one protester
is quoted (Di Justo 2004). Through this unexpected usage of TXTmob practice, the protest itself and the community building process of which the user
is part of are only revealed on cellphone displays. The TXTmob developers
embrace this appropriation as an emergence of a new form of participation,
which seems to be even more promising. Far from being simple "voyeurism
or participation without risk," Hirsch and Henry observe "solidarity with
protesters" in this tele-present partaking, which raises further questions for
"further work":

"Does this form of participation constitute a collective identity (a sense of 'we-ness'
among participants)? [...] Is there something unique about mobile devices that en-

hance such identification (in a way that, say, email or websites don't)." (Hirsch/ Henry 2005: 1458)

The unexpected user practices clarify that TXTmob is not only a tool for protest but is itself part of a process of medial participation that becomes visible on cellphone displays by sharing of messages. Participation as a medial process cannot be reduced to merely initiating an encounter on the physical site of the protest. It takes place between users and cellphones connected by the sending and receiving of messages, in an "onscreen encounter" (Licoppe 2013). Despite of recognizing the importance of the mobile device in this process, Hirsch and Henry disregard two important points: Firstly, the process of medial participation never results in a fixed community or in a 'collective identity'. The "comparution" (Nancy 1992) of community is implemented in the media process and does not take place independently. Even the bike riding flashmob in the streets of Manhattan can only be seen as an imagined, unfinished, undetermined, and fleeting community, even by its participants on the TXTmob interface. Secondly, Hirsch and Henry do not mention the flipsides of this new form of participation: Similar to Twitter some years later, TXTmob has the problem that it is not only open to activists but also to police surveillance. Years after the New York protests Hirsch was subpoenaed by the city and asked to hand over all messages sent during the protests and to identify people who used the service (Moynihan 2008). The same technological processes that promise to transform users into political actors, and to merge those actors into an uprising collective, condition the possibility of the (legal) invocation and even interpellation of subjects. Therefore, simultaneous with every promise TXTmob keeps, it reveals the flipside of participation.

3 DISSENT (WIDERSPRECHEN)

The researchers of the project "Media and Participation: Between Demand and Entitlement" and, in particular, the researchers of the sub-project "Micropractice: Practicing Engagement and Resistance" presume that there is a contradiction in exchange processes and that it is constitutive for every process of participation. This dissent is thus understood as an interfering, interrupting modality in the media constellations themselves. It is conceived as a process that generates an inside and an outside as well as inclusions and exclusions, and it is not assigned to a place that is exempt from economic constraints and distortions. From this perspective, the contradiction of art, whose resistance is historically justified with the modernist idea of aesthetic autonomy (cf. Rebentisch 2006) and its functionlessness (cf. Adorno 1997: 320), is not conceived in an essentialist way but rather understood as a constitutive interweaving with historical-social and medial constellations.

The project "Micropractice: Practicing Engagement and Resistance" understands practices as fundamental authorities by means of which the forms of co-existence are constituted in all relationships, communities, and institutions and by means of which vice versa the forms of living and subjectifying are produced in the first place. Subjects delineate and subjugate themselves through practices. And practices are grouped in complexes, interweaving into a social fabric and forming disciplines, institutions, politics, and cultures (cf. Dieterich et al. 2015). The goal of the project is, therefore, to explore how micropractices, dissent, and community building condition and relate to one another in the field of art and socioculture. "Aesthetic micropractices" can be used to describe sensory-physical, reflexive, discursive, and, above all, experimental approaches that are formed in specific historical and sociocultural frameworks. Case studies will show how aesthetic micropractices alter ways of embodiment, break down normative patterns, and contribute to a different "distribution of the sensible" (Rancière 2004).

Whereas the specific subject fields are studied under "Micropractices in the Field of Art and Their Aesthetic Politics", practices of "doing it together" are studied within sociocultural projects like "Micropractices of Existence" and as "Politics of Participation". In both fields of research, participatory strategies are reflected upon as aesthetic politics of contradiction and resistance. Firstly, our interest is focused on how dissent is configured in relation to the circumstances of the art system and how this very contradiction of participation or non-participation, or belonging and not belonging, is formed in the process. Secondly, we focus on practices of sharing, repairing, or handcraft in open workshops as well as practices of self-organization and (re)appropriation of urban space in order to work out, under the uniform perspective of micropractice, the potential of these practices in terms of resistance and in terms of pharmacology.

The ancient Greek word pharmakon, which can be translated as "poison" or "drug" as well as "medicine", is central to the analysis of micropractices. From the pharmacological perspective (Derrida 1981), we try to capture the fundamental conflict of aesthetic micropractices and resist the simplistic juxtaposition of resistant micropractices versus power-stabilizing macropractices (cf. Stäheli 2004: 160). This approach is intended to reveal the diverse gradations of media participation and dissent (in the sense of inconsistence) as a potential of contradicting.

The multimedia project *Funk Lessons* by the artist Adrian Piper can be used as an example of micropractices (cf. Bippus 2015). The micropractices in the media of performances, texts, photographs, and a video – as interrupting and interfering modalities – contradict the affects determined by normative patterns and the identifications with funk.[11] Between 1982 and 1984 Piper undertook her *Funk Lessons: A Collaborative Experiment in Cross-Cultural Transfusion*, in an effort to combine political content with pleasurable experiences. Under the motto "Get down and party. Together", she taught the history of Afro-American funk and soul to an audience from the immediate neighborhood, the university, and the art world at the University of California, Berkeley. A fifteen-minute video, directed by Sam Samore, shows her lessons and the artist's historical contextualization of funk. In her "Notes on Funk", published in 1985, Piper theorized on funk in culture and society.

By using diverse media, Piper was reacting to the widespread racist discrediting of funk by the white middle class as black working-class culture. She employed funk as a collective and participatory medium of self-transgression and opened up the affective possibilities of this music genre by deconstructing normatively determined ideas of funk and making it possible to reflect on cultural and racist barriers (cf. Piper 1996: 232). Funk

---

11 Affect is evoked not as a simple natural-mental impulse but rather becomes recognizable in its historicity and contingent character and is explained as an effect of interpretative patterns. Affect becomes an aesthetic articulation of immanent diversity and transformability in the spirit of Gilles Deleuze, who conceptualizes affect in cinema audiences as an interruption of affectively regulated relationality, as an interstice that resists space-time definitions in its potentiality and multiple connectivity (cf. Bippus 2014).

stands for, according to Piper in her "Notes on Funk", black pop music and a dance style that became the typical form of expression in the black culture of the 1970s, a "language of interpersonal communication and collective self-expression" (Piper 1996: 195).

In her performances (and even more so by using a variety of media), physical experiences – basic elements of music and dance – mesh with information on cultural background, such as funk's relationship to other, "white" music and combines experience and reflection. The affirmation of funk thus invites us not simply to identify and join in, but rather each of the parties is challenged to take a position on his or her own role.

The performance does not "aspire to experience black culture sympathetically or through participation" (Piper 1996: 208), nor is it about participating in a work of art, as with interactive art, nor about creating a vague sense of a multicultural society of equals. Rather, those who are involved are addressed as people who have already been participating: they are part of a historical-cultural apparatus in which they subjectify themselves and form their identity, thinking, perception, ideas, and attitude. The artist formulated her goal to "restructure people's social identities, by making accessible to them a common medium of communication – funk music and dance" (Piper 1996: 198). The medium of cultural communication offered by Piper is not oriented around stereotypical patterns but rather calls into question both affirmative-identifying and aversive-racist ideas of funk. The micropractical realizations of funk in media show affects to be structured and determined by historical, cultural, or social patterns of interpretation (cf. Butler 2009: 50) and point not only to the conditions of inclusion or exclusion in the social reality of the 1970s but also to those of the field of art. By taking up funk as a "cultural benefit" and integrating it into the value system of white high culture as "an unbelievably rich and enriching art form" (Piper 1996: 203), Piper exposes conflicts – especially the common and normative image of funk and the status as a privileged member of (white) society that the artist has "attained." In their interplay, the performances, the text, and the video reflect the conditions and interrelation of inclusions and exclusions in social reality and in the field of art. The mediatisations (of funk) problematize the claims, demands and impositions associated with the respective offering of participation.

Following Gilles Deleuze and Félix Guattari, Piper's "Funk Lessons" can be related to a micropolitical critique that begins on the level of practice. *Micropolitics*, as conceived by Deleuze and Guattari, refer to a political experiment, a political commitment that reacts to the neutralization of revolutionary politics and the revolutionary subject caused capitalism since the 1970s (Deleuze/Guattari 1997: 453-454): In a society of control, norms are no longer imposed by repression; instead, they arise, mutable, from the wealth of differences and deviations and serve as guidelines that can be rejected or coveted. Individuals adjust their own behavior correspondingly. Piper seems to be especially interested in these practices of self-adjustment, since in her micropractice she focuses more on the power procedures of "governmentality" (Foucault 1997: 225) that form a physical-mental habitus.

Piper's micropractices contextualize implicit physical knowledge historically, socially, and culturally. With her practices, they interrupt internalized physical-perceptual pathways, disturb their affective efficacy, and open possibilities of affecting in new ways. The exercises can literally set in motion hardened, habituated practices of the body and thus rouse normative ideas and attributions of funk on a micropractical level. "Taking part" is staged not as participation in a (funky) community but literally realized in space and time so that a community of the "we"/"with" is called up, which Jean-Luc Nancy has described "as context and as separated and even dispersed singularities" (Nancy 2014: 24-25).

Piper's mediatizing of funk in the form of a performance, which both invites active participation and addresses receptive engagement through video and text as forms of presentation, can be problematized by recent art historical research that distinguishes pre-participatory from participatory art. Silke Feldhoff argues that participatory projects are tied to physically visible activity whereas "involvement or participation takes place on a receptive level, that is to say, an active physical involvement is anticipated, but not put into practice" (Feldhoff 2009: 41).

Claire Bishop makes an argument in her dissertation that is similar to Feldhoff's. In her view, the participatory art of the 1990s altered the relationship between the art object, the artist, and the viewer in such a way that "the artist is conceived less as an individual producer of discrete objects than as a collaborator and producer [...]; while the audience, previously conceived as a 'viewer' or 'beholder', is now repositioned as a co-producer or *participant*" (Bishop 2012: 2, original emphasis).

In art historical writing, participation is thus simplistically associated

with an action and distinguished from 'mere' intellectual, receptive participation by its mobilization, say, by calling into question the unity of the author and the work in favor of the "birth" of viewers (cf. Eco 1989, Barthes
1977). The problematic thing about this perspective is that it necessarily
presumes a subject capable of action and thus not only ignores the effects
of both practices and affects but also underestimates ways of seeing and
reading as a methodological approach.

The contrasting of active and passive seems also essential for the conceptualization of micropolitics as formulated by Brian Massumi. He speaks
of a critique that always looks for its point of departure in specific situations and which has to be critical from the inside out, out of the centre. But
Massumi only considers the body in motion. A body in motion "does not
coincide with itself. It coincides with its own transition: its own variation"
(Massumi 2002: 4).

"There is no situation of being outside a situation. And no situation is subject to
mastery. It is only by recognizing the bonds of complicity and the limitations that
come with the situation that you can succeed in modulating those constraints at the
constitutive level, where they reemerge and seriate. This is immanent 'critique'. It is
active, participatory critique. For me, micropolitical action involves this kind of immanent critique that actively alters conditions of emergence. It engages becoming,
rather than judging what is." (Massumi 2009: 14)

Our research project addresses the problematic contrasting of active and
passive by making aesthetic practices and relations (and not the actions between subjects and objects) the focus of its study. They are manifested in
many media formats and their function is worked out for participatory processes of becoming subjects and community building. Our goal is to study
how belonging and not-belonging constitute each other in media processes
of participation and how (previous) exclusion is produced in the gesture of
including (Neuner 2007).

In this way, putting micropractical processes into perspective as fundamentally pharmacological operations of participation and non-participation
sets itself the goal of calling into question the art historical and philosophical critique that asserts that participatory art neglects artistic-aesthetic criteria in favor of ethical ones (cf. Bishop 2012, Rancière 2009) and merely el-
evates "meetings, encounters, events, various types of collaboration be-

tween people, games, festivals, and places of conviviality, in a word all manner of encounter and relational invention" (Bourriaud 2002: 28) to aesthetic objects. This project presumes that ethical and aesthetic criteria do not exist as given but are rather formed in processes of media exchange in order to justify inclusions and exclusions in the field of art or socioculture and its communities as supposedly pre-existing. For that very reason, critical, aesthetic, micropractical action is confronted with the challenge of making itself recognizable in all its contradictions, at least in part, in order to resist normative and regulating positionings of and attributions to art (cf. Butler 2006: 186-187).

Section 3 "Dissent" of this chapter was translated by Steven Lindberg.

REFERENCES

Adorno, Theodor W. (1997): Aesthetic Theory, edited and translated by Robert Hullot-Kentor, Minneapolis, MN: University of Minnesota Press.

Barker, Timothy Scott (2012): Time and the Digital. Connecting Technology, Aesthetics, and a Process Philosophy of Time, Dartmouth, NH: Dartmouth College Press.

Barthes, Roland (1977 [1967]): "The Death of the Author." In: idem: Image, Music, Text, Essays selected and translated by Stephen Heath, New York, NY: Hill and Wang, pp. 142-148.

Bergermann, Ulrike (2009): "MONSTRARE. Zum Ausstellen von Dis/Ability." In: Hanne Loreck/Katrin Mayer (eds.), Visuelle Lektüren – Lektüren des Visuellen, Hamburg: textem, pp. 177-192.

Bippus, Elke (2014): "Affekt(De)Regulierung durch Affizierung." In: FKW // Zeitschrift für Geschlechterforschung und visuelle Kultur 55, pp. 16-25, http://www.fkw-journal.de/index.php/fkw/article/view/1267 (August 14, 2015).

Bippus, Elke (2015): "Adrian Pipers Funk Lessons: Eine Mikropraxis transformierender Affirmation." In: Lotte Everts/Johannes Lang/Michael Lüthy/Bernhard Schieder (eds.), Kunst und Wirklichkeit heute. Affirmation – Kritik – Transformation, Bielefeld: transcript, pp. 201-221.

Bishop, Claire (2012): Artificial Hells. Participatory Art and the Politics of Spectatorship, London: Verso.

Bourriaud, Nicolas (2002): Relational Aesthetics, Dijon: Presses du Réel.

Butler, Judith (2006): Gender Trouble: Feminism and the Subversion of Identity, 2nd ed., New York, NY: Routledge.

Butler, Judith (2009): Survivability, Vulnerability, Affect. In: idem, Frames of War: When Is Life Grievable?, New York, NY: Verso, pp. 33-62.

Coleman, Stephen/Shane, Peter M. (2011): Connecting Democracy: Online Consultation and the Flow of Political Communication, Cambridge, MA: MIT Press.

Debord, Guy (1999 [1967]): La société du spectacle, Paris: Gallimard.

Deleuze, Gilles/Guattari, Félix (1987): A Thousand Plateaus: Capitalism and Schizophrenia, translated by Brian Massumi, Minneapolis, MN: University of Minnesota Press.

Derrida, Jacques (1981): "Plato's Pharmacy." In: idem, Dissemination, translated by Barbara Johnson, Chicago, IL: University of Chicago Press, pp. 67-186.

Di Justo, Patrick (2004): "Protests Powered by Cellphone", September 9, http://www.nytimes.com/2004/09/09/technology/circuits/09mobb.html (August 14, 2015).

Dieterich, Sebastian/Furrer, Wiktoria/Bippus, Elke (2015): "Micropractice: A Work in Progress." In: Alan Roth/Dimitrina Sevova/Stevphen Shukaitis (eds.), Micropolitics of Play. Wivenhoe: Minor Compositions.

Eco, Umberto (1989 [1962]): The Open Work, translated by Anna Cancogni, Cambridge, MA: Harvard University Press.

Engell, Lorenz (2010): "Kinematographische Agenturen." In: Lorenz Engell/Jiří Bystřický/Kateřina Krtilová (eds.), Medien denken. Von der Bewegung des Begriffs zu bewegten Bildern, Bielefeld: transcript, pp. 137-156.

Feldhoff, Silke (2009): Zwischen Spiel und Politik. Partizipation als Strategie und Praxis in der bildenden Kunst. Dissertation. Fakultät Bildende Kunst, Universität der Künste Berlin, opus4.kobv.de/opus4-udk/files/26/Feldhoff_Silke.pdf (August 14, 2015).

Foucault, Michel (2007), "Technologies of the Self." In: Paul Rabinow (ed.), Ethics: Subjectivity and Truth, translated by Robert Hurley et al., New York, NY: New Press, pp. 223-251.

Fuchs, Peter (1997): "Adressabilität als Grundbegriff der soziologischen Systemtheorie." In: Soziale Systeme. Zeitschrift für soziologische Theorie 3/1, pp. 57-81.

Goggin, Gerard (2011), "Mobile Internet. New Social Technologies." In: idem, Global Mobile Media, London: Routledge, pp. 116-135.

Hirsch, Tad/Henry, John (2005): "TXTmob: Text Messaging For Protest Swarms." In: CHI 2005, April 2-7, Portland Oregon, pp. 1455-1458.

Kincheloe, Pamela (2010): "Do Androids Dream of Electric Speech? The Construction of Cochlear Implant Identity on American Television and the 'New Deaf Cyborg'." In: M/C Journal 13/3, http://journal.mediaculture.org.au/index.php/mcjournal/article/view/254 (August 14, 2015).

Knorr-Cetina, Karin (1982): "Scientific Communities or Transepistemic Arenas of Research? A Critique of Quasi-Economic Models of Science." In: Social Studies of Science 12, pp. 101-130.

Kortuem, Gerd, et al. (2001): "When Peer-to-Peer Comes Face-to-Face: Collaborative Peer-to-Peer Computing in Mobile Ad hoc Networks:" International Conference on Peer-to-Peer Computing (P2P2001), August 27.-29., 2001, Linköping, Sweden, http://comp.eprints.lancs.ac.uk/1570/1/P2P-2001.pdf (August 14, 2015).

Latour, Bruno (1991): "Technology is Society Made Durable." In: John Law (ed.), A Sociology of Monsters: Essays on Power, Technology and Domination, London: Routledge, pp. 103-131.

Licoppe, Christian (2013): "Merging Mobile Communication Studies and Urban Research: Mobile Locative Media, 'Onscreen Encounters' and the Reshaping of the Interaction Order in Public Places." In: Mobile Media & Communication 1/1, pp 122-128.

Mandiberg, Michael (2012) (ed.): The Social Media Reader, New York, NY, and London: New York University Press.

Massumi, Brian (2002): Parables for the Virtual: Movement, Affect, Sensation, Durham N.C.: Duke University Press.

Massumi, Brian (2009): "Of Microperception and Micropolitics: An Interview with Brian Massumi by Joel McKim, 15 August 2008." In: Inflexions: A Journal for Research Creation 3, http://www.inflexions.org/n3_Of-Microperception-and-Micropolitics-An-Interview-with-Brian-Massumi.pdf (August 14, 2015).

Moynihan, Colin (2008): "City Subpoenas Creator of Text MessagingCode." In: NewYorkTimes, March 3 http://www.nytimes.com/2008/03/30/ny region/30text.html?_r=0 (August 14, 2015).

Nancy, Jean-Luc (1992): "La comparution/The Compearance. From the Existence of 'Communism' to the Community of 'Existence'." In: Political Theory 20/3, pp. 371-398.

Nancy, Jean-Luc (2001): The inoperative community, Minneapolis, MN: University of Minnesota Press

Nancy, Jean-Luc (2007): Listening, New York, NY: Fordham University Press.

Nancy, Jean-Luc (2013): "Of Struction", translated by Travis Holloway and Flor Méchain. In: Parrhesia 17, pp. 1-10, http://www.parrhesiajournal.org/parrhesia17/parrhesia17_nancy.pdf (August 14, 2015).

Nancy, Jean-Luc/Tatari, Marita (2014): "Kunst und Politik." In: Marita Tatari (ed.), Orte des Unermesslichen. Theater nach der Geschichtsteleologie, Zurich and Berlin: diaphanes, pp. 23-41.

Neuner, Stefan (2007): "Paradoxien der Partizipation. Zur Einführung." In: Das Magazin des Instituts für Theorie 31/10-11, pp. 4-6.

Ochsner, Beate/Robert Stock (2014): "Das Hören des Cochlea Implantats." In: Jan Friedrich Missfelder/Ludolf Kuchenbuch (eds.), Historische Anthropologie, Themenheft Sound 22/3, pp. 408-425.

Ochsner, Beate/Spöhrer, Markus/Robert Stock (2015): "Human, Nonhuman, and Beyond: Cochlear Implants in Socio-Technological Environments." In: NanoEthics 9/3, pp. 237-250.

OpenSource.net (2004): "Interview with Tad Hirsch of MIT and TxtMob.com", September 24, http://boston.indymedia.org/feature/display/28589/index.php (August 14, 2015).

Pickering, John (1997): "Agents and Artifacts." In: Social Analysis 41/1, pp. 46-63.

Piper, Adrian (1996): "Notes on Funk I–IV." In: Idem, Out of Order, Out of Sight, Cambridge, MA: MIT Press, pp. 195-216.

Rafael, Vicente L. (2003): "The Cell Phone and the Crowd: Messianic Politics in the Contemporary Philippines." In: Public Culture 15/3, pp. 399-425.

Rancière, Jacques (2004): The Politics of Aesthetics: The Distribution of the Sensible, translated by Gabriel Rockhill, London: Continuum.

Rancière, Jacques (2009): "Bild, Beziehung, Handlung: Fragen zu den Politiken der Kunst." In: Michaela Ott/ Harald Strauß (eds.), Ästhetik + Politik. Neuaufteilungen des Sinnlichen in der Kunst. Hamburg: textem, pp. 29-46.

Rebentisch, Juliane (2006): "Autonomie? Autonomie! Ästhetische Erfahrung heute." In: Sonderforschungsbereich 626 (ed.), Ästhetische Erfahrung: Gegenstände, Konzepte, Geschichtlichkeit, Berlin, http://www.sfb626.de/veroeffentlichungen/online/aesth_erfahrung/aufsaetze/rebentsch.pdf (August 14, 2015).

Rheinberger, Hans-Jörg (1992): "Das epistemische Ding und seine technischen Bedingungen." In: Idem, Experiment – Differenz – Schrift. Zur Geschichte epistemischer Dinge, Marburg/Lahn: Basiliskenpresse, pp. 67-88.

Rheingold, Howard (2002): Smart Mobs. The Next Social Revolution, Cambridge, MA: Basic Books.

Sifry, Micah (2012): "From TXTMob to Twitter: How an Activist Tool Took Over the Conventions", August 25, http://techpresident.com/news/22775/txtmob-twitter-how-activist-tool-took-over-conventions (August 14, 2015).

Stäheli, Urs (2004): "Subversive Praktiken? Cultural Studies und die 'Macht' der Globalisierung." In: Karl H. Hörning/Julia Reuter (eds.), Doing Culture. Neue Positionen zum Verhältnis von Kultur und sozialer Praxis, Bielefeld: transcript, pp. 154-166.

Tholen, Georg Christoph (1999): "Platzverweis. Unmögliche Zwischenspiele von Mensch und Maschine." In: Norbert Bolz/Friedrich A. Kittler/Georg Christoph Tholen (eds.), Computer als Medium, München: Fink, pp. 111-138.

Thom-Santelli, Jennifer (2007): "Mobile Social Software: Facilitating Serendipity or Encouraging Homogeneity?" In: Pervasive Computing, IEEE 6/3, pp. 46-51.

Vogl, Joseph (2001): "Medien-Werden. Galileos Fernrohr." In: Lorenz Engell/Joseph Vogl (eds.), Archiv für Mediengeschichte. Mediale Historiographien, Weimar: VDG, pp. 115-123.

Vogl, Joseph (2012): "Taming time. Media of Financialization." In: Grey Room 56, pp. 72-83.

Vonen, Arnfinn Muruvik (2007): "Bilingualism – a future asset in the education of socially deaf children." In: Mervyn B. Hyde/Grete Hoie (eds.), Constructing educational discourses on deafness, Oslo: Norwegian Government Printers, Skadalen Resource Centre, pp. 108-118.

Weber, Samuel (1989/90): "Upsetting the Set Up: Remarks on Heidegger's Questing After Technics." In: MLN, pp. 976-991.

Whitehead, Alfred North (1929/1978): Process and Reality, New York, NY: Free Press.

Winkler, Hartmut (1999): "Die prekäre Rolle der Technik. Technikzentrierte versus 'anthropologische' Mediengeschichtsschreibung." In: Claus Pias (ed.), [me'dieni]i Dreizehn Vorträge zur Medienkultur, Weimar: VDG, pp. 221-240.

Contributors

Abend, Pablo, is a postdoc at the DFG-Project Modding and Editor-Games (Priority Program 1505 Mediatized Worlds) at the Institute for Media Studies and Theater, University of Cologne. Between 2008 and 2012 he held a scholarship at the Graduate School Locating Media, University of Siegen. Recent Publications: "Geo-browsing Google Earth und Co. Nutzungspraktiken einer digitalen Erde", Bielefeld: transcript 2013. "The Map Becomes the Gamer's Territory – Kartographische Bildpraktiken des Computerspiels", in: Beil, Benjamin/Bonner, Marc/Thomas Hensel (eds.): *Computer-Spiel-Bilder*, Glückstadt: vwh 2014. "The Uses of Geomedia: An Object-Centered and Situated Approach", in Thomas Jekel et. al. (eds.): *GI_Forum* 2013. Creating the GISociety, Berlin: Wichmann 2013. His research interests include: game studies, location-based and situated media studies, geomedia, participative practices, media and political protest, science and technology studies.

Axer, Eva, holds a postdoctoral position in the DFG-project „Zeit und Form im Wandel: Goethes Morphologie und ihr Nachleben in der Theoriebildung des 20. Jahrhunderts / Time and Form in Motion. Goethe's Morphology and its Afterlife in 20th Century Theory" at the Zentrum für Literatur- und Kulturforschung Berlin. From May 2012 until March 2014 she was a Humboldt-Fellow at the University of Nottingham, UK, where she pursued her postdoctoral project on the political dimensions of the German ballad between the 18th and the 20th century. Eva Axer studied German Language and Literature as well as Comparative Literature at Bonn University, where she also completed her PhD on Walter Benjamin's short prose.

Bartz, Christina, is Professor of Television and Digital Media at the Department for Media Studies, University of Paderborn since 2009 and was a researcher of the DFG-Network "Media of Collective Intelligence". Christina Bartz was a visiting professor at the Stiftungs Universität Hildesheim and research assistant at the Institute for Film and Television Studies, University of Cologne and principal investigator of the SFB/FK 427 "Media and Cultural Communication" in Cologne. Her research interests include television history, semantics of the crowd, discourse history of media and feminist film theory. Recent publications are *MassenMedium Fernsehen. Die Semantik der Masse in der Medienbeschreibung* (transcript 2007) and *Spektakel der Normalisierung* (Fink 2007, edited with Marcus Krause).

Beil, Benjamin, is Assistant Professor of Digital Culture at the Institute for Media Culture and Theater, University of Cologne. His research interests include: game studies, digital film, TV series, prosumer culture, inter- and transmediality. Recent publications are *Avatarbilder. Zur Bildlichkeit des zeitgenössischen Computerspiels* (transcript 2012). *First Person Perspectives. Point of View und figurenzentrierte Erzählformen im Film und im Computerspiel* (Lit 2010) and *Game Studies – eine Einführung* (Lit 2013).

Bippus, Elke, is Professor of Theory and History of Art at the Zurich University of the Arts. She worked as guest professor and professor at the University of the Arts Bremen from 2002-2005. Elke Bippus also has been teaching art history and art theory at the University of Visual Arts Braunschweig and at the University of Hamburg. She received her PhD with a thesis on serial procedures in the art of the 1960s (*Serielle Verfahrensweisen. Pop Art, Minimal Art, Conceptual Art, Post-minimalism*, Berlin 2003). Main topics of interest include contemporary art, theory of image media, representation, interfaces and limitations of art-historic, artistic and curatorian activities; artistic methods of production and procedures; relationship between art and science. Publications include ›*MIT-SEIN*‹: *Gemeinschaft – ontologische und politische Perspektivierungen* (Springer 2010, edited together with Jörg Huber and Dorothee Richter).

Cruz, Teresa, teaches at the Communication Sciences Department, in the Social and Human Sciences College of the NOVA University of Lisbon (UNL – Portugal) in the fields of Image Theory, Media Aesthetics and

Theory and Contemporary Art. She is the director of the Research Center on Communication and Language, where she also coordinated the research line on "Art and Communication" (2007-2012) and created the Journal "Interact – Art, Culture and Technology" (www.interact.com). Her research interests focus upon contemporary art and post-media aesthetics as well as cultural techniques and cultural heritage.

Dege, Martin, is a visiting fellow in political theory at Yale University, a postdoc in Sociology at Hamburg University and a Fellow of the Fritz Thyssen Foundation. He investigates the emergence of new forms of participation on the Web 2.0 and traces the roots of the participatory Internet back to the beginnings of the industrial revolution. In particular, Martin aims to show how this development was generated by changes in labor organization, social movements, and science and technology over the course of the past century. On a more theoretical level, Martin examines the concepts of technology developed by Max Weber, Martin Heidegger, as well as the early Frankfurt School.

Denecke, Mathias, is a PhD student at the Digital Cultures Research Lab (DCRL) at Leuphana University Lueneburg. His PhD project focuses on the metaphors of the stream and flow as well as its usage within a psycho-philosophical context since the late 19th century. Mathias Denecke completed his M.A. in Literature, Art, and Media Studies (Konstanz) in 2014 with a thesis on the conditions of possible formations of communities. His research interests include media theory, participation theory as well as specifically the relation of individual and community. He is associated with the research group "Media and Participation".

Dokumacı, Arseli, a *Fonds québécois de la recherche sur la société et la culture* (FQRSC) postdoctoral fellow at McGill University, Department of Social Studies of Medicine. She is also a research associate at Concordia University, Mobile Media Lab, where she has recently completed a postdoctoral research. Arseli received her PhD in Performance Studies from Aberystwyth University in 2012. The title of her dissertation is "Misfires that Matter: Invisible Disabilities and Performances of the Everyday". Her current work focuses on the histories of disability measurement in which task-performance appears as the baseline for calculation. Arseli's work has appeared in *Performance Research*; Wi Journal and in the edited collections of *Misperformance: Essays in Shifting Perspectives* (Maska 2014) and *Disability in Judaism, Christianity, and Islam* (Palgrave 2011). Arseli is the chair of emerging scholars committee and a board member of Performance Studies international.

Franz, Nina, is a member of the *Image Knowledge Gestaltung* Cluster of Excellence in Berlin where she works on a doctoral thesis about problems of vision and visibility in times of unmanned military technologies. Since 2012 she is a researcher within the Chair of Cultural Theory and Aesthetics at the Institute for Cultural History and Theory at Humboldt-Universität zu Berlin. In 2004 Nina Franz obtained her B.A. in Liberal Studies at the Grand Valley State University in Allendale, Michigan. During her studies she spent a semester at the East China Normal University in Shanghai and at the University of California, Berkeley. She completed her M.A. in Cultural History and Theory with a thesis on concepts of community in architecture and urban housing in Berlin. Her research interests include the political dimensions of design; sketch, plan and ichnography in architectural and cultural theory; machine theories and the cultural history of technology and technics.

Ganzert, Anne, is a PhD student at the University of Konstanz, Germany. Her dissertation focuses on contemporary North-American TV series and their „Serial Pinboarding". Her advisors are Prof. Dr. Beate Ochsner (Konstanz) and Prof. Dr. Jennifer Gillan (Boston, MA) and she received a full scholarship from the Friedrich-Naumann-Foundation for Freedom (2012-2015). Her main research interests are TV Studies, Visual Culture Studies, Diagrammatic Reasoning, Participation Theory, Reality TV, Fan Studies, Transmedia Storytelling & Convergence Media. Recent publications are "SyncNow. Fernsehen und das Versprechen von Teilhabe" (AugenBlick 58, 2013) and "We welcome you to your Heroes community. A Case Study in Transmedia Storytelling" (IMAGE 21, 2015).

Hörl, Erich, is Professor of Media Culture at Leuphana University of Lueneburg. Here he is also Senior Researcher at the Digital Culture Research Lab (DCRL). Erich Hörl studied philosophy in Vienna and Paris and received his PhD from Humboldt University Berlin. Later, he was a member of the research project "Bild-Schrift-Zahl" at the Helmholtz-Zentrum für Kulturtechnik at Humboldt University and Assistant Professor of Techno-Philosophy at the Department of Philosophy at ETH-Zurich in 2004-2006. Afterwards he was Junior Professor for Media Technology and Media Philosophy at Ruhr University at Bochum where he became Associate Professor in 2012. His publications include *Die technologische Bedingung. Beiträge zur Beschreibung der technischen Welt* (Suhrkamp 2011); *Die Heiligen Kanäle. Über die Archaische Illusion der Kommunikation* (Diaphanes 2005); A Thousand Ecologies: The Process of Cyberneticization and General Ecology, in *The Whole Earth. California and the Disappearance of the Outside*, ed. by Diedrich Diederichsen and Anselm Franke (Sternberg Press 2013); Variations on Klee's Cosmographic Method, in *Grain, Vapor, Ray: Textures of the Anthropocene, Vol. III: Ray*, ed. by Kathrin Klingan et al. (MIT-Press 2014).

Kaun, Anne, is an assistant professor at the Department for Media and Communication Studies at Södertörn University, Stockholm. Being interested in the relationship between crises and social critique, her current project concerns historical forms of media participation that emerged in the context of economic crisis. Furthermore she is working in a collaborative project on European Narratives. She has previously published in peer-reviewed journals such as Participation; Communications – The European Journal of Communication Research; Information, Communication and Society and the International Journal of Qualitative Methods. Based on her PhD thesis, which she successfully defended in June 2012, Anne has published the book *Being a Young Citizen in Estonia – An Exploration of Young People's Civic and Media Experiences* (2013).

Manning, Erin, holds a University Research Chair in Relational Art and Philosophy in the Faculty of Fine Arts at Concordia University (Montreal, Canada). She is also the director of the *SenseLab*, a laboratory that explores the intersections between art practice and philosophy through the matrix of the sensing body in movement. In her art practice she works between painting, dance, fabric and sculpture. Current iterations of her artwork explore emergent collectivities through participatory textiles. Her writing addresses movement, art, experience and the political through the prism of process philosophy, with recent work developing a notion of autistic perception and the more-than human. Publications include *Always More Than One: Individuation's Dance* (Duke University Press 2012), *Relationscapes: Movement, Art, Philosophy* (MIT Press 2009) and *Politics of Touch: Sense, Movement, Sovereignty* (Minnesota University Press 2007).

Mitchell, Christine, is a visiting scholar (Quebec) and FQRSC Postdoctoral Fellow in Media, Culture and Communication at New York University. In 2013-2014 she was a postdoctoral fellow with SpokenWeb, a digital poetry archive at Concordia University in Montreal. In 2015 she co-edited, with Jason Camlot, *The Poetry Series*, a special issue of Amodern (amodern.net), oriented around poetry readings and recordings. Her published work has focused on the materialities and histories of language and media in relation to speech, text, Artificial Intelligence, machine translation and scenes of instruction. She is currently working on a manuscript that develops a media theory of translation through examination of language laboratories, machine translation, translation bureaus, and gamified language learning.

Niederer, Sabine, is director of CREATE-IT Applied Research, the R&D center of the School of Digital Media and Creative Industries at the Amsterdam University of Applied Sciences, where she is launching the Citizen Data Lab (www.citizendatalab.org). As a PhD researcher, she is part of the Digital Methods Initiative at the University of Amsterdam. She is board member of Amsterdam Data Science, a research institute for data science in Amsterdam, and free-lance curator of new media art. Until 2012, Sabine Niederer was the managing director of the Institute of Network Cultures, with Prof. Geert Lovink, coordinating various publications (such as the INC Reader Series and Network Notebooks) and events as Urban Screens, Society df the Query, New Network Theory and A Decade of Web Design. In 2011, she was visiting scholar at the Annenberg School for Communication at the University of Pennsylvania.

Ochsner, Beate, is Professor of Media Studies at the University of Konstanz since 2008. She received a Phd in Romance Languages and Literature and Media Studies from the University of Mannheim where she worked for several years as a research assistant. In her habilitation thesis she analyzed representations of monsters and monstrosity in literature, film and photography (2009). Recent publications are *Andere Bilder. Zur Produktion von Behinderung in der visuellen Kultur* (Bielefeld 2013, edited together with Anna Grebe), "Translations of Blind Perception in the Films Monika (2011) and Antoine (2008)" (InVisible Culture 2013, with Robert Stock) and "Von intermedialer Konvergenz zu *produsage* oder: Die neue Partizipa-tionskultur im Musikvideo" (Nadja Elia-Borer et. al.: *Blickregime und Dispositive audio visueller Medien*, transcript 2011). Her main research interests are media theory and aesthetics, disability studies and visual culture.

Otto, Isabell, is Professor of Media Studies at the University of Konstanz. She was visiting professor of Media Studies at the Ruhr-Universität Bochum and a fellow of the Center of Excellence "Cultural Foundations of Social Integrations" allowing her to work on her second book about digital temporalities. She was the coordinator of the DFG-Network "Media of Collective Intelligence". Selected publications are *Aggressive Medien. Zur Geschichte des Wissens über Mediengewalt* (transcript 2008), *Das Planetarische. Kultur – Technik – Medien im postglobalen Zeitalter* (Fink, 2010, edited with Ulrike Bergermann, Gabriele Schabacher), AugenBlick Special Issue „Bilder in Echtzeit. Medialität und Ästhetik des digitalen Bewegtbildes" (51, 2012, edited with Tobias Haupts). Her research interests are discourse history of media, media in history of the sciences, digital media and temporality.

Pias, Claus, is Professor for History and Epistemology of Media at the Institute for Culture and Aesthetics of Digital Media (ICAM), Director of the Institute for Advanced Study in Media Cultures of Computer Simulation (mecs), the Centre for Digital Cultures (CDC) and the Digital Cultures Research Lab (DCRL) at Leuphana University in Lueneburg. In 2015 summer term Claus Pias was a senior fellow at the Institute for Advanced Study "Cultural Foundations of Social Integration", Konstanz. Main areas of interest are the media history and epistemology of computer simulations, the history of media studies, and the history and epistemology of cybernetics. Publications include: *Computer Game Worlds*, Amsterdam 2015 (in print); edited with I. Baxmann und T. Beyes: Soziale Medien – Neue Massen, Zürich 2014 (English version forthcoming with Chicago University Press, 2015); *Was waren Medien?*, Zürich 2012; edited with T. Brandstetter and S. Vehlken: Think Tanks. Die Beratung der Gesellschaft, Zürich 2010.

Schramm, Samantha, was a scientific staff member at the department of Media Studies, University of Konstanz from 2010-2015. She received her PhD in 2012 with a dissertation about concepts of site and media in Land Art and was then a visiting professor for the History of Art at the Staatliche Hochschule für Gestaltung in Karlsruhe. After having studied in Stuttgart and at the University of Kansas where she received a Fulbright scholarship, Samantha Schramm was member of the graduate centre "Bild-Körper-Medium. Eine anthropologische Perspektive" and fellow at the Terra Summer Residency 2008 in Giverny, France. Her research interests are picture theory, media theory, art and location, pragmatics of the image.

Simons, Sascha, is a research fellow at Leuphana University's Digital Cultures Research Lab (DCRL) and a member of the editorial collective of the web journal *spheres*. He currently writes a doctoral thesis on the aesthetics of authenticity and the social testimony of web videos. He is interested in the aesthetics, theory and history of social media and the interplay of media and social morphology. He recently published "Das Ornament der Mass Customization" in *Soziale Medien – Neue Massen* edited by Inge Baxmann, Timon Beyes and Claus Pias (Zürich 2014).

Stock, Robert, is a research assistant at the University of Konstanz where he coordinates the research initiative "Media and Participation". He holds a Master's degree in cultural anthropology from the Humboldt-University of Berlin. In his dissertation at the International Graduate Centre for the Study of Culture (Gießen) he analyzes postcolonial memory politics in documentary films from Mozambique and Portugal. His main research interests are media studies, visibility, critical disability studies and postcolonial memory politics. Publications include "Translations of Blind Perception in the Films Monika (2011) and Antoine (2008)" (InVisible Culture 2013, with Beate Ochnser) and "Retina Implantate. Neuroprothesen und das Versprechen auf Teilhabe" (AugenBlick 2013).

Stramskas, Arnoldas, is a PhD candidate at the Department of Political Science and Diplomacy, Vytautas Magnus University, Kaunas, Lithuania. He has a Master's degree in social and political critical studies, and earned his bachelor in gender, women and sexuality studies from the University of

Minnesota in 2009. His research and practice deals with collective experimentation, micropolitics, and urban restructuring, as well as other subjects.

Vehlken, Sebastian, is a junior director of the Institute for Advanced Study in Media Cultures of Computer Simulation (mecs) at the Leuphana University Lueneburg. After having studied media studies and economics at Ruhr-University Bochum and at Edith Cowan University, Perth he was a DFG scholarship holder in the graduate school "Media of History – History of Media" at Bauhaus-Universität Weimar. Since 2007 he worked as a research associate in Media Philosophy, University of Vienna. In 2010, he finished his PhD thesis on a media history of biological and computational swarm research at Humboldt University Berlin. Then, he was a research associate (PostDoc) at the Institute for Culture and Aesthetics of Digital Media, Leuphana University Lueneburg. His main research interests focus on a media history of agent-based modeling and simulation, computer simulation in the Atomic Age, the history and epistemology of supercomputing, and oceans as media environments.